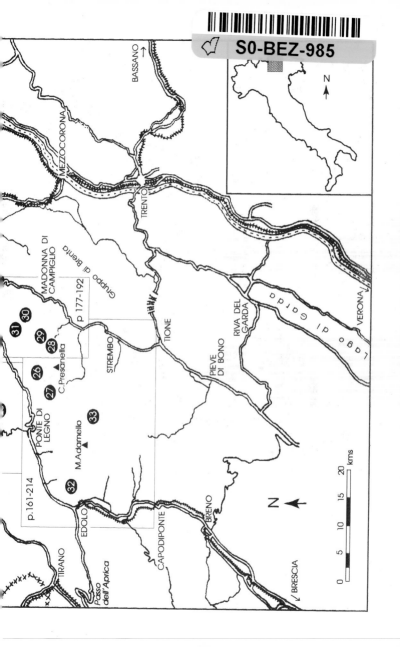

WALKING IN THE
CENTRAL ITALIAN ALPS

Precarious plank crossing near Rif. Segantini (walk 28)

WALKING IN THE
CENTRAL ITALIAN ALPS
Vinschgau, Ortler, Adamello and their Parks

by

Gillian Price

CICERONE PRESS
2 POLICE SQUARE, MILNTHORPE

© Gillian Price 1995
ISBN 185284 183 4
A catalogue record for this book is available from the British Library

To Nicola, with all my love.

A special mention for my parents Betty & Dave, together with walkers-to-be Kathryn, Morgan and Giacomo.

Thanks to Nicola Regine for all his incredibly patient work on the maps and diagrams, to walking companions Egidio, Paola, Piero and Nicola, as well as Cinzia and Marta for technical assistance.

All the photographs were taken by Gillian Price and Nicola Regine.

Other books by the same author:
Walking in the Dolomites

Front Cover:
During the descent towards Rif. Bédole and Val Genova (walk 27)

CONTENTS

Advice to Readers

Readers are advised that whilst every effort is taken by the author to ensure the accuracy of this guidebook, changes can occur which may affect the contents. A book of this nature with detailed descriptions and detailed maps is more prone to change than a more general guide. Waymarking alters, there may be new buildings or eradication of old buildings. It is advisable to check locally on transport, accommodation, shops etc. but even rights of way can be altered, paths can be eradicated by landslip, forest clearances or changes of ownership. The publisher would welcome notes of any such changes.

INTRODUCTION

THE AREA

Walking through this border region means following in the footsteps of Stone Age hunters, Holy Roman Emperors, salt smugglers, German migrant miners, Venetian merchants and First World War troops, not to mention dwarves and giants.

A vast area in the central part of north Italy is covered, namely the Italian side of the Rhaetian Alps. From the borders with Switzerland and Austria, it is delimited by Meran, Bozen (South Tyrol) and Trento (Trentino) in the east, across to Valcamonica at the western edge, and up through Bormio (Lombardy). Most of the itineraries run through protected areas - the Stelvio National Park and the Provincial Nature Parks of Texel and Adamello - and include everything from meadows and woods through to snow fields, glaciers and spectacular summits.

The incredibly varied natural landscape, with an essentially metamorphic rock base, is the result of modelling by glaciers combined with weathering by wind and rain. The retreat in stages of ancient ice masses left tell-tale signs in ridges of glacial debris (moraine), U-shaped valleys and polished and grooved rock surfaces. There are still several sizeable glaciers (notably Adamello and Forni), not to mention remnants, hanging glaciers, left in armchair-like cirques. Countless small lakes (tarns) have formed where abandoned rubble obstructed a valley and waterfalls are plentiful.

Each different zone has a rich history. Prehistory has left treasures in the form of rock engravings in Valcamonica and the Similaun "Iceman". After Roman colonisation came turbulent medieval times starring Margaret of the Big Mouth and Frederick of the Empty Pockets. Lombardy, South Tyrol and Trentino were variously under Bavaria, France and Austria.

During the First World War, the front (dividing Austria's weakening Hapsburg Empire and Italy) ran along mountain ridges from Stilfser Joch south to Monte Adamello, curved southeast to Lago di Garda, before heading northeast to the Marmolada. Though very few actual battles took place on this impervious terrain (even the ice-bound 3905m Ortler peak was occupied and equipped with cannons), enormous numbers of lives were lost to avalanches and the treacherous cold. There are modest war museums at Vermiglio in Val di Sole and Temù in Valcamonica, but walkers will often come across crumbling fortifications and rusty relics given up by the retreating ice masses.

At present, Lombardy together with Trentino are "Italian" areas, culturally (and gastronomically) speaking. South Tyrol, on the other hand, consists of two-thirds native German speakers, with the rest Italians and a tiny fraction ($^1/_{20}$) speakers of Ladin, an ancient Rhaetian dialect.

HOW TO GET THERE & PUBLIC TRANSPORT

As the map shows, the area lies in the central part of northernmost Italy on the borders of both Austria and Switzerland, and can be approached from many directions.

It is served extensively by public transport. (This entire guide was in fact researched using local means.) As well as rendering walking holidays more relaxing, using public transport means making a worthwhile and substantial contribution to keeping the roads quieter and the air more breathable. Timetables are free at the Tourist Offices.

For access by train, as well as the important Brenner Pass-Bozen-Verona line, useful lines run Bozen-Meran, Trento-Mezzocorona-Malé, Venice-Bassano-Trento, Brescia-Edolo, and St. Moritz-Tirano-Milan. The Austrian railhead of Landeck has a coach line via Nauders to Meran. In the summer there are also connections by long-distance coach from major cities in north Italy.

Following is a list of relevant coach and private rail companies:

- S.A.D. coaches cover the area north and east of Meran, including connections to Austria. Tel:1678-46047 (toll-free).

- F.T.M. is a private electric railway that links Trento to Malé. Its coaches then continue west as far as Passo del Tonale, and link with Madonna di Campiglio. There's also a direct summer coach to Milan. Tel:0461/822725 (Trento), 0463/901150 (Malé).

- the ATESINA coach company services the valleys west of Trento, and includes many Adamello-Presanella accesses. Tel:0461/983627.

- private railway (S.N.F.T.) connects Brescia with Edolo, in upper Valcamonica. Tel:030/980061.

- the BUSTI company connects Edolo with Ponte di Legno, and also has a direct Milano-Malé line. Tel:035/244429-248474.

- the PEREGO coach company covers the Bormio area and further afield southeast to Milan (via Valtellina). Tel:0342/905090-910105 (Bormio bus station).

WHEN TO GO

The weather varies tremendously year by year, but the walking season usually extends from June through to October. While the high altitude routes are dependent on refuge opening periods (July-September for the most part), lower itineraries (such as those in Vinschgau touching on farms and Waalwegs) are feasible even as early as Easter. July is probably the most suitable month overall, featuring wild flowers at their best. Storms and even snow, however, are not unknown in midsummer. The first three weeks of August, on the other hand, are high season for Italian visitors (meaning fully booked valley accommodation). September tends to be quiet and animals are easier to observe as they start to descend towards the valley in search of food. The air is crisper and clearer, making for better visibility. The days, however, are shorter by then (Italy goes off Daylight Savings at the end of September). With the start of autumn and October, vegetation colours can be superb. Though most refuges will have closed by then, plenty of low-altitude day walks are possible, even after the first snow falls.

WALKS & WALKING

The itineraries described follow well-marked and numbered paths for the most part, though they range from wide easy tracks through woods to tiring moraine debris and snow crossings. Waymarking (usually red and white paint stripes) and path maintenance is the responsibility of Alpine Clubs or local Councils, if not Park authorities. Preference has been given to circular routes or traverses connecting different valleys - as well as the psychological satisfaction they provide, they can be split up into individual sections as short day walks. Alternative accesses and exits are given where possible.

As far as timing goes, only "bare" times are given, *not including* stops for rests or meals, so always add on extra time. Walking times are for reasonably fit walkers and, on average, mean in 1h you cover 5km on level ground, 300m in ascent and 500m in descent. Descent times tend to be two-thirds of ascent times.

Cable cars and chair lifts are occasionally referred to as alternatives. Reductions are often available for children, the over 60s, and Alpine Club members.

Some Important Do's and Don'ts:

Read the walk description beforehand to get an idea of what to expect and select an itinerary that suits your state of fitness. Never set out when the weather is uncertain, particularly at high altitudes. Routes that are straightforward in good weather can be treacherous in low cloud or a storm, making orientation very difficult.

Always carry warm protective and waterproof clothing, even if you leave the refuge in shorts and a T-shirt. Remember that on average the temperature drops 6°C for every 1000m you climb.

It's a good general rule to start out on mountain walks early in the morning, as clouds tend to form later on, spoiling visibility and threatening storms. Furthermore, it means extra time in case of unforeseen circumstances such as a wrong turn, late-lying snow making progress slow or covering the path, or even detours where paths have washed away.

Find out what weather is forecast. Advice can be obtained from Tourist Offices or refuge staff. Italian and German speakers can consult local newspapers, radio or television, or telephone 191 (recorded message). An altimeter is also useful - for example when a known altitude, such as that of a refuge, goes up, walkers should plan on going down as the pressure has dropped and the weather will probably worsen. Should you be caught out in an electrical storm, don't be tempted to shelter under trees or overhanging rocks, and keep away from metallic fixtures.

Learn the international rescue signals: the call for help is SIX visual (such as waving a handkerchief or flashing a torch at night) or audible (whistling or shouting) signals per minute, to be repeated after a minute's pause. The answer is THREE visual or audible signals per minute to be repeated after a minute's pause. Anyone picking up a call for help is obliged to contact the nearest refuge as soon as possible. The following arm signals could be useful for communicating at a distance or with a helicopter.

Both arms raised diagonally:

> * help needed
> * land here
> * YES (to pilot's questions)

One arm raised diagonally, one arm down diagonally:

> * help not needed
> * do not land here
> * NO (to pilot's questions)

Don't pick any wild flowers, light fires or leave any trace of your presence. Walkers should not stray from marked paths, to avoid damaging vegetation, disturbing wildlife (such as ground nesting birds) and causing erosion. Alpine areas are not renewable resources.

Please take all your rubbish back down to the valley. The lack of rubbish containers is part of the attempt by Parks and refuges alike to phase them out, so as to free their staff and funds for more worthwhile purposes. As far as toilet stops go, avoid areas near water courses and PLEASE don't leave any unsightly paper lying around.

Last but not least, make an attempt to address local people in their own language. It will undoubtedly be appreciated. English is starting to be more common among young people, especially in the larger ski resorts, but it's a good idea to go equipped with a German or Italian phrase book.

Greeting other walkers along the way is another pleasant habit. You'll hear "Buon giorno" from the Italians and "Grüß Gott" (which sound more like "scot") from most German-speaking walkers.

REFUGES & ACCOMMODATION

Mountain refuges make walking immensely easier and mean the mountains are accessible for a greater range of people. They inevitably occupy superbly panoramic positions and act as a base for important traverses, climbs or glacier routes. They mean you don't have to carry sleeping gear and a tent, and provide a hot meal and bed for the night. A refuge nowadays means anything from a hotel-restaurant at a road pass to a modest alpine farm. Some are even served by cable cars (for winter skiing as well). Others, such as the traditional family-run farms in Vinschgau, offer basic accommodation (an attic with mattresses on the floor), while meals feature fresh butter and cheeses or home-made sausages and salamis (usually on sale as well). Don't expect any mod cons like hot water (or even an indoor bathroom when it comes to that), but charges are always reasonable and the atmosphere friendly. On the other hand, there are some farms and refuges that exploit meltwater flow from higher glaciers by converting it into power by way of a turbine - the significance for walkers being a good chance of free hot water.

The majority of refuges in this guide are run by various Alpine Clubs - CAI (Club Alpino Italiano), SAT (Società Alpinisti Tridentina, a CAI branch), AVS (Alpenverein Südtirol) and DAV (Deutscher Alpenverein, the German Alpine Club). You'll have the option of a bunk bed in the dormitory ("dormitorio" in Italian, "Lager" in German) complete with blankets or continental quilt (in 1995 this cost 11,000 Lire for members and 22,000 Lire for non-members) or a room, usually with fresh linen, at a slightly higher charge. The members' rates are also applicable to people from other Alpine Clubs, including those from English-speaking countries which have reciprocal agreements. Note that CAI refuges plan to introduce a surcharge of 3000 Lire for non-members as from 1995 (to go towards refuge maintenance). Food-wise, these huts guarantee hot meals (usually a hot pasta dish and "minestrone", vegetable soup, followed by second courses of meat and various accompaniments), as well as regional specialities. Prices are very reasonable considering the effort and organisation required for transporting supplies - by jeep, mechanised cableway, the occasional helicopter drop, horseback or even backpack.

Relevant refuges (but *only* those with accommodation) and guesthouses are listed at the end of each walk description, along with their sleeping capacity and opening period. These dates (in brackets) will vary year to year, depending on local conditions, so if in doubt at the start or finish of the season do check (by phoning the refuge itself or checking with the nearest Tourist Office). Booking (by phone) is only really necessary on July-August weekends for refuges on mountaineering or glacier routes. Once you have booked, however, should you change your route, *do* phone again to cancel as rescue operations (at your expense) might be set in motion when you don't show up.

Refuge guests should always sign the register and indicate their next destination (or tell the guesthouse staff their planned route for the day), as it could point rescuers in the right direction in a search.

Remember to change enough foreign currency before setting out on walks, as refuge staff cannot be expected to accept anything but Italian Lire in cash.

Some other basic "rules" for refuges:

* Lights out 10pm-6am when the generator usually goes off. Exceptions are refuges on important glacier or summit routes, where the majority of guests may be served breakfast as early as 4am.

* Walking boots, together with bulky ice and mountaineering gear, should be left in the hallway in appropriate racks. Slippers are often provided.

* Dogs and smoking (unless there is a separate room) are not allowed.

A note on drinking water: in some refuges you'll see the sign "Acqua non potabile" or "Kein Trinkwasser", meaning the water is unsuitable for drinking purposes. This is not necessarily because of dangerous bacteria, but could be due to the lack of mineral salts if the water comes from a glacier (ie. distilled water), or to a low temperature (Italian law puts the minimum temperature for drinkable water at 14°C). While drinking a small amount will not necessarily be harmful, stomach cramps and diarrhoea can result. Refuge water is analysed regularly by local health authorities. As an alternative, safe bottled mineral water is on sale everywhere.

Bivouac huts are free and always open, unless mentioned otherwise. Facilities vary, but a bunk bed and roof over your head are guaranteed, not to mention the peace of an isolated setting.

As far as camping is concerned, the National and Nature Parks forbid it, except in the specially designated areas, though these are few and far between. Otherwise most main valleys have camping grounds and caravan parks.

MAPS

An excellent road map covering the entire area is "Trentino-Alto Adige 1:200,000" by the Touring Club Italiano (TCI).

For walking, the TABACCO maps, available in 1:50,000 and 1:25,000, have been preferred for their clarity and graphics. They give names in both Italian and German. However parts of the Vinschgau are better covered by the KOMPASS series. These are available in scales ranging between 1:50,000 and 1:25,000 but only give the German version of place names in the South Tyrol. Graphically they are rather crude, with bright colours, and the thick light blue line they use to show ski touring routes is easily confused with water courses. Furthermore their larger scales are sometimes photographic enlargements of smaller ones. However the points in their favour are that they are often updated and show the bus stops - 'H' (Haltstelle). They can be used as alternatives to TABACCO maps in all cases, but have not all been listed to save space. One particularly useful map that covers the entire Stelvio National Park is KOMPASS NO.072 (1:50,000).

In order to follow even the easiest itinerary walkers must carry the relevant map. The sketch maps that accompany the walk descriptions are only intended as rough guides, and due to limitations of space cannot show all the paths, numbered or otherwise, that exist in any given zone. The "official" maps, while not always perfectly accurate, do show contours and natural features, essential for orientation. Easy paths are unbroken red lines, slightly difficult ones are broken red lines, and difficult stretches (particularly steep, exposed or simply unclear) are red dots. Crosses indicate an aided climbing route which necessitates experience and suitable equipment. The Glossary at the end of the book includes geographical terms commonly found on these maps.

Both TABACCO and KOMPASS maps are widely available in northern Italian cities as well as the mountain resorts. In fact a good map, properly used, is all that is needed to explore an area on foot. The itineraries described in this guide will hopefully serve as "antipasto" and stimulate walking appetites.

As far as the SKETCH MAPS go, together with the walk descriptions, to save space place names have been given in German for the South Tyrol zone, and Italian for the rest (Trentino and Lombardy). For the former, this has sometimes meant oversimplification. Most South Tyrol refuges, originally built by the Austrian-German Alpine Club, were renamed (in Italian) when transferred to or rebuilt by the Italian Club. Zufallhütte, for example, is Rif. Corsi for its present Milan CAI owners. The matter of actual place names is a little more complicated. Many original Ladin names were translated into German during the various periods of German-language settlement or influence. Then, in a 1934 attempt to "Italianise" the area, place names were translated into Italian. Many of these versions exist merely on paper still today. The refuge Hochganghaus is referred to in Italian guidebooks and on maps as (literally translated) Casa del Valico, though this name never appears on signposting in the area itself. Recent news from the Bozen Province tells of an attempt under way to settle on a single version of place names, probably the most used or most historical.

Signposting in the meantime is bilingual, with the addition of a third, Ladin name in the relevant valleys.

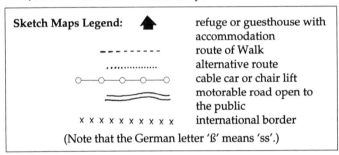

Sketch Maps Legend:	
▲	refuge or guesthouse with accommodation
– – – – – – –	route of Walk
....	alternative route
o–o–o–o–o	cable car or chair lift
～～～～	motorable road open to the public
x x x x x x x x x x	international border

(Note that the German letter 'ß' means 'ss'.)

EQUIPMENT

A few suggestions to be prepared for all eventualities:

* Sturdy walking boots, already worn in to avoid blisters, made of leather (synthetic models tend to lose their waterproofing faster), better for snow routes, combined with a good gripping sole.
* Training shoes to change into for evenings.
* T-shirts and shorts.
* Long warm walking trousers, or the popular continental version cut off at the knee (thus leaving it freer), worn with long socks. Jeans are totally unsuitable.
* Pullover and down jacket.
* Lightweight rain gear such as a poncho, to cover your rucksack as well.

* Sunglasses, sun barrier cream, hat and chapstick. (Remember that for every 1000m you ascend, the intensity of the sun's rays increases by 10%, further enhanced by lower levels of humidity and pollution. Moral: use a cream with a much higher protection factor than you would at sea level.)
* Gaiters are recommended for early season walking or for those routes that cross snow fields. They are particularly efficient for avoiding boots full of snow and soaking wet trouser legs when walking on overgrown paths after rain or wet by dew.
* Lightweight sheet sleeping bag - compulsory in all SAT refuges as from 1995 and encouraged in CAI refuges. A good idea anyway if you're squeamish about refuge blankets.
* Mineral salts are extremely useful to combat salt depletion, caused by excessive sweating in hot weather, and manifest in undue weariness and symptoms similar to heat-stroke.
* Ski poles (preferably telescopic for convenience of transport when not needed) are a great help for steep descents. They have become popular for actual walking and studies show that they are actually helpful in reducing the load on legs.
* Compass, altimeter and binoculars.
* Torch and extra batteries.
* First aid kit.
* Water bottle.
* Extra food for emergencies.

FLORA & FAUNA

Due to the variety of terrains and habitats, from low-lying meadows through woods and scrub to high-altitude rock and icescapes, this vast area offers an incredible range of flowers and wildlife and some astonishing examples of adaptation to harsh environments. Helpful posters with illustrations of local flora and fauna, protected and otherwise, are posted in refuges and villages. Guided walks with rangers or local guides are organised throughout the summer - contact the Tourist Offices.

Following are brief notes on flora and fauna most commonly observable.

Apparently barren rock surfaces host a myriad coloured lichen which break down the rock in preparation for hardy cushion plants

Glacier crowfoot

such as saxifrage, another "rock breaker" due to its penetrating roots.

Among the first flowers to appear on the very edge of the snow line is the dainty fringed blue-violet alpine snowbell. It is said to melt the snow around it with the heat released by the breakdown of carbohydrates. Another early bloom is the perfumed sticky primrose. The white or rarer pink glacier crowfoot, however, holds the record for height, having been found at 4200m in the Alps. The leaf cells contain a rich fluid that acts as an antifreeze. A lover of siliceous scree, it grows close to glaciers, hence its name.

On the other hand stony grasslands with calcareous soil (from limestone or dolomite rock) are ideal terrain for delicate yellow Rhaetian poppies. Often found growing nearby are white star-shaped edelweiss, with leaves equipped with fine felty hairs which trap heat. On similar terrain is another favourite, the gentian, not always in the brilliant blue trumpet or stemless form, but also in a larger pale yellow spotted variety.

A common sight in the Stelvio and Adamello Parks are the clumps of yellow, daisy-like chamois ragwort (with serrated leaves). Arnica, very similar (but with rounded leaves) is found at slightly lower

17

Edelweiss

levels, and is well known for its effectiveness (in cream or tincture form) in treating sprains and bruises. Alpine moon-daisies share the same rock-strewn terrain. Rhododendrons in miniature, alpenrose, are a delight of July, in dwarf, hairy or "rusty" forms. Usually on the upper edge of woods and often interspersed with larch or dwarf mountain pines, the shrubs transform mountain sides with their pink blooms.

Common to marshy lake sides is fluffy white cotton grass, as well as the occasional sundew.

Pasture slopes and meadows are dotted with precious specimens such as the unpretentious triangular-headed black vanilla orchid, which smells like cocoa, wine-red martagon lilies, purple orchids and columbines.

Avid mushroomers comb the woods, especially after rain. Unless you are familiar with the culinary end-results of the dubious-looking fungus types, and equipped with the necessary permit and wicker basket (to let the spores drop back to the ground), you won't even be slightly tempted (nb. "commestibile" means edible, "velenoso" is poisonous). It's advisable to try them in the refuges or valley restaurants, prepared by experts (ask for "funghi").

*Yellow alpine
pasque flower*

Wild fruits, however, are plentiful in late summer. Raspberries, tiny wild strawberries and bilberries are the most common.

Rodents and burrow dwellers, the delightful marmots are plentiful and easy to spot with a little practice. The adults, on the lookout for their main enemies, the eagle or fox, have a shrill whistle which helps locate them. On similar terrain but with a preference for higher, seemingly inaccessible rocky outcrops is the shy, acrobatic chamois, a type of mountain goat. Its short horns and white patches on face and rear distinguish it from the heavier ibex, which has long ring-grooved horns. Easier to approach but rarer in general, one exceptional herd now populates Val Zebrù (Stelvio National Park) after being reintroduced there in 1967.

The thick woods of mixed conifer that cover most valley sides are home to pretty roe deer and larger red deer. Both are extremely timorous, but can occasionally be spotted in the early morning or around sunset when grazing.

Woods in late summer usually mean hordes of squirrels feeding on Arolla pine cones, along with squawking nutcrackers. This brown speckled bird, about the size of a starling, also buries the cones but often forgets where, and thus helps the spread of the tree.

19

Young marmot

Other interesting birds include woodpeckers, easier to hear drumming on tree trunks than actually see, and song birds. Birds of prey (which necessitate binoculars) include the golden eagle (symbol of the Stelvio National Park), reportedly on the increase. It is not unusual to see it in aerial territorial battles with flocks of the jet-black crow-like alpine choughs, which frequent refuges and passes for food. Not to be mistaken for an eagle (rounded tail when seen from below) is the lammergeier or bearded vulture (wedge-shaped tail), the largest bird in the Alps (with a wing span up to 3m). Reintroduced to neighbouring countries, sightings are slowly increasing, and posters request visitors to report them. There are several types of partridge and grouse. The ptarmigan is noteworthy for its white camouflage and unusual hairy "snow shoes" that prevent it from sinking as it hunts for food.

Skimming over alpine lakes in summertime are crag martins, a type of light brown swallow with a squarish tail.

Believe it or not, a fascinating inhabitant of the surface of glaciers, snow fields and moraine between 2500m and 3800m is the so-called glacier flea. Said to be amazingly agile and an active leaper, the hairy or scaly mottled brownish 1-2mm creature feeds on organic debris such as conifer pollen carried up and deposited there by the wind. When present in large numbers it gives the appearance of a widespread dark stain.

20

A brief note on snakes: the occasional dry grassy mountain side, especially where buildings have been abandoned, may mean an encounter with a poisonous viper. As a rule they do not attack people, and will slither quickly away if surprised sunning themselves on the path. *Do* give them time to escape though. If walking through an overgrown zone a good rule is to keep your legs covered and walk heavily. Familiarise yourself with their appearance from the clear wildlife posters in refuges and villages. Greyish brown, they have a darker zigzag pattern down their backs. Opinions on treatment of snake bite vary enormously. A serum is currently available from most chemists, but it requires refrigerator storage so is not suitable for rucksack transport. Extensive bandaging and immobilisation of the affected limb are the most widely accepted at present, though some suggest a small hand-operated suction device for venom removal.

Ibex

Vinschgau

INTRODUCTION

This section covers the northern side of the Vinschgau valley and a northwestern zone, whereas the southern part belongs to the Stelvio National Park, described in the second section.

Once part of Raetia, an Alpine province of ancient Rome, the Vinschgau had its own road that connected further south with the Via Claudia Augusta. Running west from Meran, nowadays the wide valley, seat of the Etsch river, is a continuous orchard watered by full-time sprinkler systems. The water supply has always been of primary concern here. On record as early as the 13th century, ingenious wood and rock channels, "Waale", were constructed by local people to carry water from glaciers in the upper reaches to where it was needed for crops, lower down. The name comes from the Latin "aquale" which means jug (presumably the idea was a water container). A keeper was paid to ensure an unimpeded flow and fair distribution, and a path, "Waalweg", built alongside the channel for this purpose. The final stage of Walk 6 follows one that has been maintained in good condition, but there are plenty more to discover.

Directly northwest of Meran stands the horseshoe-shaped Texel Group and butterfly-like Nature Park, instituted in 1976 and bordered in the north by Austria's Ötztaler Alps. (The Park's Information Office at Naturns, tel:0473/88201, has a useful English brochure.) The name Texel came from the German "Dachs", used for both badger and the hoe-like tool used for opening up their setts. The dark mountain sides are not particularly inviting, however the long ascents are worth the effort for the amazing variety of landscapes. Included are some delightful lakes which formed in glacial cirques obstructed by moraine. They are witnesses to previous glacial activity, now reduced to a handful of hanging glacier pockets.

A 100km walking circuit, the Meraner Höhenweg (waymarking n.24) effects a complete circuit of the Park in 5 days, with accommodation mostly in farms and small guesthouses. Though not described here, it can easily be followed with a map.

Branching northwest off Vinschgau is the Schnalstal running

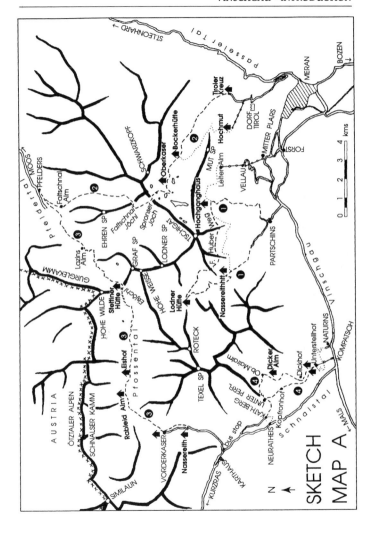

SKETCH MAP A

along the southwest edge of the Texel Park, its arid flanks enlivened by ancient large dark timber farmhouses known as "hof". At the end of its road is Kurzras, a small ski resort (year-round glacier skiing at 3000m) with incongruous and pricey hotel-apartment complexes which sprang up in the 1970s in conjunction with the cable car.

Back in Vinschgau, continuing west, are some elegant castles and Romanesque churches. A veritable jewel in the upper valley is the tiny walled medieval town of Glurns, with its own Hamlin-like rat story but without the gruesome ending. Nearby is Mals with an unusual collection of towers. The valley heads decisively north from here to the nearby border with Austria, while to the west is the Sesvenna Group, shared with east Switzerland.

As far as the geological make-up of this Vinschgau area goes, it began as sedimentary deposits from as far back as Precambrian times (the period immediately following the consolidation of the Earth's crust). Much later on, during the upheavals that led to the formation of the Alps, they underwent metamorphism. Successively intrusions of magma caused further transformations. Today, then, the area's main ingredients are metamorphic, dominated by gneiss and mica-schist in sparking sheets. There are also fascinating examples of dazzling white marble banding, as in Lodner Spitze, not to mention the multicoloured rock layers long forced into harmonious folds.

WALK 1 (see sketch map A, p.23)
TEXEL GROUP - Franz Huber Weg

---

via Partschins - Hochganghaus (3h30mins) - Franz Huber Weg - Lodnerhütte (4h) - Nassereith Hütte (2h) - Partschins (2h)
Total walking time: 11h30mins - 2-3 days suggested
MAPS: TABACCO No.011 scale 1:25,000 or No.5 scale 1:50,000

This walk is more suitable for early summer or autumn as it starts at a low valley location (631m) and the initial ascent can be unbearably hot on a muggy summer's day. However you can still expect to find some snow on sheltered stretches in July.

Note that Stage Two (the Franz Huber Weg) is a long traverse on

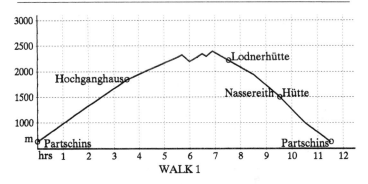

WALK 1

a particularly narrow, cliff-hugging path with extended exposed stretches, aided when necessary. Even though it is not strictly categorised as a climbing route, it should not be attempted in bad or unsettled weather by beginners or anyone without a good head for heights. As well as its wide-ranging views, the beauty of the Franz Huber Weg (named after an early president of the South Tyrol Alpine Club) is that it provides convenient access to the Lodnerhütte, and consequently the possibility of doing an excellent round trip with a return to Partschins. A well-trodden alternative is, however, given following Stage Two.

ACCESS: the starting point, the village of Partschins (631m), lies in the easternmost part of Vinschgau. It is only 7km from the sedate township and spa resort of Meran, which is connected by frequent trains with the city of Bozen SE. From Meran there is a local bus run (leaving from the railway station) west via the suburb of Forst and its famous brewery, to Partschins. The bus stop is just uphill from the main car park in the lower part of the village.

Stage One: to Hochganghaus (3h30mins)

From the bus stop, walk straight on uphill and follow signposting for the Niedermair guesthouse. You'll soon come to a shrine with a madonna, crowned with red roses in summer. Turn right out of the built-up area and follow the black sign for a "Waalweg" (a path following an ancient man-made irrigation channel). Some 10mins along the narrow road among laden grape vines is a turn-off left for

25

Hochganghaus. Path n.7a starts its climb gradually through a light wood of hazel and chestnut. 10mins on, the "Waalweg" turns off left at a small cascade, and 7a continues upwards with clear and fairly frequent red and white waymarking (marked AVS). There is a stretch in common with a white gravel vehicle access track for the mountainside farms. After 1h total walking, the path becomes n.7 and turns up left to climb for some 20-30 steep mins through scrubby undergrowth and wood. The path may occasionally be obscured due to timber cutting work and debris, so don't go too long without checking for waymarking. The steep climb is rewarded by a good rest stop - the clearing and modest buildings of Oberhaus (1163m), with views SE to Meran, the Etsch river and further to the Dolomites.

After passing a small shrine and ruins of a building left of the Oberhaus, the path goes straight up into a cool tall pine forest, over a narrow gushing stream, then into the official Nature Park area (notice-board). 50mins or so later is the first of three path junctions - stick to n.7 going unerringly straight up, under the refuge's overhead cableway line. There is a final clearing before you arrive at the refuge, and ringing cow bells will mean you're in the vicinity. The Hochganghaus (1839m) is also called Schutzhütte (Schutz means shelter, refuge) Casa del Valico and Rif. del Valico. It is also a busy dairy farm run by a hard-working family. Food and accommodation are basic (cold water tap outside for washing) and prices reasonable. Remember to be outside for sunset on the far-off Dolomites in the SE. Uphill from the refuge are good spots for chamois watching.

Alternative access: from Mitterplars via Vellau (1h30mins-3h)
A local Meran bus line goes NW to the villages of Plars and Vellau. As well, the village of Mitterplars (400m) has a chair lift to Vellau (908m), from where a gondola car runs up to near the Leiteralm (1522m) (refreshment stop). These lifts usually operate in summer, but fringe-of-season walkers should check. Then it's 1h30mins on path n.24 west to Hochganghaus (add 1h30mins if by foot from Vellau as well). Several sites in the proximity of Leiteralm are thought to have been inhabited in prehistoric times.

Stage Two: via the Franz Huber Weg to Lodnerhütte (4h)

From the Hochganghaus looking uphill, take path n.7b left (west),

Lodnerhütte at the head of Zieltal

destination Lodnerhütte, across the meadow and into the wood. 10mins along is a path junction where the circular high-level route, the Meraner Höhenweg (path n.24), continues straight on (see alt. route following). The Franz Huber Weg (recommended for experienced walkers only) bears right in gradual ascent. 50mins of sweet wood and alpenrose later, the path climbs up out of the trees and reaches a shepherd's hut and grassy clearing, probably populated with cows. The next long section is regularly waymarked with red and white paint on rocks. It proceeds over loose rocks at first, then follows a series of corners and crests with brief ups and downs, cutting across the southern flanks of the Tschigat. The path has a firm earth base though narrow and exposed to a steep slope dropping down left.

Early summer walkers may find snow lying in the inturned valleys. Wild flowers are plentiful and could include gentians, pasque flowers, pink or purple primroses, depending on the time of year. Herds of nimble goats graze on these slopes watched over by very shy shepherds.

You're approximately half-way when you reach the signpost for a detour (which rejoins the main path later) to the top of the Sattel Spitz (20mins, for climbers). The Franz Huber Weg continues with lengths of well-anchored chain in the cliffside and several stretches of "hands-on" rock clambers. You soon climb up to a wide grassy space having rounded the point, with views up the Zieltal (or Val di Tel) across which (SW) is the peak of the same name. For a while the going (NW) is easier, but there are more ups and downs with numerous stream and rock slab crossings and the chance of late-lying snow.

Further on are two brief successive descents of rock faces (steep but not exposed) aided with metal rungs and accompanying cable - best taken one person at a time. The path is in gradual descent, and is soon joined by n.7 (from Halsl Joch). Abandoned dairy farm buildings can be seen down left in the valley as well as the path, but you won't catch sight of the refuge and its small chapel until the very last stretch. Lodnerhütte sits on a rock "island" at 2262m perched in the middle of the valley at the intersection of two torrents. The path (n.7 now) curves around and across the torrent, either over a thick bank of snow or, after it's melted, a small wooden bridge. Sheep and cascades and torrents all around punctuate the otherwise desolate and rather featureless landscape here, and a flourishing marmot colony keeps up a chorus of cries on the hillside SW of the hut. This pleasant and well-run refuge dating back to 1891 is named after the Lodner, the 3224m mountain flanking the valley to the NE, though it is better viewed from the Spronserjoch pass (see Walk 2, Stage Two) for its beautiful SE aspect.

Alternative to Nassereith Hütte (2h30mins)
This is a more straightforward lower traverse from the Hochganghaus and is suitable for inexperienced walkers or in uncertain weather. The only disadvantage is that it comes out at the Nassereith Hütte at 1523m which means a further 700m (ar.d 2h30mins) in ascent to reach the Lodnerhütte - and the same return route in descent.

Leave the refuge as explained above at the start of Stage Two, and continue on path n.24 (known as the Meraner Höhenweg and the AVS Jugendweg). It goes via a couple of dairy farms and has only slight ups and downs, apart from the final descent to cross the torrent to the refuge and farm at 1523m.

Kesselsee just before Spronserjoch
Stettiner Hütte from Eisjöchl

Katharinaberg, Schnalstal
Bilstöckeljoch looking south-west

Stage Three: descent via Nassereith Hütte (2h) to Partschins (2h)

This stage consists of a long 1600m descent but involves no technical difficulties. It could easily take up the best part of a leisurely day as it follows the delightful Ziel Tal, once known aptly as the Katrauntal, "valley of waterfalls".

Path n.8 goes straight down from the refuge building to cross a feeder stream and descends on the right-hand side of the main valley for the first stretch, and past a couple of abandoned farms. There are endless carpets of alpenrose wherever you look (best in July) as well as Dolomite views again SE. Stretches of the path are paved.

A good 1h down from the refuge after a solitary hut (1944m) is an easy aided part, followed by a climb around the crest (right) leaving the upper valley. There's a lovely waterfall soon and it's mostly grassy slopes and low bushy undergrowth the rest of the winding way down to the dairy farm and refuge Nassereith Hütte (1523m). Like many other farms in this lower part of the Vinschgau valley, it has its own private cable car and, among other things, uses it for transporting livestock.

(If your knees have had it by now, make your way east from here to Maso Steiner at 1442m, where they'll probably let you ride down in their cable car, cutting about 400m off the descent. It arrives slightly uphill of the Wasserfall guesthouse.)

Follow the signposting (next to the pigsty) for the Wasserfall and Birkenwald guesthouses. Go through the gate and straight down the valley into the thick wood (still on path n.8), with the torrent, swollen in early summer, crashing away hidden by trees. Turn left off n.8 at the next signposted path junction and across the newly timbered bridge. A bitumened road is soon crossed - keep straight down on a walled-in path then stone steps. Overhead is a network of cables from the higher farms' goods cable cars. After approx. 1h from the refuge, you come out at the Wasserfall guesthouse at about 1000m. A road starts here, but the path cuts straight through the damp wood to a good (though deafening) viewing spot for the Partschins waterfall with its 98m drop into huge potholes. The next landmark is the Birkenwald guesthouse and parking area. Another 45mins or so via the road and various short-cuts will see you back at the hospitable village of Partschins.

It boasts several lovely (and reasonably priced) guesthouses for a well-earned rest. Curiously enough it was also the home of the inventor of the typewriter, Peter Mitterhofer. As well as his grave, there is a stone typewriter memorial on the other side of the church.

(This stage takes some 5h in the opposite direction.)

HOCHGANGHAUS/RIF. DEL VALICO tel:0473/43310. Private, sleeps 30 (1/5-1/11)
LODNERHÜTTE/RIF. CIMA FIAMMANTE tel:0473/967367. CAI, sleeps 43 (25/6-30/9)
NASSEREITH HÜTTE/RIF. NASSERETO tel:0473/968222. Private, sleeps 15 (1/5-1/11)
TOURIST OFFICE ALGUND tel:0473/48600
TOURIST OFFICE MERAN tel:0473/35223
TOURIST OFFICE PARTSCHINS tel:0473/97157

WALK 2 (see sketch map A, p.23)
TEXEL GROUP - The Ancient Way of the Dead

via (Dorf Tirol) Tiroler Kreuz - Bockerhütte (3h15mins) - Oberkaser (1h15mins) - Spronserjoch (1h15mins) - Faltschnaljöchl (30mins) - Pfelders (2h)
Total walking time: 8h15mins - 2 days suggested
MAPS: TABACCO No.011 scale 1:25,000 (except very last stretch) or No.5 scale 1:50,000

This easy walk crosses some fascinating landscapes in the heart of the Texel Nature Park and features sparkling mica-flaked terrain and dazzling marble intrusions. It passes a series of delightful lakes in cirques. As local grazing rights were not revoked when the Nature Park was instituted, you share paths and slopes with cows, sheep, goats and their shepherds as well as wild marmots. The route is said to have been in use since ancient times. According to local folklore, the villagers of Pfelders in the northernmost valley used to set out every spring, snow permitting, on the long crossing to Dorf Tirol (in the south). They had no priest and so would carry all the newborn babies for christening at the parish church of St Peters, as well as the

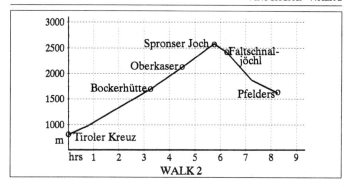

Spronser Joch
Faltschnal-jöchl
Oberkaser
Bockerhütte
Pfelders
Tiroler Kreuz
WALK 2

dead for burial. Small guiding fires were probably lit in the cup-shaped rock hollows still seen today in the area below the Pfitschjöchl (upper Spronser Tal), which is also said to have been a prehistoric site of worship.

Other curiosities are to be found at the starting point of this walk, the village of Dorf Tirol. Its famous castle (worth a visit - Mondays closed - take the "Schloßweg" path) is said to have started off as a Roman watch tower called "Teriolis" (evidently an even earlier, Illyrian word). The main castle was constructed by the Vinschgau counts in the 12th century, and gave its name to the whole Tyrol region, officially created in 1248.

Meran in fact was the capital of Tyrol until 1420 when Innsbruck took over. In the vicinity of the castle are some unusual tall "earth pillars" (Erpyramiden) like elongated mushrooms. Rain has eroded the clay columns, leaving each with a boulder perched on top.

Foodwise, as well as the assortment of tasty cereal breads known throughout the region, there's "Kaminwurzen", a sort of smoked salami, and "Speck", smoked pork.

ACCESS: from Bozen take the train NW to Meran. The year-round local bus for Dorf Tirol (5km to the north) leaves from the railway station. It is sometimes met on arrival in the small square at Dorf Tirol by a smaller bus which continues up past the cable car station to the Tiroler Kreuz guesthouse. Parking is very limited and car owners would be better off parking down in the main village area to lessen congestion here.

At Pfelders at the end of the walk, there is a year-round service to Moos with connections via St Leonhard in the Passeier valley for Meran.

Stage One: from Tiroler Kreuz to Bockerhütte (3h15mins)

(If you walk from the Dorf Tirol's village square (640m) up to the Tiroler Kreuz guesthouse (806m), add on 30mins.)

From here clear signposting for the Bockerhütte (n.6 for the entire itinerary) indicates the unsurfaced track (barred to unauthorised vehicles) as it enters the Park and proceeds up the left-hand side of the Spronsertal. It is tall forest at first with ferns as undergrowth, and can be muggy in summer. About 45mins up (where the access track to the Longfallhof restaurant turns off), a long slender waterfall down high dark rock walls comes into sight on the opposite side of the valley.

N.6, now a path, keeps left, and for the rest of the way up is paved with stone flags, uneven at times. At a clearing with a hut and aerial cableway for the dairy farms up-valley, the path turns up left and climbs more steeply through raspberries and ferns to a wide rock passage with a timber railing. The wood thins gradually and you start to get views back down and across SE to the Sarntaler range. The valley widens at the farm buildings of Lungfall Alm (1470m) with its sawmill and double-barrelled cableway. You follow the fence along, then the path zigzags up the next rise with the goats, eventually to emerge at the old timber huts of the Spronser Alm.

Just a little further up is the wide amphitheatre housing the hospitable private refuge and active dairy farm Bockerhütte (1700m) with its livestock. You are put up in the cosy attic dormitory supplied with continental quilts, and the reasonable charge includes breakfast (with home-made butter). As there is no electricity, dinner is candle-lit and a torch is useful elsewhere.

Alternative access via cable car and Mutkopf (2h30mins)
Take the cable car from upper Dorf Tirol to the Hochmut guesthouse (1361m) on the southern slope of the Mut Spitze which dominates Dorf Tirol. Follow path n.22 in ascent northish to a junction not far above a restaurant, Mutkopf (1684m). Turn up left (NW now) on a stretch in common with n.23 (to the Mut Spitze summit, 2294m), then take the Bockersteig (path n.22).

Keeping on a constant high level coasting up the Spronsertal it eventually comes out at the refuge. Total time is 2h30mins, but there are only brief ups and downs, compared to the 900m ascent in Stage One. This could also be used as an alternative descent to make a round trip.

Stage Two: ascent via Oberkaser (1h15mins) to Spronserjoch (1h15mins)

From the refuge go down (n.6) to cross the stream, then the path climbs up past the Unterkaser (lower dairy farm) and keeps to the right-hand side of the torrent. It now follows a wide, old winding track, recently painstakingly repaved. The path climbs up gradually in a northwesterly direction, with cascades to the left. As the conifers thin out, heather, juniper and alpenrose shrubs take over. After about 1h the path levels out and enters a lush valley. Keep right at the path junction (the Jägersteig path, left, could be used as an alternative return route to make a round trip). The first lake, Kaser Lacke, a lovely green, has fluffy cotton grass growing along its marshy edges. Set back from the shore is the Oberkaser (upper) dairy farm (2131m), good for hearty meals but only limited accommodation (authorisation pending. No phone). Drinking water here is supplied by a nearby spring, which also drives the unusual water-driven butter churn you'll see just past the buildings.

Narrower and steeper now, the path winds up next to a lovely waterfall. Surrounding hilltops are dotted with silent sentinels of heaped-up stones. There are some interesting rock formations here with shiny micas, conglomerates of pure white and grey chunks cemented together, huge artistic folds and surface coverings of grey, green and rusty lichen. At the top of the waterfall is a lookout point (Rötel Spitze south), and smooth rock slabs flank the valley, evidence of previous glacial modelling.

Above the next marshy, murky-sounding lake, Müchensee (it actually means mosquito lake) is a dry-stone dam wall and tiny hut (possible emergency shelter) leaning against a huge boulder. This is on the daisy-studded shore of steep-sided, greenish-blue Grünsee (2338m). It is fed by two of the higher lakes and separated by morainic debris from the Langsee (the largest in the group), to the SW.

Follow signposting for "Spronserjoch/Pfelders" along the right-hand side of the lake. You climb up a smooth rock slope to join the cows on their grassy panoramic ridge. The path continues virtually due north across tracts of late-lying snow and into a filled-in cirque. Left is one of the loveliest lakes, bluish Schiefer (slate) See. You follow an old wall along the lake edge then climb a brief rock face with a couple of wooden rungs. This stretch is marked as "difficult" on the maps but improvements have made it completely trouble-free. The delightful bowl-shaped Kesselsee is down left.

Two enormous cairns ahead mark the pass you're heading for, but a myriad hardy eye-catching flowers such as saxifrage in pink cushions, white and yellow glacier crowfoot, purple sticky primroses and tiny intense blue gentians will slow you down. The wide Spronserjoch pass (2581m), strangely enough, isn't named on maps despite the fact that it has been used for many generations (its suffix is said to be pre-Latin). As well as glimpses north over to the mountains (the Ötztaler Alpen) in nearby Austria, this is a good point for appreciating the graceful form of Lodner to the west and its unusual wide layered bands of marble. The Italian name "Cima Fiammante", "Flaming Peak", was translated thus from the original German name "Lodner", believed to derive from "lodern", to blaze or flame, as the rays of the setting sun are captured by the ice and seem to set alight the peak. The line-up continues towards north with the triangular peak of its light-coloured twin Hohe Weiße, the (lower) Graf Spitze, then the imposing darker reddish Hohe Wilde. NNW on a prominent ridge at the foot of a glacier, you can make out the shape of the Zwickauerhütte.

Stage Three: descent via Faltschnaljöchl (30mins) to Pfelders (2h)

Clear waymarkings (n.6 and painted arrow for "Plan") point you right in an easy gradual descent (N) with the Lazins valley opening up below (path n.42 - turn-off 5mins down - is a longer alternative descent to Pfelders). You cross rock surfaces pitted with intrusions of white marble which look deceptively like snow patches, and glittering slopes with flaky surface scales of mica, to the grassy saddle of Faltschnaljöchl (2417m).

The Faltschnal valley is over the ridge north, and descends below the steep eastern flank of the Ehren Spitze. 15mins down to a prominent boulder you cross to the right-hand side of the torrent. The path is earth at first through unspoilt pasture land with thistles and bell flowers. From the pass it's 1h30mins to a bench and path junction (left to Ehrensee and Lazins) as you enter the main Pfelderer Tal valley. The path curves right and widens into a dirt track to the Faltschnal Alm dairy farm (1871m) just around the bend. Turn down left ("Pfelders") over stepping stones through a lovely larch wood with ferns and alpenrose. It crosses a rough road and 25mins down reaches the valley floor. Turn right for the final 5mins to the peaceful village of Pfelders (1628m) with guesthouses, tiny Tyrolean church, shop and bus stop.

Total walking time 5h from Bockerhütte. If done in the opposite direction, allow more time as the initial ascent is longer.

BOCKERHÜTTE/RIF. DEI BECCHI tel:0473/945544. Private, sleeps 30 (30/4-31/10)
GASTHOF HOCHMUT (DORF TIROL) tel:0473/93578
GASTHOF TIROLER KREUZ (DORF TIROL) tel:0473/93304
TOURIST OFFICE DORF TIROL tel:0473/93314
TOURIST OFFICE MOOS tel:0473/643558

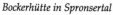

Bockerhütte in Spronsertal

WALK 3 (see sketch map A, p.23)
TEXEL GROUP - An Icy Pass

---

via Pfelders - Lazins Alm (1h) - Stettinerhütte (3h) - Eisjöchl (10mins) - Eishof (2h) - Vorderkaser (1h10mins) - bus stop in Schnalstal (1h10mins)
Total walking time: 8h30mins - 2 days suggested
MAPS: TABACCO No.04 scale 1:25,000 (except the very start), No.5 scale 1:50,000 (except the last stretch), or KOMPASS No.043 scale 1:35,000

This interesting itinerary consists of another long but easy traverse through the Texel Nature Park. The ancient route once used to connect two valleys runs just south of and parallel to the Austrian border. The paths were "rebuilt" as mule-tracks in an army exercise in the late 1920s, and are popular with intrepid mountain bikers nowadays. The Meraner Höhenweg also goes the same way. The highest point, Eisjöchl at 2895m, may live up to its name, so expect ice and snow cover, particularly on the eastern side, well into the summer.

ACCESS: Pfelders can be reached by year-round bus from Meran via St Leonhard and Moos in the Passeier Tal valley. The finishing point below Karthaus in Schnalstal is served by a bus line which runs SE down to Vinschgau (Hotel Schnalstal bus stop) and hence east to

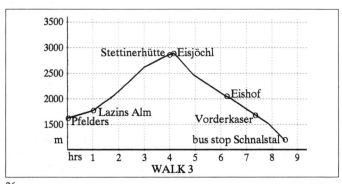

Meran. Whereas up-valley from Karthaus the line terminates at Kurzras.

Stage One: via Lazins Alm (1h) to Stettinerhütte (3h)

Head SW out of Pfelders (1628m) on the wide dirt track (n.8) on the left-hand side of the valley above the village. It's a stroll through larch wood with alpenrose, bilberries and delicate bearded bellflowers. After 20mins a wooden bridge crosses a raging torrent with deep pools flanked by enormous inclined slabs of slate. Your attention is drawn far ahead to the right-hand side of the valley, to the unusual contrasting dark rock and light marble banding in the Hohe Wilde peak and the Gurgle crest.

It's another 20mins to the footbridge detour for the picturesque, isolated hamlet of Lazins (1772m), featuring a minuscule whitewashed chapel, bee hives, and old dark timber houses with bright flower boxes. A sign announces it as a "Jausenstation", meaning possible meals and refreshments.

The valley widens and cows and horses graze on an ancient rockslide cone strewn with enormous boulders. A short climb takes you up to Lazins Alm farm (1880m, meals only).

Briefly above it is a path junction - n.42 turns south up the Lazinstal to the Spronserjoch. Continue up the regular zigzags and stone reinforcing of the ex-military track, only trodden by goats and walkers these days. The terrain is stone-embedded grass with plenty of laden bilberry shrubs. 300m and 50mins up is a cairn and path junction (turn-off left for Milchseescharte) - the depression of the Spronserjoch with its glittering mica surrounds can be clearly seen SE.

N.8/24 bears right and climbs to a wide rock and earth ledge. Minor rock falls and crumbly tracts have necessitated several path detours. Flora includes splendid white and pink saxifrage and alpine mouse-ear. You will also notice rocks with small rusty-looking bumps - on closer inspection they turn out to be brownish-red embedded garnets (specimens up to 6cm in diameter are said to be found on the northernmost reaches of the Gurglekamm crest). Higher up you enter a curious white "corridor" of marble, bordered by patchy grass where sheep graze. The smoothed surfaces with downward grooves were the result of ancient glacier movement. The path climbs gradually in wide curves up to a ruined hut (2571m) and the wooden pylons for the refuge's cableway are on your left. Soon, at the foot of the Graf Spitze and its hanging glacier, there's an immense boggy amphitheatre with enormous scattered blocks of dark rock. The stark and desolate surrounds are brightened by the purple and orange flowers of alpine toadflax.

Keep left at the signposted path junction (right is the narrow exposed path to the Zwickauerhütte). With just under 1h to go, the refuge is soon visible ahead. Gliding birds of prey are often sighted in the vicinity.

The Stettiner Hütte, alias Eisjöchl Hütte and Rif. Petrarca all'Altissima (2875m), was built in 1897 by the German Alpine Club, then transferred after the First World War to its Italian counterpart - the Padua branch decided to rename it after the poet Petrarch. The original run-down building has recently been supplemented by a new, much needed two-storey section. The setting, beneath the 3480m Hohe Wilde (or Altissima in Italian, N), is magnificent.

Stage Two: via Eisjöchl (10mins) and descent to Eishof (2h)

Follow the clear track south on a level above a small lake. The short tunnel ahead (now obstructed) was excavated by alpine soldiers in 1927. Keep left and up to the great panorama that awaits you at the 2895m saddle Eisjöchl. The Pfossental now runs down due west. The new sights, SE include: in the foreground Schnalsberg, Graf Spitze behind it, then sheer-sided Hohe Weiße, and Lodner further south. A dark ridge runs SW to Roteck and Texel Spitze, whereas west, behind a ridge of ice, is the point of the Similaun.

Once you leave the pass on rocky path n.39/24, there is the astounding sight (to the south) of the near-vertical rock sections of the Kleine Weiße. It seems a play of light and shade at first, but the effect is due to the structure and composition of the mountain - recrystallised limestone (marble) interposed with dark, fragile schist.

It's 45mins down to a junction (n.8 branches left to a difficult passage via Johannes Scharte to Lodner Hütte). You keep on the right-hand side of this wide valley and cross numerous side streams with cascades. There are pasture slopes with marmots, crickets and thistles, then juniper shrubs, alpenrose and purple monk's hood flowers, before the first occasional trees appear - reddish squat Arolla

In upper Pfossental with Hohe Weiße and Kleine Weiße

pines and feathery larches. After a shed in thin wood is an enclosed grazing area with horses (the sign says "Please don't feed the horses because they bite. Thank You"), then the modern and pleasant Eishof farm-cum-guesthouse (2071m). The site is known to have been inhabited year-round until the end of the 1800s (evidently a record for the Eastern Alps). It has a good restaurant and modest attic sleeping arrangements, not in great demand due to the relative proximity of hotels in the Schnalstal. As at other farms further down the valley, electricity is generated by a water turbine.

It's a good place for watching wildlife. There are playful wagtails in the meadows, and south across the valley the flanks of the Texel Spitze (3317m) are reportedly frequented by sizeable herds of roe deer, chamois and ibex.

Stage Three: via Vorderkaser (1h10mins) to bus stop in Schnalstal (1h10mins)

The track, for farm vehicles, is wider now through meadows, larch wood and cow gates in gentle descent. A wide landslide and avalanche area littered with boulders and fallen larches is crossed, then the

Pfossental opens up into pasture again. After 20mins you reach the Rableid Alm dairy farm (2004m), possibly dating back to prehistoric times. Barley, oats and wheat crops were grown here until recently. The buildings have been tastefully restored with some marvellous dry-stone work. Old techniques also continue to be used for cheese-making and curing hams and sausages, which are on sale. Accommodation and meals are also available.

Lower down, soon after the Mitterkaser farm (1954m) (meals) is an old wooden crucifix and depiction of a dramatic scene from 1877 when the body of a young boy, swept away by an avalanche, was miraculously recovered a month later, with the help of an angel.

There's a fresh deep-sided gorge before the final stretch out of the Nature Park area to the hamlet of Vorderkaser (1693m) and the Jäggerast guesthouse.

(From here to Pfelders in the opposite direction takes about the same time.)

Unfortunately there is no public transport here and it's another 9km down to the bus line in Schnalstal. So you can either try your luck at hitchhiking or head across the car park to the signposted path (n.24).

After a brief drop to cross the torrent, the first stretch coasts through mixed wood high above the stream before descending to a curve in the road just below the Nassereith guesthouse (30mins). From here you're obliged to proceed on the narrow asphalt for the remaining 3.5km (40mins) to the main Schnalstal road. You come out at the bus stop 1.5km below the intersection for Karthaus (1327m), the site of an ancient Carthusian monastery.

EISHOF. Private, sleeps 26 (1/6-31/10)
JÄGERRAST GUESTHOUSE (VORDERKASER) tel:0473/89230. Private, sleeps 14 (Easter-31/10)
NASSEREITH GUESTHOUSE tel:0473/89233
RABLEID ALM C/O Naturns tel:0473/87229. Private, sleeps 20 (15/5-31/10)
STETTINERHÜTTE/RIF. PETRARCA ALL'ALTISSIMA. CAI, sleeps 80 (30/6-30/9)
TOURIST OFFICE MOOS tel:0473/643558
TOURIST OFFICE KARTHAUS tel:0473/89148

WALK 4 (see sketch map A, p.23)
SCHNALSTAL - Traditional Farm Life

---

via (Kompatsch) Unterstellhof - Dickhof (1h15mins) - Dicker Alm (1h15mins) - Obere Mairalm (25mins) - Unter Perfl (1h15mins) - detour to Katharinaberg (1h return) - Kopfronhof (30mins) - Unterstellhof (1h)
Total walking time: 6h40mins - 1-2 days suggested
MAP: TABACCO No.04 scale 1:25,000

A glimpse into traditional pastoral life at high altitudes. A life-style that seems unaltered by the passage of time. A curious combination of genuine hospitality and reserve in taciturn farm dwellers who want to keep their culture intact and resent outside influences.

A couple of farms provide accommodation (at modest prices). Guests are welcome from Easter through to October. Others display a "Jausenstation" sign meaning they serve drinks and/or meals. Try "Graukäse" (literally grey cheese), a rather lumpy, strong type often served seasoned with oil, vinegar, salt and pepper, and accompanied by raw sliced onions. "Knödel", light dumplings made of bread flavoured with bacon, are a common mainstay.

Note that "hof" refers to a permanent farm, whereas "alm" is a hut or zone for summer pasture only.

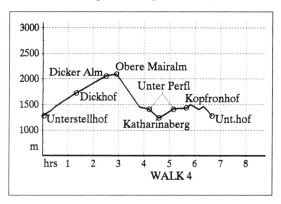

This walk is suitable for all the family, and several variants are possible. One convenient alternative entrance/exit, particularly for car users, is the village of Katharinaberg some 9km into Schnalstal. This cuts out the Kompatsch-Unterstellhof cable car.

Midsummer is not the ideal time as the weather can get very hot and muggy with haze which spoils visibility.

Before starting out: nearby Naturns is worth a quick stopover for its well-stocked shops - don't leave without at least a slice of Mohnstrudel (poppy seed pastry). The more spiritually inclined can visit the church of St Prokulus decorated with 8th century frescos, but said to have been built by a local giant.

ACCESS: Kompatsch is one bus stop (1.5km) west of Naturns in Vinschgau (13km by bus from Meran railway station in the east). The actual starting point, Unterstellhof farm (1282m), can be reached from Kompatsch (581m) by way of a private cable car (year-round), just off the main road and near the power station (limited car parking). It's unmanned, but a sign in German suggests you call the uphill station on the old-style phone when you want to leave. You pay (a very reasonable charge) on arrival, 700m later, at Unterstellhof.

Katharinaberg is a branch on the Schnalstal line, but only infrequent buses venture up there.

(Should you opt to walk as far as Unterstellhof, take path n.10 starting out from the top northwestern corner of Naturns. It climbs an escarpment on Sonnenberg, a south-facing flank, suffocatingly hot in summer, as well as monotonous. 2h30mins should do, and some 1h40mins in descent.)

Stage One: from Unterstellhof via Dickhof (1h15mins) to Dicker Alm (1h15mins)

The motto of sun-drenched Unterstellhof (meals only) is "Sonne ist Leben" (sun is life), and it has sweeping outlooks over Vinschgau. Wanderweg (path) n.10 ascends to cut over a dirt road several times and 20mins will see you at the hospitable modern guesthouse-cum-farm Patleidhof (1386m). N.10 resumes its climb to nearby Linthof (1464m, accommodation), an important point of passage for the Meraner Höhenweg (n.24). After a brief stretch in common, west, n.10 heads off up right, along a south-facing flank characterised by dry rocky terrain with scrubby cricket-infested vegetation and light wood. 45mins later (from Linthof) and you're at the sprawling buildings of Dickhof (1709m), the name apparently a reference to thick woods in the vicinity. Inhabitants of this permanent farm include squawking peacocks. Drinking water is available indoors, while meals and refreshments are served at scenic benches in the shade of an enormous crucifix.

Up past the barn, Schnalstal opens up with snowcapped Weißkugel at the end (NW), and the Ötztaler Alps spreading out north. Turn right on the uphill variant of n.10 for Dicker Alm. In conjunction with the new direction, the vegetation changes noticeably - these lush, shaded, west-oriented flanks are covered with larch trees and rich pasture. The path is steep at times but in good condition. Dicker Alm is an old, small-scale summer farm, busy with cows and goats, and has the ubiquitous mechanised cableway like its umbilical cord to the valley. It occupies a well-chosen open position at 2060m. More expansive now, the views take in nearby dark crests north belonging to the Texel Spitze, beyond which, NW, are the glistening glaciers of the Similaun and surrounding peaks, then triangular icy Hasenöhrl (Hare's Ear) SSW on the other side of Vinschgau.

Splendid specimens of edelweiss bloom in the rock garden by the outdoors eating area where modest meals are served accompanied by mountains of home-churned butter. This traditional family farm, the summer branch of Dickhof, offers basic accommodation (no electricity).

Stage Two: via Obere Mairalm (25mins) and descent to Unter Perfl (1h15mins)

Woodpeckers and nutcrackers screech off through the larch trees on your approach north (n.10) to picturesque Moar Alm (2095m) (panoramic refreshments), called Obere Mairalm or Maralm on maps, and believed to date back to the 15th century. The mountain sides are alive with clanging cows.

N.10 descends to abandoned barns, then zigzags through woods again to a stream crossing (raspberries and stinging nettles). Soon around to the right, after a fork, is a rocky balcony path with a wooden handrail and this ultimately leads to exemplary traditional farms at Unter Perfl (1417m), where a surfaced road terminates (just outside the Texel Nature Park). Don't neglect to peek inside the tiny whitewashed chapel (near the intersection with n.24) for its exquisitely decorated interior.

Detour to Katharinaberg (1h return)
Literally fenced in, you proceed NW in common with n.24, but keep left on lower branches at path junctions. The route is wooded and there are wild cherries and rowans. Lower meadows are the scene of traditional wheat harvesting and haymaking in late summer. 25mins later, Katharinaberg (1245m) stands on a dominating spur overlooking Schnalstal, but apart from an alternative entrance/exit point, it only offers a modernised church, upmarket guesthouses and a shop. Transport-wise, should your arrival not coincide with a bus, via a signposted path (n.32) you can reach Neuratheis (960m) on the main valley road (more buses) in a further 30mins.

(In ascent from Katharinaberg to Unter Perfl allow 35mins.)

Stage Three: via Kopfronhof (30mins) to Unterstellhof (1h)

From the junction at Unter Perfl, the next section is in common with n.24. It first drops to cross a stream, then heads south, with plenty of ups and downs. You pass a series of farms, every other one displaying the "Jausenstation" invitation, though whether or not you'll find anyone to serve you anything will depend on the demands of farm work. One of the larger establishments is Kopfronhof (1436m), some 30mins along. Soon afterwards you pass an interesting hamlet (Waldhof), complete with its own chapel. Enormous rotating sprinklers water the surrounding meadows and unwary walkers.

Further south, from the Innerunterstell's scenic terrace, the fertile patchwork and orderly rows of apple and pear trees in Vinschgau stretch out. At the nearby fork, you part ways with n.24 and descend gradually beneath the Linthof and Patleidhof, to Unterstellhof and its cable car once more.

DICKER ALM C/O DICKHOF tel:0473/89192. Sleeps 9
LINTHOF tel:0473/87884. Sleeps 8
PATLEIDHOF tel:0473/87767. Sleeps 14
TOURIST OFFICE NATURNS tel:0473/87287
TOURIST OFFICE KARTHAUS tel:0473/89148

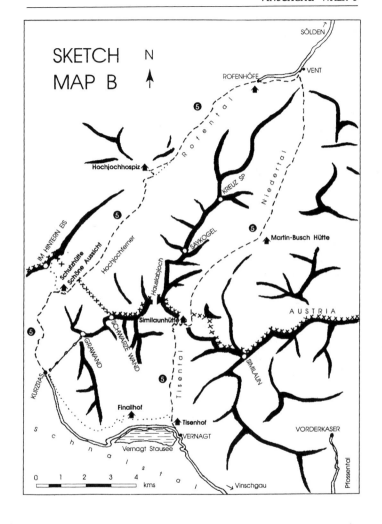

SKETCH MAP B

N ↑

SÖLDEN

VENT

ROFENHÖFE

Rofental

⑤

Niedertal

Hochjochhospiz

KREUZ SP

SAYKOGEL

Martin-Busch Hütte ⑤

IM HINTERN EIS

Schutzhütte
Schöne Aussicht

Hochjochferner

Hauslabjoch

⑤

Similaunhütte

Tisental

⑤

SCHWARZE WAND

GRAWAND

AUSTRIA

KURZRAS

⑤

SIMILAUN

Finailhof

Tisenhof

VORDERKASER

Schnalstal

Vernagt Stausee

VERNAGT

0 1 2 3 4 kms

Vinschgau

Pfossental

WALK 5 (see sketch map B, p.45)
ÖTZTALER ALPS - An Age-Old Stock Route and the Iceman

---

via Kurzras - Schutzhütte Schöne Aussicht (2h15mins) - Hochjochhospiz (2h) - Vent (2h) - Martin-Busch-Hütte (2h30mins) - Similaunhütte (2h) - Tisenhof (2h) - Vernagt (15mins)
Total walking time: 13h - 2-3 days suggested
MAPS: TABACCO No.04 scale 1:25,000 (except middle section) or KOMPASS No.52 scale 1:50,000

The people of Schnalstal are on record as having settled Vent, to their north, back in the 14th century. Contacts were regular, and in fact there are legends about local people perishing in snow storms during the crossing (though the deaths were attributed to dwarves, said to inhabit the high icy reaches). Even though Vent became an Austrian dominion in the 1800s, the former colonisers have retained grazing rights in the two communicating valleys. Every year without fail in mid-June processions of up to 3000 sheep are shepherded out of Kurzras and Vernagt and across a high-altitude international snow and ice border to rich summer pasture, with the return trip mid-September. (The Schnalstal Tourist Authority includes the relevant dates in its annual calendar of tourist events.) Interestingly enough, the valley's name comes from the Latin "Cascinales", alpine farm buildings.

This itinerary follows in the tracks of the sheep. It proceeds over north to the Austrian village of Vent, then returns to Italy via a beautiful valley and problem-free, short, almost level tract of glacier (Niederjochferner). In the vicinity is the site (near the Hauslabjoch) where the mummified body of a Stone Age hunter-herdsman was discovered in 1991 with some fascinating artefacts. "Homo Tyrolensis", carbon dated as 5300 years old, is the subject of study at Innsbruck, but will when research is complete be back in South Tyrol and hopefully on display. As he was trapped in ice, scientists think he may have been caught out by adverse weather, and later, as the climate became colder, covered by a pocket of a growing glacier.

As a whole this is not a difficult walk, and the paths are good. The

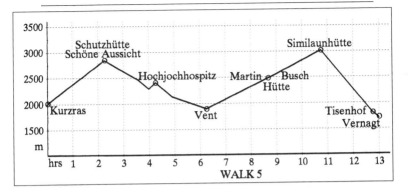

WALK 5

short stretch of glacier crossed in Stage Three is both well-trodden and problem-free under normal weather conditions (gaiters are optional). Apart from the high elevation involved, Stage One is suitable as a return family day trip. Stage Four too but the ascent is somewhat monotonous and the top stretch narrow and steep.

NB. For payments on the Austrian side, schillings are preferred (banks at Kurzras and Vent).

ACCESS: Kurzras is the end point (39km) of the year-round bus line which, from Meran via Vinschgau, services Schnalstal. Vernagt, the exit point, is some 7.5km down the valley.

As an alternative entry or exit point, the Austrian village of Vent can be reached by bus from Sölden in the NE (connections to Innsbruck and beyond).

Stage One: ascent to Schutzhütte Schöne Aussicht (2h15mins)

From Kurzras (2011m) and the bus stop at the cable car departure station (shops nearby), the walk heads uphill past the (very helpful) Tourist Information Office and tennis courts, to signposting for the refuge, north. Path n.3 is wide and well-trodden and swings up to a large grassy bowl, having left behind the lone larch trees. It plods upwards on rather uninteresting scree, past the turn-off left (at about 2700m) for the Weißkugel (west). A final curve around right leads up to the saddle and Schutzhütte Schöne Aussicht (Rif. Bellavista, 2842m), old-style but comfortable (hot showers included). Chilly winds blow

47

Bridge crossing near Hochjochhospiz

off the nearby Hochjochferner glacier. Grawand (SSE) emerges from the ice with the cable car, while SW are the twin peaks Lagaun Spitze (left) and Saldur Spitze (right), and WSW is Schwemser Spitze.

(For views of the Weißkugel (west) and vast icescapes, experienced walkers can take the path NW from the refuge for the Im Hintern Eis summit (3269m). A total of 2h30mins return time means 1h30mins in ascent with faint waymarking and only the occasional guiding cairn. Reportedly rough going.)

Stage Two: descent via Hochjochhospiz (2h) to Vent (2h)

N.3 leaves the refuge NE across a desolate landscape, mostly smooth grey-brown surfaces with a glint of mica and streaked fiery red. Keeping high on the left-hand side of the valley, over many side streams, it descends gradually alongside the breathtaking expanse of the Hochjochferner. 15mins will see you at the official Austrian border, but the guard's hut is rarely occupied, so you easily "slip over".

You'll see Schnalstal sheep enjoying their free meals as the valley narrows and greens - the only vegetation thus far having been sparse saxifrage. About 1h20mins down is the turn-off over the torrent (to Martin-Busch-Hütte via Saykogel, experts only). Around the corner the next refuge comes into view across the next valley north, a box on a bare mountain side. N.3 bears left and soon descends to a turbulent torrent crossed by a suspended rickety bridge, strung up with overhead wires and propped up from underneath with equally dubious timbers. From the nearby path junction it's a 15mins (120m) climb to the Hochjochhospiz (2412m) refuge.

(If, however, you want to detour the refuge, saving yourself the extra climb, take the right fork, signposted "Vent".)

From the peaceful refuge, which has its supplies backpacked up, cross the grassy hillsides inhabited by marmots. The path (n.902) is soon joined by the detour, and heads in a northeasterly direction down narrowing Rofental. After a low (and wet) plank bridge crossing (40mins from Hochjochhospiz) are stretches of fixed cable as the path (Titzenthalerweg) proceeds on the plunging edge of a deep gorge. This ends at a hut and cableway point, and you proceed on a dirt jeep track for 15mins to the hamlet of Rofenhöfe (2014m, guesthouses and restaurants). Turn right for the "Hängebrücke" suspension bridge over the Rofentaler Ache. On the other side of the valley is a series of benches and picnic areas, and 20mins down through the herds of horses at pasture, you meet the dirt track in ascent from Vent. (If the village doesn't interest you, you can take this track straightaway, and thus cut a good 20mins off the access time for the Martin-Busch-Hütte.)

Keep left and down to Vent (1896m). It has shops, a bank, inexpensive guesthouses and perfectly chilled beer. In the lower part of the village near the church are the Tourist Information Office and bus stop (possible alternative entry or exit point).

Stage Three: via Martin-Busch-Hütte (2h30mins) to Similaunhütte (2h)

Back up past the bridge over the Niedertal Ache and towards the ski lift, you'll find signposting for Martin-Busch-Hütte (or Haus). A jeep track (to supply the refuge) winds upwards but walkers can short-cut the initial curves by keeping straight up left. Light wood includes Arolla pines and upright dwarf mountain pines (which are more commonly prostrate). Back on the wide track, it's a slow climb along south-oriented Niedertal, goats and sheep grazing on grassy terraces. A shepherd's hut at 2230m is just over halfway. There are several ups and downs and only at the last moment do you curve right to Martin-Busch-Hütte at 2501m, also known as the Neue Samoarhütte, a neat stone building with red and white shutters. Only on high season weekends should its 150 beds be in short supply.

From here up the scenery becomes more interesting and previously glimpsed glacier landscapes now become close-ups. Uphill (SW) follow the clear pointers for the Similaunhütte (unnumbered path). A pleasant, ample pasture valley is followed, on the right of the stream. The wide floor of scattered pebbles interspersed with grass provides an ideal camouflaged nesting and feeding ground for rock partridge.

30mins up is a signpost where you go right to climb a consolidated moraine crest, well above the vast Niederjochferner. Delicate white alpine mouse-ear bloom. The path makes its way up the magnificent valley, guided by cairns and frequent waymarking. You eventually move onto moraine, then swing around left onto the uppermost tongue of snow-covered ice. In July-August, under normal conditions, it's a simple snow traverse in well-trodden tracks near to the rock face. Gaiters are especially recommended when blazing midsummer sun turns the snow to slush. You pass the unmanned Austrian-Italian border and head towards a large cairn. Some 20mins in all and you're back on rock and earth again at the Niederjoch (3016m), a real "yoke", where the old but very hospitable Similaunhütte (Rif. del Similaun) occupies a splendid setting. It is the base for snow-ice ascents to clearly visible Similaun, SE, and Finail Spitze, NW. Views even extend to the Ortler Group, SW. Magnificent pink masses of unusually large glacier crowfoot grow in the vicinity.

Stage Four: descent to Tisenhof (2h) and Vernagt (15mins)

The descent (path n.2) takes a steep valley ending in turquoise Stausee Vernagt (artificial lake) in the Texel Nature Park. The first narrow stretch cut into the rock face could be tricky with late-lying snow and ice in early summer, also slippery when wet. Weathered rock sections like upended bread knives stand on your left. You soon wind down to an earth and scree base, and interesting earth colours, red shale and dark folded rock with black and green lichen cover. The route is marked by a series of small standing stone slabs, like mini-menhirs, and goes easily down grassy terraces, the domain of marmots.

A refreshing larch wood threaded through by streams is the last leg before Tisenhof farm (1814m). Refreshments and meals (such as "Knödel" dumplings or freshly baked apple strudel) are served at the scenic outdoor tables. You can also stay in this hospitable farm, in traditional-style rooms whose tiny windows are edged with delicate lace curtains. Like the other farms, it has a poppy patch as the seeds are widely used in local dishes.

The village of Vernagt (1711m) awaits down the signposted path to the road. Further along left, at the lakeside parking area, is the bus stop.

(From Vernagt, the ascent time to Similaunhütte is 3h30mins.)

Alternative exit:
The indefatigable can complete the circuit on foot and return to Kurzras as follows: from Tisenhof take n.9 west via nearby Raffeinhof farm, then Finailhof (1952m, 45mins, accommodation), hence n.7 bearing north for Kurzras (1h30mins). It reportedly involves several exposed stretches and more ups and downs.

FINAILHOF tel:0473/89644

HOCHJOCHHOSPIZ (AUSTRIA) contact C/O VENT tel:05254/ 8108. DAV, sleeps 70 (1/6-1/10)

KURZRAS refuge-type accommodation C/O APPARTHOTEL ZIRM tel:0473/88388

MARTIN-BUSCH-HÜTTE (AUSTRIA) contact C/O Vent tel:05254/ 8130. DAV, sleeps 150 (30/6-30/9)

GASTHAUS ROFENHOF (AUSTRIA) tel:05254/8103

SCHUTZHÜTTE SCHÖNE AUSSICHT/RIF. BELLA VISTA tel:0473/ 662140. Private, sleeps 65 (20/6-10/10)

SIMILAUNHÜTTE/RIF. DEL SIMILAUN tel:0473/89711. Private, sleeps 60 (20/6-30/9)

TISENHOF (VERNAGT) tel:0473/89674. Private, sleeps 12 (1/6-31/ 10)

TOURIST OFFICE KURZRAS tel:0473/662177

TOURIST OFFICE VENT (AUSTRIA) tel:05254/8193

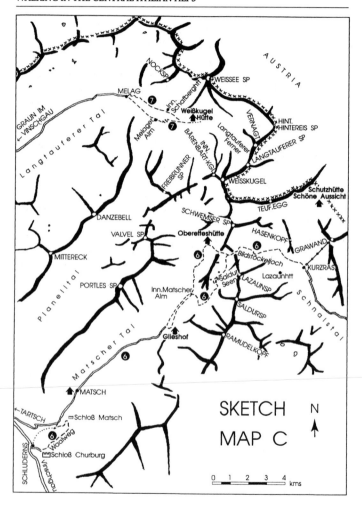

SKETCH
MAP C

N

0 1 2 3 4 kms

WALK 6 (see sketch map C, p.52)
SALDURKAMM - A Saint, a Waalweg and a Castle

---

via Kurzras - Bildstöckeljoch (3h30mins) - Oberetteshütte (1h) - Innere Matscher Alm (1h10mins) [Alt. Bildstöckeljoch via Saldurseen (1h30mins) - Innere Matscher Alm (1h20mins)] - Glieshof (30mins) - Matsch (1h30mins) - Leitenwaal - Schloß Churburg (2h) - Schluderns (10mins)
Total walking time: 9h50mins (Alt. 10h30mins) - 2-3 days suggested
MAP: KOMPASS No.52 scale 1:50,000

A solitary traverse, steep at times, to a pass presided over by St Bernard, the Apostle of the Alps and patron saint of mountaineers. A snow field, desolate lakes, a quiet farming valley and village are followed by a fascinating ancient route along an irrigation channel (Leitenwaal), all ending at a 13th century Swiss castle (Schloß Churburg). Quite an incredible kaleidoscope of landscapes and history.

Some experience is recommended for Stages One and the Alternative, long and tiring, as well as gaiters and good weather.

Instead of the complete traverse, two shorter round trips starting from the Vinschgau side are:

a) interesting, but rather long, adapt the relevant parts of Stages Two, Three and the Alternative. From Glieshof (car park), via Innere Matscher Alm, Saldurseen lakes, Oberetteshütte then Glieshof (allow 6h).

b) shorter and essentially a delightful stroll, start from Schluderns and link into the Leitenwaal-Berkwaal circuit, including the castle (about 3h, see Stage Four).

ACCESS: Kurzras is the terminal of the year-round Schnalstal bus line via Vinschgau from Meran (39km). At the end point of the walk, Schluderns in Vinschgau, regular buses can be caught east to Meran or NW to Mals.

Stage One: ascent to Bildstöckeljoch (3h30mins)

This long stage involves an ascent of almost 1100m. From the year-

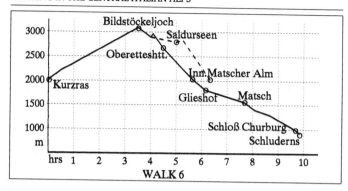

WALK 6

round ski resort of Kurzras (2011m), follow the road uphill a short way to the path junction - turn left for path n.1 and Bildstöckeljoch. Across heathered hillsides, on the right-hand side of a torrent, a good 30mins up is a crossing (turn-off for Hasenkofel). You go decidedly west (left) cutting diagonally up an alpenrose and juniper shrub slope, swarming with marmots and butterflies.

Some 20mins more, at about 2300m, is a signpost for Lazaunhütte (11a, pointing left to a bridge) but n.1 goes straight uphill on the right-hand side of the torrent. Faint red and white waymarking soon resumes and the path becomes fairly obvious, meandering its way up the Langgrubtal valley. Towards the end of the pasture (goats and cows), you veer right to zigzag up a rock outcrop. The going quickly gets much steeper, and crumbly terrain requiring sure-footedness alternates with good sections. Slippery when wet, it needs to be taken with care at all times. Alpine moon-daisies flower amongst the grey-red rocks.

At around 3000m, a small hanging glacier (Schwemser Ferner) is skirted and you head south. A steep gully, possibly snow-choked, is negotiated next, then n.1 levels out for the final stretch along a wide ledge to the Bildstöckeljoch (3097m), marked by an obvious cairn and spelt in a variety of ways on maps, sometimes with the inclusion of Matscher. The curious box on the pole houses a painting (the "Bild") of St Bernard. It comes complete with dog and "Pray for us" - useful perhaps to counterbalance Hell Pass (Höllerscharte, NNW) and Devil's Hump (Teufelsegg, on a crest NE).

Back over ENE is the Schöne Aussicht hut in its saddle to the left of Graue Wand and cable car from Kurzras. The opposite western side of Bildstöckeljoch is covered by a permanent snow field, bordered by dark crests. Even the village of Matsch is visible way down in its valley SW, and beyond it, the majestic Ortler Group. A pair of jet-black, yellow-beaked alpine choughs might drop in on you here, hoping for a titbit.

Stage Two: via Oberetteshütte (1h) to Innere Matscher Alm (1h10mins)

N.1, recently repaired on this side, is now a good path, but timing will depend on snow depth. You bear right in gradual descent over the snow field, guided by red and white paint splashes, frequent and well-placed. Some 30mins west is a path junction (at approx. 2900m). (For the downhill fork to the lakes on n.1, see the longer Alternative following.) Take n.1-4 uphill for the Oberetteshütte. There's a short climb toward a couple of cairns on a crest (2974m), with cushions of pink moss campion. The path plunges down a steep gully in tight zigzags, then turns right at the bottom, with the refuge in sight. 30mins should suffice to new AVS Oberetteshütte (2670m), which offers mod cons and a peaceful stay. Its history began in 1882 when the Prague branch of the DAV built the Karlsbaderhütte (later called Höllerhütte) on a nearby site. In the aftermath of the First World War it was transferred to the Italian Alpine Club who renamed it Rif. Diaz after a general, and it thus lasted until 1945. Views SW take in the Stilfserjoch snow fields and the Ortler peak is just visible left.

The descent route (n.1) is grassy at first as far as a terrace, then becomes monotonous loose earth and scree, with the occasional crumbled-away tract. In a total of 50mins of wide curves you reach the valley floor and hut for the refuge's cableway (about 2200m). It's a further 20mins due south now on a wide vehicle track through banks of alpenrose. Down the valley into larch wood, just past a torrent crossing, are the ruins of a farmhouse, Innere Matscher Alm (2022m), and the junction for Glieshof.

(Ascent time from here to Oberetteshütte is 2h.)

Alternative: from Bildstöckeljoch, descent via Saldurseen (1h30mins) to Innere Matscher Alm (1h20mins)

From the previously described path junction (at approx. 2900m),

30mins from Bildstöckeljoch, take n.4 (signposted "Saldurseen"). Longer, more tiring but less frequented and through more beautiful landscapes, it goes south down the desolate red debris valley towards the lakes. The background SE now is magnificent as the Lazaun Spitze, Saldur Spitze and Ramudelkopf peaks have come round into full view with their modest glaciers. Plenty of cairns and red and white paint indicate the easy descent. After an initial, mostly rock-base stretch, the path curves briefly right into a scree-filled side valley to skirt a small lake beneath the Spitzar (west). Further down is an old stone wall not far above the Saldurseen. In a setting of brown moraine, the greenish waters reflect the shrunken glacier (Nordl Saldur-Ferner). (1h from last junction.)

Having forded the lake outflow (at approx. 2800m), you are confronted with two choices for the next stretch on n.4 to Glieshof: the right variant is "schwierig!" (difficult), whereas the "normal Weg" climbs (only briefly) over a crest, then descends over grassy terrain, and is soon joined by the variant. The knee-jerking path enters a narrower valley flanked with great slabs of blue ice (Ramudler Ferner) beneath the peak of the same name (SE). Behind the Unt. Saldurkopf mount, lovely cascading streams emerge from the rocks underfoot. Up and down over old low moraine ridges, the valley floor suddenly comes into view. On the left of a cascade, keeping clear of the rapidly eroding edge, the descent proceeds NW in zigzags through alpenrose, then Arolla pines and larch. N.4 finally comes out at the ruins of Innere Matscher Alm (2022m) and rejoins the main route in descent for Glieshof.

(In ascent from here via the lakes to the 2900m junction, allow 3h.)

Stage Three: to Glieshof (30mins) and Matsch (1h30mins)

From the abandoned farm building at 2022m, either a) take the wide track the rest of the way as it's more restful for weary legs - in which case cross over to the right-hand side of the torrent where you may have to compete with tractors, or b) move onto the more pleasant and slightly longer path that continues down the left-hand side through wild roses and shady wood. Both come out at the hamlet (1807m) with the pleasant Glieshof guesthouse (accommodation best booked in advance) and parking area.

There are at least three ways to cover the 7km down to Matsch:

'Waalweg'

a) try hitchhiking in late afternoon when the car-equipped day walkers leave, b) ask the Glieshof staff to call a taxi from the village, or c) shanks's pony. The road is only asphalted for about 3km and passes through woods frequented by roe deer. Along the right-hand side of the wide green valley, you stroll through meadows being constantly watered by huge rotating sprinklers to be dodged, or the site of family haymaking in late summer. Farmhouses dot the hillsides. Some way down, from a comfortable bench beneath a crucifix, excellent views south, including the massive Ortler again, can be enjoyed. Just on the outskirts of the village is the chapel of St Florian, the patron saint, said to have changed water into wine. Matsch (1561m) also boasts a nice guesthouse, a shop (tasty local cheeses), and a summer festival (July) when the narrow road is lined with decorated beer stands and crammed with participants.

(From here the shortest exit route is by way of the road, some 6km SW to Tartsch (1029m) in Vinschgau for buses. But it would be a pity to miss the next stage.)

Stage Four: via Leitenwaal to Schloß Churburg (2h) and Schluderns (10mins)

Take the road downhill. Just over 2km (25mins) from the village, soon after a tiny church and meagre ruins of the Schloß Matsch castle atop an isolated rise to the left of the road, is a signposted fork - go left. N.18 for Schluderns is a country lane, then path through dry wood. Some 20mins down at the junction with n.17, turn left onto "Leitenwaal".

(At this point n.18 continues right with lots of bends to Schluderns. It can also be used in ascent from the valley floor - about 1h15mins - for a day trip, linking in with the following itinerary.)

Mostly on a level you follow a narrow romantic path (Waalweg) alongside the ancient Waal channel, originally constructed to supply dry valley settlements and crops with water ingeniously channelled from the glaciers. The rushing water occasionally disappears beneath protective stone slabs and wooden gratings filter out leaves and other debris that could obstruct the flow. Signs request walkers, in fact, not to throw anything into the water, tempting though it may be. There is a brief passage beneath a hillside prone to falling stones ("Steinschlag"). About 20mins on, both the path (via a bridge) and the channel (overhead piping propped on old stone pillars) cross the dramatic Saldurbach torrent. A pretty spot. There are several turn-offs, but follow signs for n.20 and Churburg, "Berkwaal" (sometimes written as Bergwaal) or Vernalhof. All sorts of traditional devices to aid and check the water flow can still be found along the way - a clapper fixed up a tree, hollowed-out log crossings, and gates and locks to deviate flow on demand.

Once you reach farm buildings in an open position overlooking Vinschgau, go down sharp right (for Schluderns). The path is soon covered by a canopy of trees, then through apple orchards turns right briefly on asphalt and around the castle walls to Schloß Churburg (999m), called Castel Coira in Italian.

The castle was built in 1260 by the bishops of Chur in Switzerland, hence the name. It served as a defensive position against the powerful Matsch counts up-valley. Interesting guided visits (end March to beg. November, closed Mondays) are usually in German and Italian, but an English version is available on request. An important collection of historic arms is included.

10mins down the road is Schluderns (921m) with lovely fountains, and bus stop down on the main road.

GASTHOF GLIESHOF tel:0473/82622. Private, sleeps 40.

KURZRAS refuge-type accommodation C/O APPARTHOTEL ZIRM tel:0473/88388

OBERETTESHÜTTE/RIF. OBERETTES tel:0473/80280. AVS, sleeps 90 (30/6-30/9)

GASTHOF WEISSKUGEL (MATSCH) tel:0473/82600

TOURIST OFFICE KURZRAS tel:0473/662177

TOURIST OFFICE MALS tel:0473/81190

TOURIST OFFICE SCHLUDERNS tel:0473/615258 seasonal

WALK 7 (see sketch map C, p.52)
LANGTAUFERERTAL - A Pope and a Glacier

via Melag - Melager Alm (25mins) - Weißkugelhütte (1h50mins) -
Innere Schafberghütte (45mins) - Melag (1h)
Total walking time: 4h - 1 day suggested
MAP: KOMPASS No.52 scale 1:50,000

In one of the northernmost corners of Italy, on the edge of Austria, the Langtauferer Tal branches off Vinschgau to run east, culminating in a barrier of ice-bound peaks. Icescapes and a graceful sweeping glacier characterise this easy day trip, popular with walkers of all ages.

ACCESS: from Mals in upper Vinschgau, a bus (except Sundays) goes north via "new" Graun, then east off the main road and 11km along Langtauferer Tal to terminate at Melag.

A curiosity: the original village of Graun was submerged in the early 1950s for hydroelectric purposes, but its solitary clock tower still emerges from the lake.

Stage One: ascent via Melager Alm (25mins) to Weißkugelhütte (1h50mins)

The road finishes at Melag (1915m) (guest-houses but no shops) and

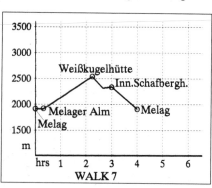

you walk through the hamlet to path n.2. As a farming track, it goes along the valley floor through meadows on the left-hand side of wide Karlinbach. 20mins along is the turn-off (right) across the torrent for an optional detour to Melager Alm, a refreshment stop (the

Uina Schlucht gorge rock passage

During ascent to Madritschjoch, view back down to Zufallhütte, backed by
Venezia Group

At Schluderscharte looking over Martelltal towards Zufrittspitze
Zufallhütte backed by glacier and the twin Cevedale peaks (right)

Weißkugelhütte in upper Langtauferertal

track rejoins the path further up). N.2 keeps left and narrows, through alpenrose and flowered banks. Further on, after a signpost, it starts climbing in wide zigzags up a grassy and stoney slope to a crucifix and first scenic point. Over a ridge, the Langtauferer Ferner comes into view, with the refuge perched on a moraine crest, left. Past the junction (with path n.3) and it's not far to old, friendly Weißkugelhütte (alias Rif. Pio XI alla Pala Bianca) at 2544m.

The refuge, constructed in 1893 by Frankfurt Alpine Club members, was later transferred to the Desio (Milan) CAI branch who extended it in 1936. They considered Weißkugelhütte a "primitive" name, so renamed the hut in honour of Pope Pio XI, a native of their town and keen mountaineer.

Weißkugel (Pala Bianca, 3739m), the highest peak in the southern Ötztaler range, is just visible with its pyramidal point SSE, behind the Innere Bärenbartkogel, from which another glacier flows down. To its left (SE) on the high barrier is Langtauferer Spitze, then the Vernagt peak further around (ESE). For a better view, continue up the high moraine ridge on the left-hand side of the glacier, going as far as you feel safe as the path becomes progressively narrower and more exposed. You look down into the crevasses formed as the body of ice is dragged down a steeper slope and loses its even surface as cracks open. Grandiose. The barren, clayey side slopes above the path are anchored by lovely cushions of livelong saxifrage. (NB. timing for the stage does not include this extension.)

Stage Two: descent via Innere Schafberghütte (45mins) to Melag (1h)

This variant is only slightly longer than the ascent route, but more panoramic as it stays higher longer. A little way back down from the refuge on n.2, after a small lake, is the fork right for n.3 - narrower but problem-free with just the odd crumbly tract where heavy rain has sent rocks and earth sliding valleywards. The Innere Schafberghütte (2340m) (shepherds' hut) is set in an idyllic green side basin fed by a stream. To its immediate north is rounded, grey-green Nockspitze, whereas NW is Weißsee Spitze, on the border with Austria.

Leave the area on the lower path 3A (not the higher one marked by a large '3'). It coasts high above the picturesque valley along a grassy hillside where the rare reddish version of the (protected) triangular-headed black vanilla orchid grows - close up it smells strongly of cocoa or vanilla. After a crucifix, the last stretch zigzags steeply down to sweet-smelling hay fields, and heads right along an old stone wall. There's a bridge and turnstile, then 5mins back to the village on the main path.

(In ascent on this variant allow 2h30mins.)

WEISSKUGELHÜTTE/RIF. PIO XI ALLA PALA BIANCA tel:0473/
    633191. CAI, sleeps 45 (1/7-30/9)
TOURIST OFFICE ST VALENTIN A. D. HAIDE tel:0473/634603

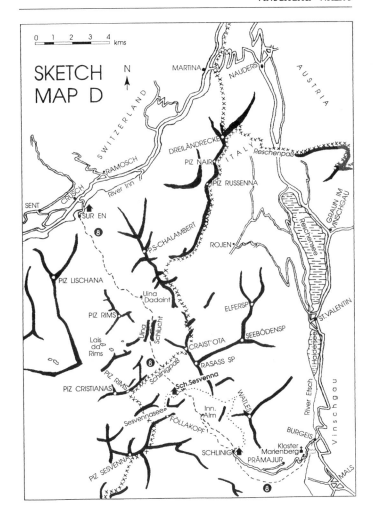

> ## WALK 8 (see sketch map D, p.63)
> ## SESVENNA GROUP - The Smugglers' Gorge

via Burgeis - Schlinig (1h45mins) - Schutzhaus Sesvenna (1h45mins) - Schlinigpaß (30mins) - Uina Schlucht (40mins) - Sur En (Switzerland) (2h20mins)
Total walking time: 7h - 2 days suggested
MAP: KOMPASS No.52 scale 1:50,000 (except for the very last stretch, but is sufficient)

The central section is an ancient smugglers' path hewn out of the sheer side of the dramatic dolomite Uina Schlucht gorge, and evidently used as late as the 1960s for cigarette contraband. Furthermore, for at least 450 years, the earlier sections of the route have been the scene of the summer "migration" of sheep from Mals and neighbouring farms. This still takes place on a night in early July, and they are herded through Schlinig and across into Swiss pasture. Should you happen to be there when the flocks and shepherds arrive, you'll find a scene akin to a country fair, with customs officers (to count the heads and exact the appropriate tax), vets and hangers-on.

The walk itself is straightforward on good, well-trodden paths. The only "delicate" point is the Uina gorge itself - in a sheltered position facing north, it is infamous for "attracting" bad weather, and may have icy passages at the start of summer or immediately following storms.

After the ascent and a visit to the Uina gorge, if you opt not to proceed all the way down to Sur En, it is feasible to do a loop via a slightly longer variant - see the Alternative return to Schlinig. It makes a worthwhile, if long, round trip from Schlinig (you can drive this far), and can just be fitted into 1 day (approx. 6h total).

ACCESS: to do the complete traverse and round trip, start walking from Burgeis in the northern arm of Vinschgau, some 3.5km beyond Mals. Buses heading for the Reschenpaß (and Austria) will drop you off on the main road just outside the village.

For the return trip, from Sur En in the Inn valley (Unter Engadin)

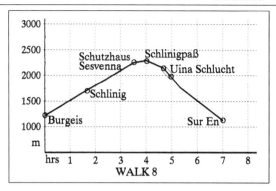

in Switzerland, take the Postauto (PTT) bus - it crosses the River Inn by way of a lovely covered bridge - to the main road 2km away at Crusch (just south of Sent). There are connections NE via Martina, where you cross into Austria via a pass to Nauders. Here the SAD (South Tyrol, Italian) company goes back south via the Reschenpaß to Vinschgau. (At the time of writing, the 3.45pm daily bus from Sur En had good through connections all the way.)

NB. on the first Swiss section, ticket payment should be in Swiss francs, then Austrian schillings are also accepted on the line to Nauders. Back to Italian lire for the final return stretch!

An interesting extra visit from Burgeis is to the vast, majestic white Benedictine Kloster Marienberg monastery and abbey, founded in the 12th century. Guided tours include the oldest part, the crypt, decorated with Romanesque frescos. (Closed Saturday afternoons and Sundays.)

Stage One: via Schlinig (1h45mins) to Schutzhaus Sesvenna (1h45mins)

From the bus stop on the main Vinschgau road near the church of St Nikolaus, walk downhill across the Etsch river and around to the Burgeis (1216m) village square and fountain (10mins). Do any food shopping here, as there are no possibilities in Schlinig - the flat rounds of fennel-seeded rye bread travel well in rucksacks, and are best filled with local Speck (smoked pork).

Follow signs for Schlinig, along the narrow road uphill in a

65

*Ex Rif. Rasass (near Schutzhaus Sesvenna) and views southeast
to Ortler Group*

southerly direction, past the old Fürstenburg castle (left). Soon high above the road, clinging to the hillside, is the Kloster Marienberg, reminiscent of a Himalayan monastery.

At a wide curve (30mins this far) is the tiny church of St Stefan. Turn left off the road here (signposting n.1), past the church and onto an old cart track SW. It gradually swings around westish and is equipped with several lookout points over the vast expanses of Vinschgau and its cultivated patchwork of fields and settlements such as Mals SW with its characteristic towers. The light wood is rich in wild strawberries, raspberries and hazelnuts. Continue past a couple of turn-offs and in brief descent to the torrent - keep right. Up to open meadows below farms, the track crosses to the left side of the stream for a little while, to re-cross at the sawmill (Säge). The village is visible ahead now, and you come out onto the main asphalted road by an old mill, just below the Aniggl Hof guesthouse. Even if you don't stay there, take a look in the bar - it has an incredible wooden sculpted interior and some marvellous hand-crafted locks (good food too). Schlinig (1738m) is essentially a quiet farming community.

(Park here if you drove the 6km from Burgeis.)

Just outside the village, past the ex Italian Customs building (presumably abandoned due to lack of smuggling), signposting indicates the wide track (n.1) up the left-hand side of the valley. However the middle route (n.1A) straight ahead through the meadows is just as valid, and has stations of the cross. The two routes join a good 40mins up-valley, before a small farm (Inn. Alm, 1923m) and the refuge's cableway loading point. On the tree-covered left-hand side of the valley, roe deer can often be seen. The 4WD (and mountain bike) track climbs more steeply now in zigzags to the right of a waterfall. The flowered banks have bell flowers and alpine pinks, as well as marmots, whereas on the rock crests west around the Föllakopf a herd of magnificent ibex is often seen. Once up into the upper valley, a picturesque old stone building, ex Rif. Rasass, stands on a lake side, not far from modern Schutzhaus Sesvenna (Rif. Sesvenna), ably run by the AVS (2256m). A wide panorama of the central part of the Ortler Group with snowcapped peaks can be seen SE.

(An optional side trip: take n.5, signposted (west at first) for Sesvennasee lake at 2629m. Allow 2h30mins return time.)

Alternative return to Schlinig (2h)
Near the lake (the one near the refuge), n.8 heads off in an easterly direction climbing across the grassy hillside to a stretch mostly along the crest (SE). Take n.8A (right). It ends with a rather steep last-minute drop to the village.

Stage Two: via Schlinigpaß (30mins) to Uina Schlucht (40mins) then Sur En (2h20mins)

Path n.18 leads to a wide passage NW, then through swampy land colonised by cotton grass and frogs. It's 30 easy mins to Schlinigpaß (2295m), marked by a marble boundary stone and a fence (electrified presumably for the animals), where you cross into Swiss territory (unguarded border, not even a flag). Two curious stone walls form an open-ended wedge through which the Italian sheep are channelled and counted to calculate grazing taxes. This point is also the watershed for major rivers - the Inn (north) and Etsch (south).

The obvious path (still n.18) leads down to shepherds' huts and meanders through fertile pasture land punctuated by marmot burrows, golden cinquefoil, delicate spring gentians and tiny bird's-eye primroses. 40mins from the pass the valley narrows, the rock is lighter (dolomite) and the Uina gorge begins, with a passage cut into its dramatic right-hand flank. The path winds in and out around the precipices in slight descent, and where exposed has a protective handrail or fixed cable. 20mins will see you out of the gorge itself.

The descent is on loose scree at first, but soon improves in mixed conifer wood. A beautiful valley. 20mins down is the Uina Dadaint (1770m) farm (drinks and snacks available). From now on you're on a wide track back and forth across the torrent in a squirrel-infested forest. Further down is another deep gorge gouged out by the torrent. The last legs are somewhat monotonous, but after some 3h30mins walking from Schutzhaus Sesvenna (and off the 1:50,000 map now), you reach a parking zone on the outskirts of Sur En (approx. 1100m), on the Inn (En) river. Straight down the road is a fountain and bus stop (PTT-Postauto timetable on display). A further 1min downhill, for a cool beer in the garden while you wait for the bus (or an overnight stay if you missed it) is Gasthof Val d'Uina, whose friendly staff can sometimes be persuaded to sell Swiss Francs for the bus.

GASTHOF ANIGGLHOF (SCHLINIG) tel:0473/81210
GASTHOF EDELWEISS (SCHLINIG) tel:0473/81441
SCHUTZHAUS SESVENNA/RIF. SESVENNA tel:0473/80234. AVS, sleeps 70 (15/6-30/10)
GASTHOF VAL D'UINA (SUR EN, SWITZERLAND) tel:084/93137
TOURIST OFFICE BURGEIS tel:0473/81422

Stelvio National Park

INTRODUCTION

The "Parco Nazionale dello Stelvio", instituted in 1935, is the largest of Italy's national parks and offers spectacular scenery and wild valleys. It is spread over Lombardy in the west, where it has a common border with Switzerland's Engadine Park, South Tyrol in the north and Trentino in the southeast. The Park's headquarters and main Visitors' Centre are at Bormio (tel:0342/905151), while many valleys have several seasonal ranger posts which usually organise guided walks and evening slide shows during the summer. As far as the thriving wildlife goes, the best valleys to visit are Val Zebrù, Martelltal and Valle di Rabbi.

While the northern part of the Park is reached via agricultural Vinschgau, the main access valley for the southern side is Val di Sole, whose mainstay is tourism. The name "Sun Valley" could be a reference to the sun cult believed to have been practised there.

An outline of the area's geology gives a base consisting of metamorphic rock dating back to the Palaeozoic (600-230 million years ago) and beyond. This was covered by a sedimentary layer, and the formation was then subjected to the widespread violent earth movements that forced fractured sections upwards into mountains, and left many layers exposed, giving the area its present complex configuration. Noteworthy peaks in the northern part are the unusual light-coloured Ortler and König-Spitze, actually dolomite for the most part, confirmed by the presence of flowers such as edelweiss and Rhaetian poppies. The hardy glacier crowfoot, on the other hand, indicates metamorphic rock such as schist. These predominant darker rocks, often interposed with intrusions of magma, are less resistant to weathering so have eroded faster and less attractively. Other points of interest are the sizeable marble layers in the Laas valley, and the mica-schists further south around Monte Vioz.

Mining (iron, copper and zinc, to mention a few) was an important activity in the 13th-19th centuries, in virtually every valley. Furthermore, there are numerous renowned mineral spas (resorts at

Bormio and Peio for example), thanks to geological faults.

The Park's nucleus is comprised of the Ortler-Cevedale Group, an awesome chain of summits, topped for height by the Ortler at 3905m, but by the König-Spitze for elegance. Ice and snow dominate and in fact there is a total of 116 glaciers, though the majority are the hanging type, isolated remains of larger bodies. One exception, the Forni glacier, second only in extension to the Adamello glacier in this eastern part of the Alps, never fails to impress. As can be expected, there is widespread proof of ancient glacier passage in the form of U-valleys and "roches moutonées", not to mention the myriad (over 100) high-altitude lakes. Furthermore, the present-day towns of Santa Caterina Valfurva and Peio, just to give two examples, occupy sites consisting of ancient moraine.

The actual heart of the area, consisting mostly of glaciers, is impenetrable to inexperienced walkers, though local guides and ice equipment can be arranged through Tourist Offices and many refuges. However it is possible to effect a circumnavigation of the Ortler with only a couple of brief bus connections, by joining up (anticlockwise) and adapting Walks 24-25-23-21-20-19-18-16-15-12-11-9.

This vast area offers some superb walking opportunities in a fascinating range of both natural and human landscapes, each valley with its own individual flavour.

WALK 9 (see sketch map E, p.72/73)
TRAFOIERTAL - Goldseeweg

via Stilfser Joch - Drei Sprachen Spitze (15mins) - Goldsee (35mins) - Furkelhütte (1h50mins) - Trafoi (1h20mins)
Total walking time: 4h - 1 day suggested
MAP: TABACCO No.08 scale 1:25,000

A brilliant way to start (or a rewarding way to finish) a walking holiday in the area. Beginning at the dramatic Stilfser Joch (alias Passo dello Stelvio, 2757m) a good path descends gradually with simply magnificent scenery, opposite the line-up of glaciers and peaks culminating in the massive Ortler SE. High above the Trafoi valley, the itinerary follows its NE flank, beneath the spine of the Fallaschkamm.

Though the pass had long been in use, the actual road across the Stilfser Joch was constructed between 1820-1825 under the Austrians with the aim of connecting the Tyrol with Milan. Until 1936 it was the highest road pass in the world. There are 48 hairpin bends and an average gradient of 100:9 above Gomagoi (1273m) on the eastern side and 38 bends, a couple of tunnels and a 100:13.5 gradient from Bormio (1217m) on the other. Until 1859 it was kept open during winter for horse-drawn sleighs but nowadays is only passable June-October. As well as being the delight of cyclists it provides access for summer skiers to extensive fields around the pass, well served by lifts. A trip (especially by bus!) to the pass is an experience in itself. The pass further constitutes an important watershed between the River Etsch, which descends via Verona to end up in the Adriatic south of Venice, and the Adda, which flows via Lake Como and eventually joins the Po.

The only restrictions for this walk are those posed by the weather - low clouds mean no views, and snow could close the historic road to traffic (the buses are necessary for access or return to the start point). Once the snow has melted on the higher sections of the path, the itinerary is within the reach of the whole family and is justifiably popular. It is, of course, worthwhile in the opposite direction (in ascent - details at the end), but in descent you are freer to admire the

71

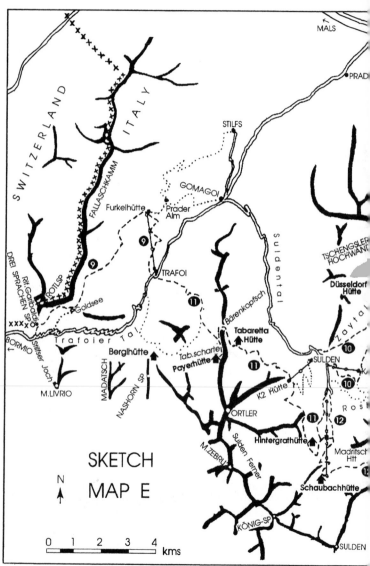

SKETCH

MAP E

0 1 2 3 4 kms

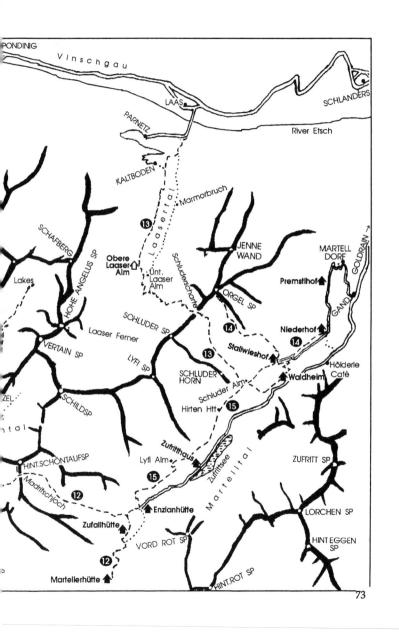

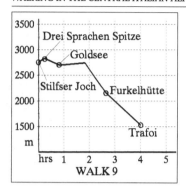

Drei Sprachen Spitze
Goldsee
Stilfser Joch
Furkelhütte
Trafoi
WALK 9

surrounds and don't have to worry about missing the last bus back.

Note that neither of the two refuges touched on, Rif. Garibaldi, Furkelhütte, offers accommodation.

ACCESS: from the start of July to mid-September, Stilfser Joch is served by buses from three sides: from the spa resort of Bormio (Lombardy) in the SW via the Braulio valley, from Santa Maria Val Müstair (Switzerland) in the north, then in the east a line originates at Spondinig (Vinschgau) and climbs via Gomagoi and Trafoi. Drivers should check on road conditions beforehand as avalanches and landslides often make these roads impassable, as does subsequent road work.

Note that for the alternative exits, year-round buses also serve the villages of Gomagoi and Stilfs (infrequent service).

Stage One: via Drei Sprachen Spitze (15mins) to Goldsee (35mins)

Plenty of accommodation is available at the pass itself, as are indescribable souvenirs. Head (north) up the easy path to fort-like Rif. Garibaldi (2838m, refreshments only) on the Drei Sprachen Spitze (the Italian version of which is Cima Garibaldi). The German name refers to the fact that this was once the meeting place of three nations (now two) and thus three languages: Romansch-speaking Switzerland still a few metres away to the north, Italy SW (province of Lombardy) and Austria east (now the Südtirol region of Italy). Views are breathtaking, especially over the Ortler-Cevedale complex, and even take in Piz Bernina not so far away SW.

From the refuge follow (still north) yellow and red paint splashes (n.20 all the way) and signposting for "Tartschl Alp", though a yellow dot in a white circle soon takes over. You pass through an area with ruined stone buildings and scattered timbers, evidence that the area was a First World War (Austrian) stronghold with ample barracks, a hospital and even electricity. Round a point the path descends

74

Late-lying snow on the Goldseeweg, with Ortler behind

gradually, bearing left then coasting eastwards across red detritus, on the lower reaches of Rotlspitz. Early summer walkers have a good chance of finding late-lying snow on sheltered inside path curves. Instead marmots will greet later walkers.

Some 45mins from the pass will see you at a path junction in the vicinity of pond-like Goldsee (2708m). Keep left on n.20 (the NE branch of path n.21 descends more directly and less interestingly to Trafoi).

Alternative access
Should local reports give the upper section of the itinerary as impassable, you can slot in here by leaving the main Stelvio pass road at its 38th bend (2564m). Path n.21 climbs diagonally NE via summer pasture land and takes about 40mins. Note though that there is no official bus stop or space for parking at the start point, so be prepared to have to walk a good stretch of asphalt, depending on where the bus will let you off.

Stage Two: to Furkelhütte (1h50mins)

The scenic route proceeds on a level for some way amidst skittery sheep. Even though there may still be extensive snow cover ahead, the slopes are gentle and crossing presents no problems. Vinschgau backed by the Ötztaler Alps and the Weißkugel (NE) come into view.

The terrain varies between loose rock, earth and grass cover, and likely wild flowers are rose-tinted glacier crowfoot, chamois ragwort and plenty of gentians. From the large anti-avalanche barriers soon reached, Furkelhütte is visible far below. This area affords an excellent vision of the now due south line-up of glaciers and mountains: outstanding features, starting from the westernmost end, are M. Livrio, Geister Spitze (Ghost Peak, so-called due to the legend in the Trafoi valley about a shepherd-ghost wandering around the summit at night), the massive dark Madatsch outcrop, then the curious bulbous Nashornspitze (supposedly named thus by the children of a Trafoi innkeeper), above which in profile, left, is Trafoier Eiswand, its ridge culminating in Thurwieser Spitze. To the SE is the Ortler, probably with roped groups of climbers on its white slopes.

The final 50mins or so are much steeper and descend into a rich and varied conifer wood with a wonderful variety of wild flowers. Unusual scented black vanilla orchids grow on sheltered sunny grass-rock terrain. On the last leg a curious tree-sculpted figure stands guard by the path. Cows and slopes cleared for winter skiing indicate the vicinity of Furkelhütte (2153m, meals only, no accommodation) and its chair lift.

(In ascent from here to the pass, allow a good 3h30mins, but remember to check on return bus times beforehand.)

Stage Three: descent to Trafoi (1h20mins)

Like the refuge, the chair lift (a 10min trip) operates early July-end September. Otherwise on foot, from the refuge take the wide track down to the war fortifications, where a signpost (n.17) points down into wood. Blue columbines and the wine-red variety can be seen along the way. The direction is essentially south and the well-trodden good path crosses beneath the chair lift several times to the village of Trafoi (1532m). (In ascent allow 1h45mins.)

Alternative descent to Gomagoi (1h30mins)
Past the war positions bear left 5mins to panoramic Prader Alm farm (2051m). N.12, clearly marked and not often used, leads through the buildings into quiet wood. It drops quickly in tight zigzags and can be hard on the knees with several crumbly, gravelly stretches, exposed at times. There's also a brief passage around a rock face with fixed cables down the Obergrimm about halfway. Continuing east, it eventually emerges from the wood in view of an old fort at Gomagoi (1273m) (2h in ascent).

Alternative descent to Stilfs (2h)
As for the Gomagoi descent, proceed to Prader Alm then keep on the wide track (n.2) with short cuts for the wide curves. This easy-going pleasant descent ends up in the village of Stilfs (1302m) (3h in ascent).

TOURIST OFFICE STILFSER JOCH (PASSO DELLO STELVIO) tel:0342/903030 seasonal
TOURIST OFFICE TRAFOI tel:0473/611677

WALK 10 (see sketch map E, p.72/73)
ZAYTAL - Roches Moutonées

---

via Sulden - Düsseldorfer Hütte (2h30mins) - side trip to upper lakes (2h return) - Kanzel (1h10mins) - Sulden (45mins)
Total walking time: 4h25mins (+ 2h for side trip) - 1 day suggested
MAP: TABACCO No.08 scale 1:25,000

An easy day walk suitable for all the (fit) family. As well as some interesting, glacially produced scenery, there are sweeping views over the Sulden valley dominated by the majestic Ortler peak.

ACCESS: from Mals or Spondigna in Vinschgau, take the Stilfser Joch bus line (July to mid-September) and change at Gomagoi for the resort village of Sulden (1906m).

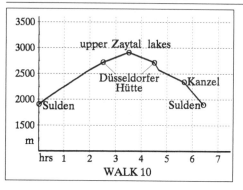

WALK 10

Stage One: to Düsseldorfer Hütte (2h30mins)

Get off the bus at the beginning of the village (shops and Tourist Information). Cross the torrent and cut up right to rejoin the road for a very brief stretch. Signposted path n.5 turns uphill at a small guesthouse just before Hotel Cristallo. It weaves in and out between the old houses and up to a painted arch and sign telling you whether the Düsseldorfer Hütte is "geöffnet" (open) or not (5mins to here). Marked by red and yellow paint splashes, the path now climbs up the left-hand side of the Zaytal next to a frothing torrent. It's some 30mins to the first bridge where you cross to the right, then several backs and forths follow. The valley opens out into well-grazed pasture, and shortly afterwards a path joins up from the right. The refuge is soon visible way above. The path bears left to ascend a boulder-strewn slope of ancient moraine spattered with green lichen. After a little over 2h total walking you reach the next path junction (n.12 from Kenzel joins up). Just a little further up at 2721m is the restored building originally called the Düsseldorfer Hütte (after the club that founded it in 1896). Now under the CAI, it is also known as the Zaytal Hütte or Rif. Serristori (after a member of the Florence section).

The building stands on a shelf of smooth rock, modelled, polished and incised in the distant past by slow downhill glacier advance, also responsible for the batches of "roches moutonées" in the vicinity. Literally "sheep rocks", they are so-called for their resemblance to large recumbent sheep. Normal-sized live specimens usually graze here among scattered gentians, daisies and pink and white cushions of saxifrage.

A helpful artistic diagram shows the main profiles and peaks here. You're likely to see roped climbing parties crossing the Zay

Ferner in ascent to the Hohe Angelus Spitze (east). This summit, according to ancient local credences, was the resting place for the souls of good men on their way to paradise (alias the sun).

Side trip to upper lakes (2h return)
With time to spare, a highly recommended extension is simply to continue NE up-valley for at least 1h, as far as the unnamed lakes shown on maps at 2886m. Path n.5 is clearly marked with paint splashes and the occasional heap of stones. Follow it down into the hollow, cross between the lakes and climb over the last grassy rise, coloured by yellow arnica blooms. You enter a silent but sun-warmed amphitheatre before curving left into an eerie corridor - either pick your way along the rocky left-hand side or go straight up the probably snow-filled middle. Banks of detritus tower over you. This entire upper valley area is in fact chock-a-block with higgledy-piggledy moraine, deposited by retreating glaciers, mere pockets of which remain today. The only sound that reaches your ears is from trickling snow melt. Unworldly rockscapes.

Some 1h from the refuge is a signposted junction - the left fork

Düsseldorfer Hütte and Ortler

leads up a steep gully to the Tschenglser Hochwand and its metal cross, north (aided climb). Once upon a time the souls of bad women resided there, battered by a terrible wind and hail storms caused by the passage of an infernal procession headed by Berchta (alias snow queen and baddie) riding on a goat, her retinue of witches and a goose bringing up the rear.

The first of the lakes (2886m) comes complete with a rudimentary wooden bench. Views back across the Sulden valley have improved, and the glacier on the König-Spitze appears a spectacular cascade even from this distance. Return to the refuge the same desolate way.

Stage Two: descent via Kanzel (1h10mins) to Sulden (10mins-45mins)

From the Düsseldorfer Hütte it's about 10mins down a couple of wide zigzags to the junction - keep on n.12, virtually straight ahead. It appears to be on a level, coasting leisurely south around the mountain side but actually descends nearly 400m. The first part is surprisingly tiring as the wide track is partly buried in fallen boulders. West is the magnificent mountain line-up crowned by the Ortler, and even Payerhütte is visible on the north crest.

The panoramic point and chair lift at Kanzel (2348m) (refreshments and meals) is a favourite launching point for hang-gliders. If you don't indulge in the scenic mechanised descent (10mins - late June to beg. October, reductions for children and over 60s), either follow the dirt jeep track (heading NW at first), or keep south on the level path to a junction - n.12 veers right to zigzag down through the wood. The bus stops are down on the road. On foot allow 45mins at the most.

Rosimtal Detour: at the previously mentioned junction, n.13 proceeds NE up the Rosimtal. It's worth the climb to admire the modest but multi-crevassed glacier with its steep dramatic front. Give yourself a good 1h30mins or more depending, naturally, on how high you go. You can return to Sulden via n.11, taking about 1h from the junction with n.13.

DÜSSELDORFER HÜTTE/RIF. A. SERRISTORI tel:0473/613115.
   CAI, sleeps 60 (18/6-25/9)
TOURIST OFFICE SULDEN tel:0473/613015

WALK 11 (see sketch map E, p.72/73)
ORTLER GROUP - Skirting the Giant

---

via Sulden - cable car halfway station (50mins) - Hintergrathütte
(1h20mins) - Morosini Weg - K2 Hütte (1h) - Tabarettahütte
(1h20mins) - Tabarettascharte (1h20mins) - Payerhütte (40mins
return time) - Trafoi (2h30mins)
Total walking time: 9h - 2-3 days suggested
MAP: TABACCO No.08 scale 1:25,000

A magnificent traverse coasting first above the Sulden valley, this
route takes you around the north-eastern corner of the Ortler giant
and along its northern outrunner ridge, before dropping down
1400m into the quiet Trafoi valley. In good weather there are no
difficulties, apart from the steep Tabarettahütte-Payerhütte section
with an exposed ridge (2871m-3029m). It is easily adapted into two
separate return day trips (to either Hintergrathütte or Payerhütte)
from Sulden. Late summer is the most suitable time for snowless
walking.

The Ortler, at 3905m, is the highest mountain in the Alps east of
Piz Bernina, and was first scaled in 1804 by Pichler. Ortles, by far the
oldest version of the name Ortler, is Ladin, and is thought to be taken
from that of a farmhouse high in the Sulden valley, itself named after
Ortnit or Ortwin, its founder. Furthermore "Ort" in German means
"place", and in fact the mountain was the legendary resting place for
the souls of Celtic princes and pagan gods. Ortler was also locally
known as a proud and arrogant giant. Irritated by the fact that his
neighbours the König-Spitze and Cevedale were actually taller, he
puffed himself up with arrogance and managed to gain the extra
metres necessary. In turn he was beaten by a taunting dwarf on top
of his head. His fury tired and froze him into the massive mountain.

ACCESS: from Spondinig in Vinschgau (year-round coach connections
with Meran and its railway station), take the Stilfser Joch bus line and
change at Gomagoi for the resort village of Sulden. Both of these lines
are limited to July to mid-September. For the exit at Trafoi you pick
up the Stilfser Joch line.

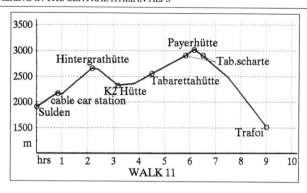

WALK 11

Stage One: via cable car halfway station (50mins) to Hintergrathütte (1h20mins)

At the southernmost end of Sulden (1906m) is the cable car (late June-early October until 5pm, reductions for the over 60s) for Schaubachhütte, and the first trunk can be used to cut 40mins (not to mention nearly 300m) off the walk time. On foot, however, from the valley floor, take the wide service vehicle track (n.2a) which follows the thundering grey torrent closely. Before it climbs up to the left, a path branches off right and later joins n.2 on the opposite bank, above the intermediate cable car station.

Passengers who start out from the station should take path n.2 down to cross the rickety bridge. In ascent the first section is mostly pebbles and earth, then it becomes grassy and populated by ground nesting song birds and marmots romping among wild flowers. Once you've reached the crest the path veers decidedly NW and it's only a matter of 150m more (20mins or so) to the Hintergrathütte. You come across it at the very last minute at 2661m on the shore of a small lake - treat the water with respect as it's the hut's principal supply. Indoor bathroom facilities are limited to a couple of WCs, let alone water for drinking. However, it is a particularly pleasant old-style hut, and has panoramic dormitories. Booking is advisable on weekends as it serves as a crucial base for climbers. The original 1892 Baeckmann-Hütte was named after a mountaineer from St Petersburg who donated it to the Sulden guides group who run the present refuge. The position is wonderful: facing the towering SW side of the Ortler

Moraine ridge below Ortler, with Hintergrathütte right
(seen from Schaubachhütte)

at the extremity of its wide SE-running ridge (the "Grat" ie. ridge referred to in the name), it provides interesting angles on the nearby glacier, M. Zebrù, König-Spitze, and all around the vast and spectacular valley.

Stage Two: via the Morosini Weg to K2 Hütte (1h), then Tabarettahütte (1h20mins)

Heading due north at first, path n.3, the Morosini Weg, climbs briefly then moves onto the right-hand side of the ridge. It continues on a level flanked by orange and purple alpine toadflax flowers. Some 20mins along is a crumbly rock passage rendered trouble-free by fixed safety cable. Soon the path bears around left and down from Scheibenkopf to cross the moraine drifts way below the remnants of the End der Welt (End of the World) glacier. Where the moraine has been levelled for the ski piste under the lift lines, a couple of cairns will hopefully have been re-heaped to show the way, diagonally down. Around the corner is a wide track down to the K2 Hütte (2330m, bar/restaurant, no accommodation).

Alternative access from Sulden (10mins-1h20mins)

The Sessellift Langenstein chair lift (beg. July to beg. October, discounts for children and over 60s) operates from near the church of St Gertraud not far from the Tourist Information Office and takes 10mins. Otherwise on footpath n.3 through wood takes 1h20mins to K2 Hütte.

Near the chair lift is signposting for Tabarettahütte NW along a wide track which quickly narrows. Start off on n.10, then opt for the higher branch (n.4a though not numbered at first) curving around left mostly on a level. It crosses open terrain with low shrub cover including snowy mespil and alpenrose, interspersed with yellow chamois ragwort. After joining n.4 (direct from Sulden - see alternative access), there is an immense stretch of old frontal moraine belonging to the Marltferner (glacier), and where the path is uncertain or under late-lying snow, metallic orange markers show the way. Across to a large boulder (about halfway now) with plaques commemorating climbers who have lost their lives on the Ortler, and the stiff zigzag grassy climb begins. Among other things such as a commanding position surveying the whole of the Sulden valley and a popular sun terrace for doing just that, modern private Tabarettahütte (2556m) is directly beneath neck-craning Payerhütte (SW) on its impossible perch on the Tabaretta crest. The name derives from "tabià", a reference to alpine pasture.

Alternative access from Sulden (2h)

As for the previous alternative access route, start out from the church but take n.4 heading right (west) up through wood. It is joined by the above route on the moraine section, and total time from the valley is 2h.

Stage Three: via Tabarettascharte (1h20mins) to Payerhütte (40mins return time)

A constantly narrowing grey scree path, slippery at times, n.4 cuts NW up a slope with a considerable drop down right. The ascent affords ever-improving sights of the thick sculpted layers of snow and ice on the Ortler, its pointed peak beyond the refuge. A series of tight zigzags leads to the first saddle in the rock ridge,

Bärenkopfscharte (Bear's Head Pass, 2871m). Due south now it keeps to the right-hand side of the crest in gradual ascent. Take care your rucksack doesn't catch on the occasional overhanging rock. The weathered light-coloured needles and towers up here testify to the dolomite-type limestone composition of the Ortler. An aided wooden plank passage and you're at Tabarettascharte (2903m). You'll see the famous road to the Stilfser Joch snaking its tortuous way up to the summer ski fields.

(At this point, should the weather look like deteriorating or the path not appeal to your sense of balance, don't hesitate to turn straight down right and start the descent for Trafoi - see Stage Four.)

The final 20min stretch along the airy crest continues to be exposed on both sides, though no "technical" difficulties are involved. Payerhütte (3029m) occupies an incomparable position and you can expect long-range northerly views towards the Swiss and Austrian mountains. Though an oldish structure, it gets top marks for hospitality and cooking. If you do opt to stay here (advance booking advisable on weekends), count on being woken up at an ungodly hour as virtually everyone else will be staying here with the aim of scaling the Ortler.

The refuge was named after Julius Payer, an Austrian officer and cartographer, the first to climb a good 36 of the peaks over 3000m in the Ortler region as well as carrying out extensive exploration in the Adamello and Presanella groups. The original hut dated back to 1875, the work of the Prague branch of the DÖAV, and was also an important Austrian base during the First World War. In fact, from 1916 until the end of hostilities the 3905m summit itself was occupied. Strategic tunnels and an ice cave to house 30 men were dug out and two cannons were somehow dragged up.

Return to the Tabarettascharte along the crest as per the ascent.

Stage Four: descent to Trafoi (2h30mins)

The clear path for Trafoi (n.185) descends NW on a scree base with occasional snow covering, and is relatively untrodden in comparison to the paths on the Sulden valley side. Some 15mins down (not as shown on maps) n.18/186 branches off west to Berglhütte and Trafoi (see alternative descent). The clumps of delicate yellow Rhaetian poppies that grow along the way are further proof of the presence of the limestone-type rock. Some 45mins down, around a rocky corner, is a ruined hut (don't count on emergency shelter as it's in very bad shape), the ex Edelweiß hut (2481m). Views south towards the Stilfser Joch and surrounding ice-plastered mountains are more expansive now.

Curving north n.19 crosses its last scree slope and descends across terrain anchored by the first trees, scraggly dwarf mountain pines. These are soon joined by larch and Arolla pines providing a soft carpet of needles, welcome underfoot. Trafoi and the valley are glimpsed. The ruins of ex Alpenrosehütte at 2029m mark the start of a long-established thick forest and though the path is easy, its roots and rocks can be slippery in wet weather. In the lower reaches you'll come across several path intersections - all will bring you out at some point in the vicinity of Trafoi, but n.19 is regularly marked. It keeps on virtually straight down to a rickety bridge over Rio Trafoi, then climbs briefly to the road, emerging near the bus stop at old-style Hotel Posta (1532m).

As well as hotels and bus connections, Trafoi offers excellent views NE to the Weißkugel and the Ötztaler Alps, then south to the dark Madatsch bastion and glacier landscapes.

The name Trafoi is Ladin, as were its original inhabitants, and sources give its meaning as either "clover" or "three springs". In fact 45mins uphill (south) from the village is a sanctuary with three wooden statues spouting "holy spring water" (Drei Brunnen).

Alternative descent via Berglhütte (1h30mins) to Trafoi (1h30mins)
From the path junction referred to above, n.18/186 leads SW in and out across grey moraine, a bit up and down. Waymarking is not always regular and though the route is a little more difficult the terrain and outlook are more varied, and the route even less frequented. Berglhütte (Rif. Borletti, 2188m) is at the lower extremity of the massive NW-running spur of the Ortler. Should you decide to stay there, an easier path (n.15/186) awaits you next day. It drops through wood in about 1h to the Drei Brunnen (1605m), where a track continues across the torrent to an Italian Police force children's holiday home and parking zone, before a side road 3km north to Trafoi.

BERGLHÜTTE/RIF. BORLETTI. CAI, sleeps 30 (20/7-30/8)

HINTERGRATHÜTTE/RIF. DEL COSTON tel:0473/613188. Private, sleeps 60 (20/6-1/10)

PAYERHÜTTE/RIF. PAYER tel:0473/613010. CAI, sleeps 120 (25/6-25/9)

TABARETTAHÜTTE/RIF. TABARETTA Contact Sulden tel:0473/613187-613035. Private, sleeps 30 (20/6-15/10)

TOURIST OFFICE SULDEN tel:0473/613015

TOURIST OFFICE STILFSER JOCH TEL:0342/903030 seasonal

TOURIST OFFICE TRAFOI tel:0473/611677

WALK 12 (see sketch map E, p.72/73)
ORTLER GROUP - Glaciers and Spirits

---

via Enzianhütte - Zufallhütte (40mins) - side trip to Martellerhütte (2h return) - Madritschjoch (3h) - side trip to Hintere Schöntaufspitze (1h return) - Schaubachhütte (1h15mins) - Sulden (1h15mins)
Total walking time: 6h10mins (+ 3h for side trips) - 1-2 days suggested
MAP: TABACCO No.08 scale 1:25,000

This is a crossover route and takes advantage of one of the few ice-free passes in the Ortler Group. Deep snow is likely, but only at the very start of summer (gaiters are handy), and in good conditions represents the only "difficulty" of the walk. The landscape is glacial for the most part, but the bodies of ice have retreated dramatically over recent decades, making it more accessible to walkers. Right from the start, at the head of glorious Martelltal (see also Walks 14 & 15), are views of undulating glaciers wrapped around high peaks. Included is an optional scramble to a 3325m summit - stunning views, needless to say. The final descent towards Sulden is devoid of colour - a series of black and white stills of a morainic valley enclosed by sombre but majestic snow and ice-covered mountains of dark rock.

The itinerary is equally feasible walked in the opposite direction, but the vision of the König-Spitze as you come up to the Madritschjoch from the eastern side is something special.

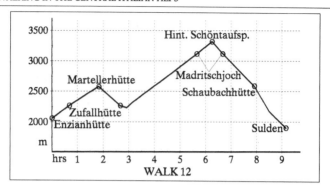

ACCESS: by coach from Goldrain in Vinschgau take the summer line (July-October) SW up Martelltal. It terminates at the Enzianhütte (2055m), in a guesthouse area known as Paradies am Cevedale. At other times of the year the bus line is limited to the village of Martell - get off at the turn-off at 1267m at Gand, 12km down from the Enzianhütte. (The valley's last shops are in this lower inhabited zone.)

The exit point of Sulden is served by a summer bus line which runs via Gomagoi to link up with Vinschgau.

Stage One: via Enzianhütte to Zufallhütte (40mins)

From the bus stop at Enzianhütte, with Zufallhütte already visible ahead, go uphill to the end of the car parking area, past signposting for the Schönblick Restaurant. At the junction, take the wide track (n.103-150) right.

(Left, n.37 "Blaue Piste" is a direct alternative access path for Martellerhütte, unless you want to drop off your gear at Zufallhütte on the way. See the following Side Trip. "Geöffnet" (open) or "geschlossen" (closed), is on clear display.)

The popular route climbs easily in wide curves through a conifer wood with bilberries and alpenrose shrubs, but this soon thins, leaving solitary larches. Ending with a wide swing round left, it soon reaches Zufallhütte alias Rif. Corsi (2265m) and its First World War commemorative chapel, above the tree-line. The area tends to get busy in the late mornings as day-trippers arrive. Early mornings and

Near Martellerhütte, twin Cevedale peaks and glacier

evenings can be utterly peaceful, in the absence of groups, as its closeness to the road means that most people tend to return to the valley for accommodation.

Comfortable, with good catering though a little pricey, this refuge is also very popular in spring as the area offers excellent ski touring. The German name Zufallhütte probably refers to the nearby waterfall, though Zufall was also the name the inhabitants of Martelltal used for the Cevedale. The lower of the twin peaks, Cima Cevedale (3752m), is now usually referred to as Zufall-Spitze, whereas the higher is Monte Cevedale (3759m). Both are visible SW. The name Cevedale comes from the Veneto dialect Zevdal. The first ascents date back to 1864-65 and the mountain ranks as third highest in the Ortler Group.

Side trip to Martellerhütte (2h return)
This side trip presents no difficulties and is recommended for the scenery. Take path n.103-150 SW up over rock and into the next small valley. After 15mins there's an old dry-stone wall damming the valley. It seems incongruous nowadays but its construction in 1893 served to prevent repeats of the disastrous mud and ice floods which

used to sweep down and block the valley. The up-valley glaciers were more than double their present size and their run-off volume was consequently much greater. Legends, however, supply an alternative explanation: the souls of good women were said to emigrate to the Cevedale and dwell in ice palaces there. Unfortunately these collapsed during the frequent visits of "Der Wilde", a sort of wild man, and the resulting water flooded the glacier and hence the lower valley.

Your path (n.103) branches off left along the dam wall, then turns up-valley again and crosses the stream (Plima Bach) and boggy areas a couple of times. There are carpets of yellow pasque flowers, whereas the steep climb in zigzags next, up the detritus-strewn hillside (left), means clumps of yellow creeping avens flowers. On the way up, detours may be necessary at several points early in the season to avoid deep snow. Chamois can often be surprised grazing in the surrounds of the Martellerhütte (2580m). The modern hut (built late '70s) is in a splendid open position before three immense glaciers with their smooth ice humps, crevasse cracks and lower dark moraine crests. As well as the Cevedale, the graceful triangular point of the König-Spitze can be seen WNW. (Due west is a rocky hump, marked "Tre cannoni" on the TABACCO map, with First World War cannons.)

The return to Zufallhütte the same way takes about 50mins.

To make this a round day trip, an alternative return direct to the Enzianhütte area is possible by keeping straight down the valley instead of turning left along the stone dam wall. The slightly steeper path (n.12-31-37) continues down the right-hand side of the valley. Timing this way, as far as the car park, is a good 1h15mins.

Stage Two: ascent to Madritschjoch (3h)

Path n.151 leaves Zufallhütte to head NW and down briefly around a crumbly earth slope. It is soon joined by the direct path from the car park before climbing over a brief rise formed of ancient detritus and into the peaceful Madritschtal valley. A flat, boggy area is negotiated with stepping stones leading over right to a wooden bridge, then you stay on the right-hand side of the valley on a clear path. At quiet times of day you'll easily hear and see the marmots that romp here. The path climbs easily with only a few steep stretches, but the brightly-coloured flowers provide excuses for rest stops - yellow alpine pasque flowers and pink hairy primroses. There are vast views back SE onto numerous small glaciers and minor peaks, but these of course improve with the ascent.

For the last 200-300m of ascent you enter a wide amphitheatre and the path turns due west. Snow is common even in early summer, but shouldn't require anything more than a stock for depth testing and gaiters to keep you dry. As the valley is very popular with winter ski tourers, you'll find the occasional marker pole and small heaps of stones, if not previous walkers' tracks, to guide you to the wide saddle, visible from some way below. When the path is clear it is a series of more direct tight zigzags up to Madritschjoch (3123m).

On arrival you're greeted by the stunning sight of the magnificent König-Spitze (alias Gran Zebrù) mountain (SW) with its cascading glacier and curious "ice nose" beneath the summit. Its imposing regal shape is thought to have been the reason for its German name meaning "King's Summit" whereas local beliefs say it was where the spirits of bad men lived. (See Walk 24 for explanation of the name Zebrù.) A 20-year-old Franciscan friar, Steinberger, is held to have been the first to scale it (solo) in 1854, and incredibly, Austrian soldiers actually occupied the summit during the First World War. To its left you can pick out the curious rock "bottle" sticking up in Königsjoch, aptly named Passo della Bottiglia in Italian. Below it and spreading in all directions is the Sulden glacier. To the right of the König-Spitze is Monte Zebrù (due west), then the highest mountain in the group, Ortler (3905m), further right again. The only thing marring the view are the ski lifts and pylons in the valley below you. Back on the side you've come up as well as a whole series of wide but short hanging glaciers, the highest mountain is Cima Venezia, 3386m (SE, actually with three peaks) and Cima Marmotte to its right.

(If you walk this stage in reverse - in descent to Zufallhütte - allow at least 2h15mins, depending on snow cover.)

Side trip to Hintere Schöntaufspitze (1h return)

Energy, weather (ie. clouds) and time permitting, an even better (6-star) and wider-ranging view is to be had from the top of the 3325m Hintere Schöntaufspitze belvedere. It is a good 30mins and 200m more upwards and involves a couple of scrambles, but all effort is well rewarded. Signposting indicates the start of the ascent due north. It climbs on the left-hand side of the ridge and is well-marked all the way. The first narrow stretch is steep and crumbly and can be slippery in parts, but is soon more gradual. The wind plays strange games around the well-heaped cairn on the 3325m top. In the sea of snow, ice and rock that spreads out around you, some interesting landmarks relatively close-by include the Martellerhütte (SE), the Fürkelescharte pass above to its right, and twin-peaked Cevedale due south, very distinct now. Closer SSW is Rif. Casati, then the Sulden line-up as mentioned earlier from the pass. Further afield, the panorama takes in mountains of the Engadine (NW), the Presanella and Brenta Groups (SSE), and even a pale spire from the main Dolomite bloc (east) if you're lucky. This is the most accessible high summit in the Park by a long shot.

Return to Madritschjoch is by the same route.

Stage Three: descent to Schaubachhütte (1h15mins) and Sulden (1h15mins)

The descent is usually punctuated by the thundering of ice, snow and rock falls from the walls opposite. It's uncanny how they echo around the valley head and amphitheatre.

The initial descent from the pass crosses snow and rock. In the name of winter skiing, this desolate valley has been disfigured with pylons, ski lifts, poles, plastic netting and sheeting, not to mention the bulldozing work to prepare the runs. The "official" path n.151 is still marked in white and red, and is probably the less strenuous route, but several more direct (and faster) alternatives are possible via the pistes or the ski lift track. Avoid the right-bearing track unless you want to drop in at modern Madritschhütte (2818m) for a meal (no accommodation).

The dark surrounds are brightened by posies of pinky-white flowers with yellow centres - glacier crowfoot, the highest blooms in the Alps.

The surprising herd of yaks you'll undoubtedly meet came from Nepal in 1985. Every summer they are brought up to this area to graze on the scanty grass. It can only be hoped that they won't pose a threat to the indigenous wildlife in this already precarious National Park. Signs lower down request you not to feed the animals.

The dark moraine crests below the Ortler peak contrast

dramatically with the light grassed areas to its right, and the Hintergrathütte is visible NW.

(To walk this section in ascent allow 1h45mins, but this will depend on snow cover.)

Orange-roofed Schaubachhütte (Rif. Città di Milano, 2581m), built on the ruins of the original German hut (1878), is not in great demand for accommodation as most people seem to prefer to stay in the valley resort. The old, rather run-down part of the hut means a grotty curtained-off cubicle, whereas the newer, more expensive part means a private room (door included) and an eiderdown.

The cable car runs down to Sulden (15mins) (see Walk 11). Otherwise path n.1 (jeep track) curves around the uphill side of the refuge before a plunge downhill on a moraine base. The easy descent gives you time to appreciate, among other things, the Sulden Ferner (west) and its flow from the Ortler, with its immense moraine ridges. 35mins should see you down at a path junction: n.2 goes left to the intermediate station of the cable car (2172m) to continue on to the Hintergrathütte - see Walk 11. Keep right, across the lower slopes of the Schöntauerwand. Soon path n.1 branches off the jeep track and comes out at the cable car arrival station and bus stop. The actual village centre of Sulden with shops and Tourist Office is some 2.5km further down the road.

ENZIANHÜTTE/RIF. GENZIANA tel:0473/730425

MARTELLERHÜTTE/RIF. MARTELLO tel:0473/621110. AVS, sleeps 56 (15/7-1/10)

SCHAUBACHHÜTTE/RIF. CITTA' DI MILANO tel:0473/613002. CAI, sleeps 80 (18/6-25/9)

ZUFALLHÜTTE/RIF. N. CORSI tel:0473/730485. CAI, sleeps 90 (11/6-23/10)

TOURIST OFFICE MARTELL DORF tel:0473/744598

TOURIST OFFICE SULDEN tel:0473/613015

WALK 13 (see sketch map E, p.72/73)
LAASERTAL - Marble and a Desolate Traverse

---

via Laas - Obere Laaser Alm (3h20mins) - Untere Laaser Alm
(25mins) - [Return to Laas (1h50mins)] - Schluderscharte (3h30mins)
- Schluder Alm (1h45mins) - Waldheim, Martelltal (1h)
Total walking time: 10h - 2 days suggested
MAP: TABACCO No.08 scale 1:25,000

Laas, a quaint township on the River Etsch in western Vinschgau, was
settled in prehistoric times. It has several well-kept 11th century
churches, one of which, St. Sisinius, is believed to be among the
valley's oldest. Another point of interest is the medieval aqueduct
which carried water from the glaciers high in Laasertal by way of
larch wood piping supported by tall stone pillars, many of which are
still standing.

However Laas's principal claim to fame is its world-renowned
dazzling white marble quarried since Roman times and comparable
in quality to that from Carrara. Visits to the marble works and quarry
(over 1600m on the eastern side of the valley) can be arranged
through the tourist offices at both Laas and Mals. A school for
sculptors also operates in the township.

As regards the walk, it comprises a long traverse, tiring at times,
through wood and wild valleys which see very few walkers, and
there are fascinating glacial landscapes. The approach to the key pass
(Schluderscharte, 2987m) more often than not means snow covering
the steep terrain. This in turn is infamously crumbly and mobile,
cause of occasional rock and landslides. Experience along with great
care are essential. This means it is not a suitable itinerary for beginners.
However an excellent and easy 1-day round trip (5h35mins) is
feasible as an alternative by proceeding as far as the Untere Laaser
Alm, then taking the return route for Laas.

Late summer is probably the best time for the complete traverse,
though the round trip can be done early summer through to autumn.

The refuge, Obere Laaser Alm, a converted dairy farm, does not
provide continuous service so don't leave Laas without checking
first, and be prepared to carry extra food.

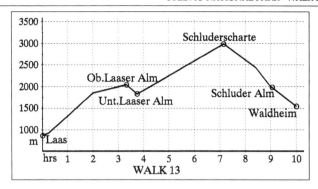

WALK 13

ACCESS: from the railhead of Meran frequent year-round buses serve the broad Vinschgau valley and drop in at the small township of Laas (not to be confused with nearby Latsch) some 40km west.

The exit points in Martelltal are connected by bus to Goldrain in Vinschgau. Outside the summer period (July-October) the service terminates at Martell Dorf, near Gand, 4km before Waldheim.

Stage One: via Wurmisionsteig to Obere Laaser Alm (3h20mins)

From the bus stop in the centre of Laas (869m), turn south down Schneidergasse (Tailors' Lane) to cross the old railway track and river. Turn left past the spacious riverside car parking area, then first right. A short way uphill in the vicinity of a Stelvio National Park signboard (934m) below the church of St. Martin, limited parking is possible (handy for day walkers). On foot this far takes 15mins.

Follow n.5/13, the wide dusty track which winds steeply to the church of St. Martin on its panoramic perch at 1052m. A little further on, turn right on n.13 in ascent for Bremsberg, the inclined hoist for transporting marble slabs. A beautiful pine forest shelters tiny sweet wild strawberries and an interesting range of mushrooms and edible fungus.

At 1359m (just under 1h this far) is the unobtrusive electric train line which connects the quarry (SSE from here) to the nearby 1929-built cog railway which drops to the township. Go right on n.14, then sharp left (before the buildings) up to join a gravel-base track. Keep left (south). Red and white waymarking and n.14 are frequently marked on trees - don't be tempted by the yellow paint markings in this maze of forestry tracks. Woodpeckers drumming contributes to the medley of melodious birdsong. On the forest floor, enormous heaps of conifer needles double as ant nests. After a steep path is the wide route known as "Wurmisionsteig" (2h total to here), then you find yourself directly over the valley from the yawning entrance to the Marmorbruch (marble quarry). Interesting glimpses of ice masses and peaks south are encouraging.

The track narrows once again and continues climbing, but less strenuously, and passes a delicious spring. Arolla pines and alpenrose dominate the vegetation. Black vanilla orchids and white alpine mouse-ear flowers are also common in the clearings. At last you climb out onto a vast clearing to the picnic tables and fountain (drinking water) at the modest refuge Obere Laaser Alm (2047m). This wonderful setting takes in icefalls and crevasses on the Laas glacier south, Schluderspitze SE, swinging around to imposing Orgel-Spitze (almost due east), then graceful Jenne Wand (ENE) with its drawn-out crest and unusual grey-white folds and marble layers. North are the Ötztaler Alps.

Alternative access via Kaltboden
From the parking area mentioned at 934m, a narrow asphalted road continues west and up past the hamlet of Parnetz, becoming a rough track, steep at times. Private vehicles are allowed through the forest as far as Kaltboden (spelled in various ways), about 1500m, from where a path connects to the main route shortly before you see the Marmorbruch. Walking time is then approx. 1h45mins.

Stage Two: descent to Untere Laaser Alm (25mins)
Down past the old cow shed and WC head right (south) towards woods where both path and waymarking reappear. Swing back around left and a couple of shepherds' huts later you reach a pasture zone alongside the torrent. You can actually cross the torrent here to join n.8A for Schluderscharte. Otherwise keep down left for the enormous shingle-roofed shed and bridge to quiet Untere Laaser Alm (1825m).

Alternative exit: return to Laas (1h50mins)

The unsurfaced vehicle track downwards from the farm buildings sports clear red and white markings for n.5 (maps show n.15). It quickly moves over to the left-hand side of the valley, and is an easy walk brightened by wild flowers such as mountain house-leeks, bell-flowers, purple orchids and monk's-hood, amidst scattered white marble and shiny mica flakes.

Some 1h later is the loading point beneath the marble quarry. (Should you be fed up with the track, a variant return is provided by n.12A which branches off down right shortly. It plunges very steeply to a wild gorge, follows the torrent bank and comes out just east of the National Park signboard referred to in Stage One.)

A couple more winds and surprisingly steep stretches and it's past the n.13 turn-off to the worthwhile detour to St. Martin's church and its welcome benches, shady in the afternoon. An excellent lookout point over the patchwork fields in Vinschgau and onto the curious alluvial cone opposite. Said to be the second largest in Europe, its volume is evidently some 1350 million m³. Buried beneath the cultivated fields is a part of the old Roman road.

The final stretch of n.5 curves down to the Park signboard and back along the road to the river and Laas.

Stage Three: ascent to Schluderscharte (3h30mins)

As mentioned in the introductory comments, the 1200m ascent ahead requires stamina and extra care due to the possibility of rock discharges. It is extremely inadvisable to set out on this traverse in unsettled weather.

The first stretch moves south past some water tanks and round several rocky outcrops. Some way along n.8A starts to climb in earnest east up a steep slope to the vegetation limit. Just above 2400m, where a path variant joins up from the west, a stream is crossed. The path snakes its way up scree flows that are usually snow covered, particularly in the higher reaches as it is sheltered by side ridges from the Orgel-Spitze. In compensation for the effort, this wild side valley is deserted and silent apart from the occasional chamois. Contemplation of the stark glacial landscape, with its moraine ridges and the ice front and tongues melting into waterfalls and torrents, constitutes a valid motive for a rest stop to break the monotony of the

Obere Laaser Alm and view north to the Ötztaler Alps

climb.

Magnificent views are the premium as you scramble up that final passage to Schluderscharte (2987m) to get your breath back. Beyond the dull grey-brown rocks of the pass where alpine mouse-ear bloom are green fields in Vinschgau NW and the white square of the Marienberg monastery at Burgeis backed by the Sesvenna Group. Then SW over the various glaciers and remnants stands a dark ridge with most notably Vertainspitze on the far left and Hohe Angelus Spitze to its right. On the other side of the pass (SE) are grandiose peaks in the Zufritt-Hint. Eggen Groups.

Stage Four: descent to Schluder Alm (1h45mins), exit to Waldheim (1h)

The initial 200m are characterised by awkward and potentially mobile detritus, but snow disappears here earlier than the previous stage due to the SE exposure. Red and white waymarking (8A) clearly indicates the start of the descent down the left-hand side of the gully to a tall pointed monolith. Soon bear right for a brief rubble traverse to more secure but steep, sparsely grassed slopes where the path as such fades out momentarily. There is occasional waymarking on the rocks. Further below you make your way down a more obvious route across scree on a soft unstable base. The floor of the immense rubble-filled bowl is reached in about 30mins from the pass and the going becomes immediately easier. Keep right at the path junction (left connects with the Orgel-Spitze - see Walk 14).

Fallen rocks are coloured with orange and green lichen. Down a series of shelf-like steps to leave the upper valley, path n.8A keeps to the left-hand side all the way. Grassy at last and dotted with tiny gentians, the valley becomes the realm of sheep and marmots, with nimble chamois on the crags and scree. A cascade adorns the imposing sheer dark wall and ridge of Lorchenwand (west) which terminates in Schluderhorn. A ruined stone hut (2440m) is some 40mins below the junction. Juniper and alpenrose shrubs precede the first larch trees, precursors of the mixed conifer wood. After an enormous boulder you swing down to enter the Martelltal near the timber huts of abandoned Schluder Alm (2005m), and join path n.8 (Walk 15 joins up here).

Briefly left (east) along the path is the signposted turn-off (n.34) for the Waldheim Hotel at St. Maria in der Schmelz down on the main road at 1550m (bus stop). While this constitutes the quickest exit route, it involves a further steep 500m in descent.

Alternative exit: via Stallwieshof (30mins) and Niederhof (30mins) to Hölderle Café (20mins)

Otherwise a scenic guesthouse is only 30mins of pleasant coasting away. Heather and stemless carline thistles thrive on this dry hillside. The clear path (n.8) traverses a wood alive with squirrels and woodpeckers. In late summer it is strewn with tell-tale gnawed pine cones from which noisy speckled nutcrackers have extracted the tasty nuts.

From Stallwieshof (1931m) continue on n.8 which turns off the asphalted road straight after the torrent crossing. Pass through wood once more to farm buildings on a surfaced road at 1851m. After n.5 turns down sharply (another route to Waldheim), n.8 keeps on east, crosses the road once again and drops easily in between woods and fields with clusters of picturesque farms. It comes out on the road close to the Volkschule. Near Niederhof guesthouse (1700m) take n.26 (south) through old farm buildings. It is soon a steep path in rapid descent to cleared areas at the bridge over the river. Uphill for 5mins via the road is the new Hölderle (elderberry) Café and bus stop (1457m).

OBERE LAASER ALM/MALGA LASA DI SOPRA contact Rudolf Hauser tel:0473/626045. AVS, sleeps 24. Open and staffed some weekends and occasional weekdays July-August. Keys available on request at other times, and blankets and firewood supplied

For MARTELLTAL accommodation details, see Walk 14

TOURIST OFFICE LAAS tel:0473/626613 part-time, seasonal

TOURIST OFFICE MARTELL DORF tel:0473/744598

WALK 14 (see sketch map E, p.72/73)
ORGEL-SPITZE - A Magnificent Peak-cum-Weather Beacon

---

via Martell Dorf - Stallwieshof (2h) - Orgel-Spitze (4h) - Stallwieshof (2h30mins) - Martell Dorf (1h30mins)
Total walking time: 10h - 1-2 days suggested
MAP: TABACCO No.08 scale 1:25,000

3305m-high Laaserspitze or Punta di Lasa is known locally as Orgel-Spitze (though you'll find any of the three names on maps). This comes from an earlier name (Arge) meaning "bad" or "evil" due to the fact that signs of approaching bad weather are first manifest on the mountain. It has long been well visited by the locals who heaped up the huge stone signal pillar on top. Despite the length of the ascent - nearly 1400m - in good conditions, any experienced and fit walker can handle the climb. The preferable period is late summer-autumn when visibility is optimum, any dangerous ice has melted but the next season's snow falls have not yet started. Waymarking is clear and frequent and the path is easy until the final 350m or so when it becomes of "average" difficulty. Effort is more than adequately rewarded as the extensive panorama is breathtaking.

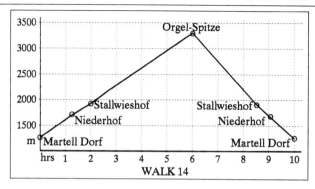

WALK 14

The actual ascent (Stage Two) starts from Stallwieshof guesthouse. Those with a car can drive that far and thus make this itinerary a feasible day trip, eliminating Stage One and the final stretch of descent. There are also several peaceful guesthouses open most of the year (listed at the end - booking advisable) along the narrow road above the village of Martell Dorf. The section of the access path between Niederhof and Stallwieshof is particularly pleasant and scenic, a worthwhile outing in itself.

ACCESS: to reach the village of Martell Dorf (1267m) catch the year-round bus from Vinschgau via Goldrain. In July-October the line is extended to Enzianhütte in the upper part of the valley, covering the Waldheim and Hölderle Café stops.

Stage One: from Martell Dorf via Niederhof (1h15mins) to Stallwieshof (45mins)

Martell Dorf (shops, post office) is 1.5km off the main valley road. From the bus stop keep on the road uphill (SW) out of the village. (Don't waste time searching for path n.8 shown on some maps cutting across fields - it no longer exists.) There are several wide curves through hay meadows and the rare short-cut. After the road has straightened out to head south, you reach the hamlet of Ennethal which stands at about 1600m with Premstlhof guesthouse. Next is a stretch of wood, with the occasional signed (n.8) path cutting up right. Some 1h15mins total will see you at the hospitable family-run Niederhof guesthouse (about 1700m) with glacier glimpses SW towards the Cevedale. (NB: a higher path signposted for Stallwieshof actually bypasses Niederhof. Though involving extra ups and downs, it is equally feasible and the two routes join up not long past the guesthouse.)

Alternative access: to reach Niederhof more directly from the main Martelltal road (5mins downhill from the summer-only bus stop at Hölderle Café), n.26 ascends in 30mins. In descent 20mins will do.

Past the now unused Volkschule, path n.8 leaves the road for the wood, noisy with birds. This route, once the sole passage for the busy farm settlements, is wide, well-marked and quiet these days as most visitors and locals use the road. Along the way are abandoned water-run mills in the fields, some still with their wheels and overhead wooden channelling. Farmers still occasionally grind their own cereals (electrically nowadays) and bake the traditional flat rye loaves (also available in local bakeries).

The path crosses the road twice and is joined further up by n.5 (from Waldheim) near Hochegg farm on the last leg. A final stretch of wood, then both path and road terminate at farm and guesthouse Stallwieshof (1931m) in its idyllic meadow setting. It looks over Zufritt See to the Venezia group of peaks beyond, SW.

Alternative access from Waldheim (1h)
On the main Martelltal road 4km after Gand (the junction for Martell Dorf) is the Waldheim Hotel (1550m). Nearby uphill is the bus stop at St. Maria in der Schmelz, so-called for the foundry that used to operate there for the minerals such as galena and pyrite mined higher up. Path n.5 crosses north over the torrent and winds and climbs via several farm buildings. The final stretch is in common with the main access route.

Stage Two: ascent to Orgel-Spitze (4h)

Just before the stream crossing to the Stallwieshof buildings, path n.5 (signposting) starts out NW. It passes a picturesque old mill and heads straight up into conifer wood. Principally there are Arolla pines and larch, then juniper and alpenrose shrubs in more open parts. With its trees berry laden in late summer, the wood provides

Stallwieshof in Martelltal

food for a veritable aviary. The path wastes no time with zigzags but climbs straight up, including grassy banks studded with stemless carline thistles. A drinking trough is passed at 2120m, and soon afterwards the path bears right through wood again. Several hollows soon reached are carpeted with bilberry plants which turn brilliant red at the end of summer. Some 45mins up is a delicious fresh spring at about 2200m. Now around left n.5 climbs out of the trees and into a desolate valley, its scattered stones green with lichen. A long climb with several terraces where sheep graze leads to even barer terrain. Stone marker heaps take over as waymarking, often painted with red and white as well.

At about 2900m you come up to a pillar-like cairn and enter yet another upper valley, this one much flatter, virtually a plateau. A curious sight, and often snow-bound late into the summer, its stone detritus base seems to have been steam-roller levelled. Due west soon is the Schluderscharte, a weathered dip in 45° angled crumbly rock strata, and beyond are important pyramidal tips in the Vertain-Hohe Angelus Group. North now you coast the SE crest of the Orgel-Spitze and the peak itself comes into view ahead. The final 350m or so (a good 1h) is steeper and tiring and involves several clambers over debris and rock (not exposed). You eventually come up to a saddle (keep below it, lower right side) then puff up the last leg to the summit (3305m). Your visit can be immortalised in the ascent book (in the metal box on the cross). Vinschgau can be admired below, in contrast to the high-altitude 360° panorama of mountains: from east moving north are the Dolomites, Großglockner (Austria), Similaun, Weißkugel, the Sesvenna Group, then Ortler (SW), M. Zebrù and König-Spitze, Cevedale, the Venezia Group, Hint. Eggen Spitze, Zufritt-Spitze, with Hasenöhrl bringing up the crest (SE). From the Orgel-Spitze itself the ridge extending northwards terminates in unusually light-coloured (marble) Jenne Wand.

Stage Three: descent to Stallwieshof (2h30mins) and return to Martell Dorf (1h30mins)

As per the ascent.

If you have spare time a longer variant is the unnumbered path that branches out as soon as you return to the stony plateau. Early signs pointing SE are easy to find, but you'll need to hunt around for successive ones. It drops into Schludertal to join n.8a - see Walk 13, Stage Four. Allow at least 30mins extra.

NIEDERHOF guesthouse tel:0473/744534
PREMSTLHOF guesthouse tel:0473/730466
STALLWIESHOF guesthouse tel:0473/744552
WALDHEIM Hotel tel:0473/744545
TOURIST OFFICE MARTELL DORF tel:0473/744598

WALK 15 (see sketch map E, p.72/73)
MARTELLTAL - Woods and Wildlife

via Enzianhütte - Lyfi Alm (45mins) - Hirten Hütte (1h) - Schluder Alm (1h) - Stallwieshof (30mins) - Waldheim (45mins)
Total walking time: 4h - 1 day suggested
MAP: TABACCO No.08 scale 1:25,000

A highly recommended itinerary moving down the NW flank of Martelltal mostly through woods but with regular scenic openings.

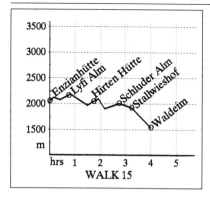

WALK 15

The route is straight-forward, with the exception of a couple of elementary though steep aided rock passages (ladders and handrail) which require due care and a sure foot. The multitude of alternative access/exit paths that connect with the main valley road and bus stops make for do-it-yourself variations. Furthermore it becomes a round trip if you take the bus to join your start and finish points.

Due to the attraction of nearby Zufallhütte and the glaciers SW, you're unlikely to encounter great numbers of other walkers. A good range of scenic picnic spots punctuate the route, but carry your own food as Stallwieshof is the first refreshment (and accommodation) point - the others are farms or simple huts, referred to only as reference points.

The vegetation band traversed (2000m-1500m) hosts thriving populations of roe deer and squirrels, as well as plentiful bird life. Deer are present but sightings are less common.

In the reverse direction (in ascent) allow around 5h30mins.

ACCESS: see Walk 12. (p.88)

Stage One: via Enzianhütte to Lyfi Alm (45mins), Hirten Hütte (1h), Schluder Alm (1h) then Stallwieshof (30mins)

Once past the tempting restaurants that serve fresh "Forellen" trout, you reach the car park and bus terminal at the Enzianhütte at 2055m. 2mins back down the road is signposting for path n.8 for Stallwies (maps show the initial stretch as n.6). It's a wide forestry track and climbs winding through conifer wood. After about 25mins it is intersected by n.20a (down to Zufritthaus at 1880m on the lake of the same name). Not much further around is the Lyfi Alm summer farm (2165m) where the track as such ends. (Another path, n.10 descends

105

to Zufritthaus.) The narrow but clear path crosses a stream maintaining the northeasterly direction. Just around the corner a strategic clearing and bench overlook the pastel green Zufritt See and afford a wonderful view SW of the twin Cevedale peaks and extensions of ice and snow backing the Zufall and Marteller refuges, whereas beyond the pines across the valley are series of peaks connected by diminishing snow fields and hanging glaciers.

Coasting above the lake you continue through dry sweet conifer wood which hosts squawking woodpeckers. After several wooden ladder descents you reach a big boulder lookout point over the northern dam wall (30mins). The view NE down Martelltal over meadows, strawberry gardens and hillside farms extends as far back as the Similaun-Texel Groups.

It continues another 10mins in descent (keep left/north at unidentified path forks) in order to pass below a steep rock flank. Eroding sections are preceded by an "Achtung Steinschlag" (beware rockfall) warning sign. It soon climbs back into wood and up to the stream in the Rosimtal and the landmark Hirten (shepherd's) Hütte (2049m). (Soon n.9, access from Schluderspitze, turns off right down for the road.) A short way further up is a grassy clearing facing SE towards the Zufrittspitze -Lorchensp.-Hint. Eggenspitze ridge cradling ice and snow.

Further climbing, east now, to yet another lookout point, soon followed by a brief descent on crumbly yellowish terrain. Be careful not to miss the turn-off, it leads to a steep passage down a rock face with stone steps and wooden handrail, before curving left to another brief aided stretch. This brings you out in the Schludertal beneath the imposing bastion (left) of the Schluderhorn. Across the torrent are several old timber huts (Schluder Alm 2005m) and the junction with n.8a.

(At this point it is possible to descend on alternative path n.34 to St. Maria/Waldheim, 1550m. It takes over 1h, barely shorter than the main route.)

The final 30min stretch to Stallwieshof (1931m) and the start of the road, is straightforward, mostly coasting through dryish wood.

Stage Two: descent to Waldheim (45mins)

From Stallwieshof follow the road briefly across the torrent and to a signposted path (n.8) down right. Some 100m down on the wide swings of the path through wood, after some farm buildings on the road, n.5 turns off sharp south for a further 300m in descent. It emerges in the valley on a wider track to cross the Plimabach to the Waldheim Hotel and bus stop. (See Walks 13 & 14 for alternative exits.)

ENZIANHÜTTE/RIF. GENZIANA guesthouse tel:0473/730425
ZUFRITTHAUS/RIF. GIOVERETTO guesthouse tel:0473/730472
See Walk 14 for other MARTELLTAL guesthouses (p. 104)
TOURIST OFFICE MARTELL DORF tel:0473/744598

WALK 16 (see sketch map G, p.116)
ZUFRITT GROUP - Soyscharte

---

via Hölderle Café - Soyalm (1h30mins) - Soyscharte (2h30mins) - Pilsberg Alm (1h30mins) - St. Gertraud (1h30mins)
Total walking time: 7h - 1 day suggested
MAP: KOMPASS No.072 scale 1:50,000

This age-old southeast-running traverse route links "wild" Martelltal to pastoral and traditional Ultental. The dwellers of the latter valley are said to descend from immigrants of the Weingarten monastery in Swabia (southwest Germany). For many years they constituted a closed community in both religious and legal senses. 17th century records referred to the valley's pastoral importance - 18-20,000 sheep from as far afield as Verona and Vicenza were sent up to graze. As well, iron, copper and sulphur were once mined in the valley. Nowadays timber is an important mainstay.

This worthwhile itinerary is normally ice-free, and though the approach to the scenic pass is long (involving a 1400m ascent), the path is good and usually problem-free - it rates an overall "average" in terms of difficulty. The walk is equally feasible in either direction - reverse timing is given at the appropriate points.

ACCESS: Martelltal is accessible by bus from the Vinschgau (Goldrain). The settlements of Gand and Martell Dorf are serviced year-round,

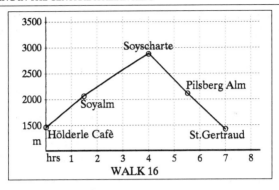

WALK 16

but the higher points (as far as Enzianhütte) July-October only. The starting point for this itinerary, Hölderle Café, is 2.5km uphill from the hamlet of Gand, so comes under the summer bus extension.

For the exit in Ultental - a year-round bus service runs from the lower part of St. Gertraud, NE via Lana to Meran.

Stage One: via Soyalm (1h30mins) to Soyscharte (2h30mins)

The bus stops right outside the new Hölderle Café (1457m), and signposted path n.4 is closeby. SE up through beautiful conifer forest carpeted with bilberries, you soon join a wider track which climbs in wide zigzags towards a waterfall, only glimpsed. This flank of the valley is shady and damp, perfect conditions for the thriving mushrooms and fungus. Just over 1h up, the cascading torrent is crossed, then a wide pasture corridor leads up out of the trees and due east to the summer farm Soyalm (2073m).

"Jausenstation" means it operates as a refreshment stop in summer. (Drinking water is available even if the building is closed.) A tranquil herd of crème caramel horses graze alongside cows. A delightful spot - up-valley views take in the moraine spread below the Soyferner and Zufritt-Spitze (known as Gioveretto in Italian) (south) as well as the pass (SSE). Even if you only come this far, it's worth the walk.

10mins further on through the last of the trees you climb up to a signposted path junction - left for Soyscharte. A ridge of alpenrose shrubs precedes a further junction (n.18 turns north and over to the next valley for the Flimseen lakes before returning to Martelltal). N.4

Soyalm, looking towards Soyferner and Zufrittspitze

keeps up the left-hand side of this open valley, crossing a couple of side streams. The path dips across a grassy hollow and up a steeper stonier crest to the last grassy basin echoing with marmot cries, at about 2500m. The final 400m and 1h15mins cover grey rubble. Waymarking is frequent, though the sun which is probably burning straight into your eyes by this time makes it hard to distinguish the painted waymarking among the glistening rocks. Keep to the path with the freshest marking (also the best path) as an older version (faded paint) disappears in spots, while heading essentially the same way.

There's a brief stretch straight up across rubble, before a move left onto mixed rock-grass terrain. Early summer could mean snow here. It becomes a rather monotonous slog but the path widens out into long curves which take the puff out of the climb. On the final leg it veers further left to emerge at Soyscharte (2888m), a silent, ample grassy pass (not a real "wind-gap", the translation of "Scharte"). Zufritt-Spitze and its glacier (SW) are now partially hidden by a dark ridge (SW). Other highlights are Ortler (due west), Orgel-Spitze (NW), Weißkugel (NNW) among the Ötztal peaks (north), and even the Brenta Dolomites (south).

(In reverse, 2h45mins should do for this stage in descent).

Stage Two: descent to Pilsberg Alm (1h30mins)

The clear path becomes n.142 and moves down the wide valley into pasture land. Via a series of terraces flowered with the lilac variety of gentian, you descend easily through occasional small bogs populated by delicate cotton grass. There are lichen-greened rocks splashed with white marble and silvery mica. The path follows the left-hand side of the valley while on the right lie several small lakes amongst smoothed rock slabs. The path is not always clear in the lower reaches - make sure you don't miss the swing down right (approx. 2200m) towards the torrent. Where fencing starts, the floor of the Ultental comes into sight with the lake Weißbrunnsee (south). A final left-bearing stretch brings you across banks thick with bilberry shrubs and the first larch, above the picturesque Pilsberg Alm shepherds' hut. Keep right (n.12) at the path junction and you soon reach the panoramic clearing (crucifix, picnic benches and drinking water) adjoining the low shingle-roofed hut inhabited by reticent shepherds (2128m).

(Allow 2h20mins in ascent from here to the pass.)

Alternative extension via Weißbrunnsee (1h) then St. Gertraud (1h20mins)
N.12 descends gradually SW into wood, soft underfoot with conifer needles. Late summer walkers should add supplementary time for inevitable bilberry picking (and consuming) stops. The path cruises across a couple of cascading torrents and in 25mins reaches a cluster of abandoned huts. Shortly, around after sturdy anti-avalanche barriers is the turn-off down left for Weissbrunn (the right branch connects to Höchsterhütte). A further easy but steep 20mins south bring you out at the lake side. On your left is restaurant-cum-guesthouse Gasthof Enzian - Ristorante da Godio (1900m), recommended for a splurge.

(Some 1h20mins in the opposite direction.)

See Walk 18, Stage Four for the final stretch to St. Gertraud.

Stage Three: descent to St. Gertraud (1h30mins)

Near the crucifix at Pilsberg Alm, a rustic wooden notice for "St.

Gertraud" points down (SE) into a predominantly Arolla pine forest enlivened by squawking specimens of speckled nutcrackers. The unnumbered path drops easily to a group of timber huts and soon afterwards crosses a road. It then cuts down to a graceful spread of traditional dark timber houses bright with geraniums and barns cluttered with old wooden equipment. Red and white marking on the corner of the buildings takes you through private property, and there are intriguing glimpses into farm life. After a shrine and bridge you pass under the wires of the hamlet's mechanised cableway - their lifeline before the construction of the road. Thick silent pine forest brings you out onto the road (about 1740m). A good 30mins (3.5km) downhill is the turn-off right for St. Gertraud proper (1519m) and church, whereas the downhill fork leads (approx. 2km) to the lower part of the village (shop and bus stop, approx. 1419m). Some accommodation is available here, and the nearest Tourist Office is at St. Walburg, 13km away.

A worthwhile side trip (30mins return time) from here is to three ancient larch trees (Urlärchen). Signposting points you over the torrent and east along a quiet road (blue and white waymarking). Though a trifle battered now, they are guaranteed 2000 years old, and the oldest is 8.20m in circumference and 28m tall.

TOURIST OFFICE MARTELL DORF tel:0473/744598
TOURIST OFFICE ST. WALBURG tel:0473/795387

WALK 17 (see sketch map F, p.112)
ULTENTAL - Three Panoramic Peaks

via St. Walburg - Marschnell Alm (2h30mins) - Peilstein (1h) - Rontscher Berg (1h) - Muteggrubspitze (30mins) - Koflraster Seen (50mins) - Riemerbergl Alm (1h) - Simian (30mins) - St. Walburg (1h)
Total walking time: 8h20mins - 1 day suggested
MAPS: KOMPASS No.52 scale 1:50,000 (except the very start) or No.052 scale 1:40,000

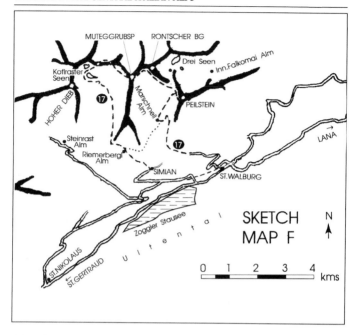

Though outside the realms of the Stelvio National Park, this is a truly worthwhile traverse of some splendid panoramic ridges and covering a great variety of landscapes. Recommended for walkers with some experience, it is awfully long and the total absence of refuges in the area makes it necessarily a 1-day trip. While the ridge traverses are reasonably straightforward (average difficulty), anything but good conditions will mean exposure to the elements and orientation problems. Furthermore, an overall climb (and descent) of 1600m is involved, added to which are the inevitable ups and downs in between.

The description is geared to car-less walkers, but can be advantageously adapted by drivers as follows:

a) with one car, drive as far as Simian. Just above Riemerbergl Alm is a link ('P') with Marschnell Alm (1h30mins from Simian), where you join the main itinerary. This cuts some 2h off walking time.

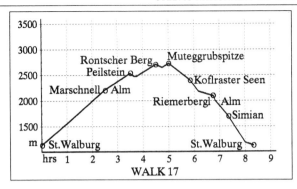

WALK 17

b) With two cars, it's feasible to leave one beforehand at Simian for the return, then drive as far as the farmhouses at 1700m in Stage One and start walking there. This means saving 2h20mins.

St. Walburg has plenty of spotless family-run guesthouses, and it's a good idea to overnight here so as to get an early start next day.

ACCESS: St. Walburg lies 20km SW of Lana, in turn 8.5km south of Meran, the starting point for the year-round buses that serve Ultental.

Stage One: ascent via Marschnell Alm (2h30mins) to Peilstein (1h)

Leave the centre of St. Walburg (1131m) heading NE via the main road. It bends left and passes a well cared for, frescoed shrine. Keep straight ahead uphill, off the main road now (which turns right to cross the torrent) - there is a faint sign for Marschnell Alm/Peilstein (n.10). After a couple of bends, take the turn-off left at a group of houses (signposted), then soon right up a dirt track. The damp mossy wood is crisscrossed by paths but n.10 is regularly marked. At a junction marked "Vorsicht Steinschlag" (careful, rockfalls) bear left to climb out onto meadows. The path is now a succession of cuts across the road, through lovely farms and across fields dotted with disused farm implements, ovens and even small water-driven mills. A final stretch of wood and you re-emerge where the road ends at farmhouses and a drinking fountain at 1700m (approx. 1h20mins this far). Walkers doing the two-car variation b) should park here.

Still heading NW, past a link path to Simian, the path soon reaches a torrent and proceeds to climb steeply up its right-hand bank, and is crossed by another track. A good 1h up on a bare hillside at a slender wooden cross, the farm access track joins up and together you curve left over the torrent and up to Marschnell Alm (2212m, drinking water) summer farm.

(As well as the access path from Riemerbergl Alm ('P'), there is a direct route to Koflraster Seen (n.10) NW over rolling hills.)

Take the right (NE) arm of 'P' for the ascent. Across stony terrain it soon follows a dry stone wall before ascending easily to a saddle. The actual Peilstein peak (2542m) is a further 10mins climb to your right, and there's a huge cross. Incredible bird's-eye views over the valley. The German name "Peilstein" means "direction finding stone".

Stage Two: traverse via Rontscher Berg (1h), Muteggrubspitze (30mins) to Koflraster Seen (50mins)

Return to the saddle and follow the NW-running crest 10mins to a path junction: a path drops down right to Drei Seen, but you take n.7 down along the left-hand side of the ridge to bypass a rocky point. Though waymarking is frequent, it's a veritable obstacle course, dodgy at times, over fallen rubble. There are several steep climbs up the rugged hillside, then compensation comes in the form of wonderful views of the Plombodensee and Drei Seen (NE). 1h should suffice as far as the triangular metallic marker on the 2711m peak of Rontscher Berg, a top lookout point. North across Vinschgau is the Texel Group.

Westward now, descend to a saddle, then up a rough detritus slope to the cairn on Muteggrubspitze (2736m). Continuing in the same direction, after a brief stretch on top, a crest is followed, then you go down the right-hand flank to a basin. A steep rubble and earth slope and tightly zigzagging path drop to the first of the picturesque and sizeable Koflraster Seen (2407m). The second is around left to a saddle and down briefly.

(From here paths descend north to Vinschgau, a good 1800m down, so not really feasible unless you've a car waiting on an access road.)

For the energetic, the ascent of nearby Hoher Dieb (Great Thief) awaits - a mere 1h to the 2730m summit. Take the path SW from the path junction between the two lakes, and head up the grass-rubble slope.

Stage Three: descent via Riemerbergl Alm (1h) and Simian (30mins) to St. Walburg (1h)

Around the right-hand shore of the second lovely lake, n.4 goes SE and down grassed terraces in about 20mins to a small hut (2187m) and fork (n.13 continues to Steinrast Alm, 1723m, hence road to the valley floor). Keep left on n.4 high along the left-hand flank of the valley with views WSW over to the Hasenöhrl and its glacier pockets. Apart from a very brief climb you mostly coast southwards into larch wood with some old gnarled specimens. About 35mins from the last fork is the junction above Riemerbergl Alm (where the 'P' access path heads east for Marschnell Alm). N.4 drops to the hut (about 2000m) then heads left into the wood. It becomes a wide old path enclosed by high stone walls and passes more small timber constructions. Simian (1712m) is a scatter of farmhouses. From here on foot either follow the narrow road down right (slightly longer route) or head off left on the likely-looking path through the fields. Unfortunately, in addition to the old footpaths which have fallen into disuse, the progressive widening and asphalting of tracks make maps out-of-date and orientation confusing at times. There's no actual waymarking at this stage but with a bit of luck (and the occasional enquiry from the locals) as well as brief stretches of road, you should reach an unusual local bar and crucifix at about 1350m, in 30mins or so. Here red and white waymarking (n.4) reappears to the left of the bar and leads diagonally through wood to the road again and bridge over the Marschnellbach torrent. A track left is signposted '4-M' for St. Walburg and, passing through a residential area, reaches the township in some 20mins.

TOURIST OFFICE ST. WALBURG tel:0473/795387

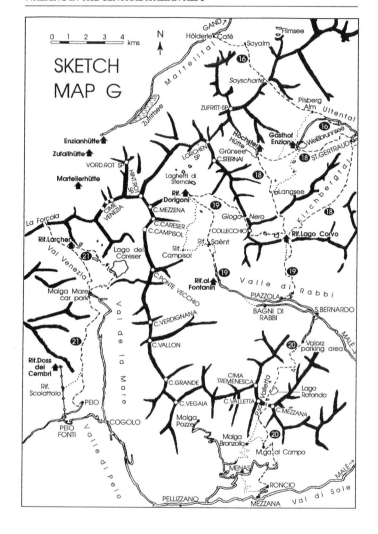

SKETCH
MAP G

0 1 2 3 4 kms

N

WALK 18 (see sketch map G, p.116)
ULTENTAL - A Circuit of Lakes

**via St. Gertraud - Rif. Lago Corvo (3h) - Langsee (2h) - Höchsterhütte
(1h20mins) - Weißbrunnsee (1h20mins) - St. Gertraud (1h20mins)
Total walking time: 9h - 2 days suggested
MAP: KOMPASS No.072 scale 1:50,000**

Ultental is a lovely valley whose tradition-oriented inhabitants earn their living from pastoral activities and timber, with tourism somewhat low key. (See also Walk 16.)

In the lower wooded zones of this itinerary, deer and roe deer are not unusual sights for quiet walkers. A further bonus is the restaurant (Gasthof Enzian - Ristorante da Godio, worth a splurge) at the lake side, before the final descent to St. Gertraud.

The first stage of this loop walk is straightforward, though the second is rather strenuous but relatively untrodden. The whole trip could just be managed in 1 day (fit walkers only) by cutting short Stage Three and descending from Langsee.

Another feasible variant is a combination with Walk 19 for traverses into southern Val di Sole.

From the start point St. Gertraud, a 30min (return time) detour can be made to the famous 2000-year-old larches, "Urlärchen" (see Walk 16).

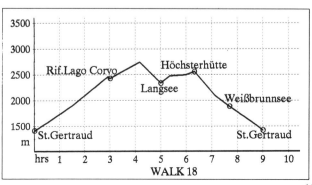

117

ACCESS: St. Gertraud is 33km up Ultental. Year-round buses leave Meran's railway station, go south 8.5km via Lana, turn SW up the long valley, and terminate at the lower part of the village where the walk starts.

Stage One: ascent via Kirchbergtal to Rif. Lago Corvo (3h)

The bus leaves you near the shop in lower St. Gertraud (1400m). Cross the stream and follow signs (right) for the Kirchbergtal. 3mins up the narrow asphalted road is a turn-off left for n.108, a dirt track (closed to unauthorised traffic). (The right branch "Zur Kirche" leads steeply to the 17th century church (1519m) near Pension Ultnerhof and a car park. From here there is a direct link back to the main route - allow 15mins extra for this detour.)

It's a peaceful pasture valley with a torrent that regularly disappears and reappears. The climb is gradual and vegetation is larch and bilberries for the most part. At long bends in the track is a short cut, marked "Kirchberg" n.108. It rejoins the track in a wide scree basin with marmots, thinning trees and a couple of huts (about 1900m, approx. halfway). Alpenrose shrubs are on the increase up the left sunny flanks, though the surrounds have otherwise become rather bare. Several tight bends and steep climbs bring you into a pleasant grassy basin. Up left is the last farm (2295m) where a path takes over. 20mins will see you at the first of a series of large stone cairns, preceding undulating terrain traversed southwards until the wide saddle of Passo di Rabbi (2467m). This seemingly unimportant pass marks the passage from the Germanic province of Bozen in the north to the predominantly Italian province of Trento, south. Culture, language and cuisine change noticeably. 5mins south is homely Rif. Lago Corvo (2425m), also known as Rif. Stella Alpina. The outlook opens up offering the Brenta Dolomites (SE), the Tremenesca Group (south), Presanella (SW) and pleasant views down the Rabbi valley.

A short stroll uphill west from the pass is rock-locked Lago Corvo (2464m), after which the refuge is named. Though it means "crow lake", it actually contains the trout-like alpine charr, a rarity for this zone.

Alternative exit to Piazzola (2h)

Path n.108 heading south descends to year-round buses from the village of Piazzola (1315m) in Val di Rabbi - see Walk 19, Stage Three.

Stage Two: traverse via Langsee (2h) to Höchsterhütte (1h20mins)

Take path n.12 north through the pass, then across the torrent. It climbs gradually over grass-rock pasture, and sheep and goats have continually to be shooed off the path. Some 30mins on, n.12 turns left (whereas an unnumbered variant continues on a level) to zigzag up the Kirchbergalm ridge, passing over it at 2740m (briefly east of the 2846m shown on maps). This seemingly desolate terrain is home to a sizeable herd of chamois. Höchsterhütte is visible NNW now on the shore of remarkably aquamarine Grünsee, sheltered by the towering mass of twin-peaked Zufrittspitze.

The steep 400m drop, monotonous at times, is on a loose red detritus base. Snow cover can be of help if firm - you can cut the zigzags and head straight down to the grassy valley floor. There, the path crosses a couple of streams that feed into nearby stomach-shaped Langsee (2339m).

(Path n.107, a lovely route, drops NE to Weißbrunnsee thence St. Gertraud and could be used as a more direct exit for a 1-day walk.)

A gradual climb through alpenrose with twittering birds follows, and is some 15mins to a marked path junction (all names in German now, painted on rocks) - keep on n.12 for Höchsterhütte. Once at the 2400m mark, the path is essentially on a level and wends its way through enormous red rock chunks. It consists of a series of slabs and steps, evidently prepared by the Electricity Commission, responsible for damming and transforming the valley. An initial impression is of desolation, bizarre somehow. However, once you actually cross the dam wall, the amphitheatre enclosed by the valley head is revealed as a simply grandiose setting with cascades thundering into the lake. It is crowned by Hint. Eggen-Spitze (WSW), identifiable by the cross on its summit, then to its right the small glacier Weißbrunnferner, then Lorchen-Spitze (west), Weißbrunnspitze and Zufrittspitze (NNW). A brief final climb and you reach Höchsterhütte alias Rif. Canziani (2561m). The original 1909 German hut is now at the bottom of the artificial lake. The quiet friendly substitute features hot water and excellent food such as the wholesome Valtellina (Lombardy) dish of pasta made from tartary buckwheat, and mixed with cabbage, potatoes and melted cheese, that comes under the name of "pizzoccheri".

Stage Three: descent to Weißbrunnsee (1h20mins)

Take n.140 downhill (SE) - it quickly becomes a pleasant rocky path accompanied by larch, alpenrose and cows at pasture. Some 45mins down at about 2100m, just before a lookout point, is a path junction.

Connection with Pilsberg Alm (1h45mins)
N.12, narrower, branches off left (NE) and passes a series of lightning-struck red-barked Arolla pines, low juniper shrubs and bilberry plants. Several small cascades are crossed, a crumbly rock point rounded, then a conduit. After the path junction (descent to Weißbrunnsee) and anti-avalanche barricades are flowered clearings featuring martagon lilies, then old timber huts (2100m). Rock ptarmigan and black grouse can occasionally be heard and spotted up here. Another 45mins will see you at the picturesque shepherds' hut Pilsberg Alm (2128m). (Drinking water available.) From here, see Walk 16 for either the traverse to Martelltal or descent to St. Gertraud.

N.140 continues directly and easily to the lake, Weißbrunnsee, and ENEL (Electricity Commission) buildings. You pass Gasthaus Alpe (meals only), then, easily identified by its incongruous gigantic metallic gentian, is the gourmet restaurant and very civilised guesthouse, Gasthof Enzian, Ristorante da Godio (1900m).

The waters of this lake once concealed a voracious dragon, fortunately lured away by an enterprising visitor who harnessed it with red leather, then rode it away down the torrent all the way to Lana, never to be seen again.

(For this stage in ascent - 2h.)

Stage Four: exit to St. Gertraud (1h20mins)

As a valid alternative to the 6km road, go over to the opposite side of the lake and follow the wide dirt track along its shore. Late summer will mean blood red, russet and golden vegetation - bilberry shrubs and larch trees - bordering sky blue water. The first intersection is on a level with the dam wall, and St. Gertraud is signposted. It is not until the fourth junction (keep left) - the route now a path (n.107) - that the descent seriously begins. The tall forest hosts roe deer which often betray their presence by dislodging stones.

Some knee-battering 300m later, you emerge onto a grazing plain. The fenced-in path goes right uphill to the 17th century church in the upper part of the small hamlet of St. Gertraud (1519m). The bus stop, however, is a further 15mins (and 100m) downhill - on the left of Pension Ultnerhof is signposting for St. Nikolaus. Follow this narrow asphalted road down past stations of the cross, houses and across the torrent to the bus stop on the main road next to the shop and Edelweiss restaurant.

(In ascent, 2h should suffice to the lake.)

GASTHOF ENZIAN - RISTORANTE DA GODIO tel:0473/790133. Sleeps 16

HÖCHSTERHÜTTE/RIF. U. CANZIANI tel:0473/790299. CAI, sleeps 60 (4/6-9/10)

RIF. LAGO CORVO tel:0463/985175. Private, sleeps 40 (20/6-20/9)

TOURIST OFFICE ST. WALBURG (13km NE from St. Gertraud) tel:0473/795387

WALK 19 (see sketch map G, p.116)
VALLE DI RABBI - Cascades and Wild Flowers

via Piazzola - Malga Stablasolo (1h20mins) - Rif. Dorigoni (3h) - Giogo Nero (1h50mins) - Rif. Lago Corvo (1h20mins) - Piazzola (2h)
Total walking time: 9h30mins - 2-3 days suggested
MAP: KOMPASS No.072 scale 1:50,000

This is the first of several itineraries through the southern section of the Stelvio National Park.

The circular walk starts in fascinating, unspoilt Valle di Rabbi. Its variety of habitats host a wealth of flora (best in July) and fauna, not to mention the witches banished to the upper part (Pra di Saènt) by the mid-16th century Council of Trent. There's a comfortable refuge followed by a high-level scenic traverse to some delightful lakes, thence return to the starting point. It is well marked and clear the whole way, unless covered in snow early summer, and is of no special

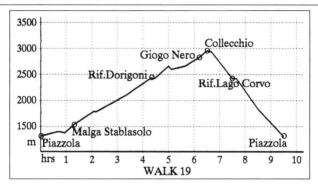

WALK 19

difficulty under normal conditions. It lends itself to plenty of adaptations, all suitable for family groups.

A feasible day trip is the ascent to Rif. Dorigoni, including the brief variant "Sentiero delle Cascate", then return by way of Rif. Campisol (Alternative Descent) - round trip timing 7h30mins from Piazzola. However by driving as far as the car park below Malga Stablasolo this can be reduced by almost 2h.

An excellent cross-over route north to Ultental is possible by combining this itinerary (as from Rif. Lago Corvo) with Walk 18.

Bagni di Rabbi has a small but interesting Stelvio National Park Visitors' Centre, not far from the bus stop. It contains an unusual photo of a brown bear (Ursus arctos) sighted nearby (Malga Fratte) in 1975, and believed to belong to the small group that inhabits the Brenta Dolomites to the south.

ACCESS: the buses from Malé (connected by train to Trento) serve alternately the small spa resort Bagni di Rabbi (also referred to as Rabbi Fonti or Terme) and the village of Piazzola uphill. There are also occasional extensions 1.5km west to the hamlet of Somrabbi.

For a return day trip, cars can be left at the final car park (approx. 1500m) just below Malga Stablasolo.

Stage One: from Piazzola via Malga Stablasolo (1h20mins) to Rif. Dorigoni (3h)

From the church and shops at Piazzola (1315m) head west along the narrowing road through the hamlet of Somrabbi (1348m). Soon afterwards (40mins this far) the road is joined by the following track from Bagni di Rabbi.

Alternative access from Bagni di Rabbi
Should the bus drop you off at the spa resort at 1222m, continue west past the spa building. Once over the torrent and after a large camping ground, the road turns into a dirt track and heads NW through tall forest. There's a water-driven Venetian-style sawmill (Segheria Veneziana) on the torrent bank, left. Soon you're on the asphalted but narrow road from Piazzola (total 40mins).

The road passes a spring (ferruginous water) and soon afterwards is a small guesthouse, Rif. al Fontanin (1380m), camping ground and the end of the asphalt. 15mins on will see you at a parking area (approx. 1500m, authorised vehicles only from here on). Not far uphill (short cuts not allowed) is a dairy farm, Malga Stablasolo (1539m), which offers meals and refreshments and an impressive line-up of cheeses. Drinking water is available here and at several more points further ahead.

"Sentiero delle Cascate" detour
Shortly there is an interesting detour (right) for the "Sentiero delle Cascate" (Waterfall Path). Only a little longer than the main route, it crosses to the eastern side of the valley and climbs close to the thundering waterfall, before a bridge leads back across the torrent to rejoin the main route near Rif. Saènt.

Otherwise the main route (n.106), a path now, climbs easily on the left of the torrent past more farm buildings, then zigzags up in the proximity of the cascades. This is a superb area for wild flowers with shady conifer wood and grassland, a veritable rock garden in fact. Common specimens are alpine pinks and mountain house-leeks. 45mins from Malga Stablasolo is a hut used by the National Park rangers, Rif. Saènt (closed to the public, 1790m) with WC and a lookout point. Patient observers should be able to spot deer or roe deer. Through the larches, north, is a picturesque valley lined with peat bog and fed by several more cascades, towering above which are the reddish flanks of the Sternai (alias Eggen) peaks.

*Lake below Rif. Dorigoni, with Cima Mezzena (left) and
Cima Rossa di Saènt (right)*

Path n.106 drops a little and follows the valley northwards, past scampering marmots, and keeping to the left-hand side of the main torrent past a small farm (1784m). There's a climb through low wood thick with purple orchids to the second waterfall. Abandoned Malga Vecchia (1890m) marks the start of the steeper stretch on "Sentiero degli Alpinisti" (Mountaineers' Path). A long series of steps leads upwards and concludes with a section fitted with a hand cable, just before a crest (2100m). With about 1h to go, the route moves NW into the upper valley through completely different terrain. Above the tree line, it's thickly vegetated with alpenrose, heather and bilberry shrubs while the flora includes the black vanilla orchid and light purple alpine aster. The delightful climb becomes gentler and soon after a signposted path junction at 2365m (connection with Rif. Campisol) the path eventually crosses the stream and marshy zone by way of slender pole bridges that require some balancing ability. It's only a matter of 100m more up to an ample platform and peaceful position of easy-going, comfortable Rif. S. Dorigoni (2437m), named after a local dignitary and Alpine Club president.

St Gertraud church, Ultental
Lago Rotondo in the "seven lakes valley"

Above: At 3645m on Monte Vioz, with Palon de la Mare (left) and the Cevedale peaks (right). Below: Last leg of ascent among First World War barbed wire to Rif. Casati, with König-Spitze

Due west across the valley is Cima Rossa di Saènt (Hint. Rot Sp.), south from which is C. Mezzena, then C. Careser.

From the refuge an interesting visit can be made due north to a series of small lakes (Laghetti di Sternai) formed in glacial cirques. The highest (Lago Nuovo, 2862m) is relatively recent - it came into being some 50 years ago following the retreat of the now extinct hanging glacier, Vedretta di Rabbi.

Alternative Descent via Rif. Campisol to Rif. Saènt (1h45mins)
Timewise, this variant takes about the same as the main route. It's definitely less frequented but nonetheless signposted and problem-free. Back down at the signposted path junction mentioned in ascent (2365m), take n.128 right off the main path. With several short ups and downs, it goes essentially south the whole way to Rif. Campisol (2126m), which belongs to the Forestry Service and does not actually function as a refuge. From here in 30mins the path drops east quite steeply some 300m to rejoin the main route near so-called Rif. Saènt.

Stage Two: traverse via Giogo Nero (1h50mins), Collecchio (20mins) to Rif. Lago Corvo (1h)

It would be unwise (not to mention disappointing) to attempt this traverse in low cloud as the rather featureless landscape could make orientation a problem. Take n.107 in descent at first, past the horse's stall and east to a small lake. Keep left at the path junction (where path n.130 provides yet another connection with Piazzola). The climb eastish cutting the flank of the Cima Sternai Meridionale is gradual but pleasant as you contemplate the valley you ascended on the last stage with numerous lakes. Grassy terrain gives way to rock and earth-detritus mixes which tend to be soft and mobile when wet. After some 40mins you reach a ridge where the path coasts for a while before steep tight zigzags up to 2825m and the Giogo Nero pass. Here are great views down NE to the lakes in Ultental, as well as SW to the Presanella-Adamello massifs.

Alternative exit
At this point path n.107 descends (NE) to Langsee (2339m, about 1h) from where you can either continue down to Weißbrunnsee in Ultental or branch off NW for Höchsterhütte - see Walk 18, Stage Two.

SE (waymarking is n.145 now) along the right-hand side of the panoramic rubble crest, with snow patches in early summer, it's only about 20mins to Collecchio (2957m). This is the southernmost point of the Sternai chain, and a renowned lookout, taking in southern vistas as well now. Apart from the occasional walker, tiny spiders and lichen seem to constitute the only life form up here.

From here on it's all in descent. There's a small pass (after 10mins), then you enter a lovely, completely different valley and head down east towards a number of glittering photogenic lakes, probably still iced-up in early summer as this is a sheltered corner. The refuge is visible just beyond them. Extra care is necessary in the presence of late-lying snow covering the path and waymarking. Normally it's trouble-free, and winds down gradually past with a series of marker pillars of heaped-up stones.

Down on the rock-slab shores of the largest lake (Lago Corvo, 2464m), which hosts rare alpine charr fish, a rest-cum-picnic stop is compulsory.

A little further down via the signposted path junction of Passo di Rabbi is Rif. Lago Corvo (2425m), facing south and the Vegaia-Tremenesca Group, not to mention the wonderful panorama of the Brenta Dolomites SSE.

Stage Three: descent to Piazzola (2h)

N.108 in descent has two variants - the more direct and steeper one goes due south straight down the narrow valley, while the other, only slightly longer but easier on the knees and more scenic, heads SE to a grassy ridge at first. It soon swings right through trees, and further down crosses a vehicle track several times. The two variants join, and Malga Palude (1835m) is passed (about half way in all). The conifer wood, much thicker now, is beautiful and silent, and you could disturb roe deer or squirrels. The path is steep but easy, and you come out at an area known as Cavallar (1420m), with a small official car park. Take the dirt track along right and down a couple of bends. Soon after the signpost for "Ret. Malga Buse" is an unmarked path which (saving you dust and traffic) brings you out at the church of Piazzola again.

RIF. S. DORIGONI tel:0463/985107. SAT, sleeps 80 (20/6-30/9)

RIF. AL FONTANIN tel:0463/902080. Private, sleeps 14 (15/5-30/9)
RIF. LAGO CORVO tel:0463/985175. Private, sleeps 40 (20/6-20/9)
TOURIST OFFICE MALÉ tel:0463/901280
TOURIST OFFICE RABBI tel:0463/985048 seasonal

WALK 20 (see sketch map G, p.116)
VEGAIA-TREMENESCA GROUP -
The Valley of Seven Lakes

via San Bernardo - Valorz parking area (30mins) - Lago Soprasasso (2h15mins) - Lago Rotondo (45mins) - Passo Valletta (1h) - Malga al Campo (45mins) - Roncio (1h15mins) - Mezzana (15mins)
Total walking time: 6h45mins - 1 day suggested
MAP: TABACCO NO.10 scale 1:50,000

Surprisingly enough, this beautiful area is not well visited, perhaps because it lies just outside the boundaries of the Stelvio National Park. No difficulty is involved, and the path (n.121 the whole way) is clear and well marked, apart from a couple of stretches in Stage Two that need a little hunting for.

Though the complete traverse is worthwhile, the itinerary lends itself to variations: one possibility is to spend a whole day just in the picturesque valley of the lakes (Stage One) and return the same way. As well, the farms and southern-oriented mountainside in the Stage Two descent can easily be explored as a return day trip - it's possible to drive as far as 1800m. While the area lacks the appeal of the lakes valley, once you're above the woods, compensation comes in the form of sweeping views of the Presanella-Adamello Group and Brenta Dolomites.

For the complete traverse, should you have access to two cars, leave one in advance at the parking area (approx. 1800m) well above Ortisé - signposting for "Passo Valletta" via a narrow dirt road west at first from the village, and where the route continues northwards for Baita Pozze, turn off right. This will save you some 900m in descent. There's a further brief saving if you start the walk from the Valorz parking area.

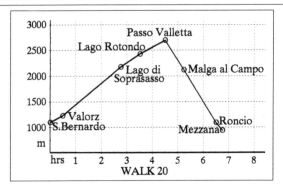

ACCESS: buses from the railhead of Malé (NW of Trento) in Val di Sole serve the Rabbi valley and San Bernardo (7km) all year round.

At the walk's end, there are even more frequent runs from Mezzana east back to Malé (12km), or west towards the Peio valley or Passo del Tonale for other itineraries.

The alternative exit point of Menas is connected to Pellizzano by a limited bus service (Tues-Fri only until 1pm at the time of writing).

Stage One: via Valorz parking area (30mins) to Lago Soprasasso (2h15mins), Lago Rotondo (45mins) and Passo Valletta (1h)

Shortly downhill from the bus stop and centre of San Bernardo village (1098m) is the signposted turn-off for n.121 (south) over the torrent. (By car, the access road is some 1km upstream.) There's an encouraging view up the valley to the Valorz waterfall. After a couple of bends to detour buildings, follow signs for "Valorz sentiero" (though "Valorz via delle malghe" is only slightly longer). A couple of asphalt winds past the houses of Valorz proper, and you join the dirt road. Lovely walking (SW) under a soft canopy of larch sheltering undergrowth of ferns and raspberry canes. At approx. 1230m the track is closed to unauthorised traffic with a parking area (30mins). Still as a wide track, n.121 proceeds to a pleasant picnic/bbq area (toilet block, drinking water and shelter, 1364m).

From here, where the valley seems impenetrable due to a sheer rock barrier, a path zigzags steeply to the right of the waterfall, and includes a short rock tunnel. Squirrels scamper in the last trees which

128

On a glacially modelled 'wave', during the ascent to Lago Soprasasso

give way to green alder shrubs for the most part. There's a wide curve SE, past a ruined farm (1958m), then you climb through alpenrose and purple monk's hood flowers and an unusual glacier-moulded rock "wave", to Lago Soprasasso (2177m). This is the first of a series of pretty lakes set in a similarly delightful series of platforms staggered all the way up to the pass.

There's a further abandoned farm (2207m) sheltered by "roches moutonées", then west, you enter a marshy side valley threaded through by a crystal-clear stream. (The dominating peak west is not Cima Tremenesca as the maps erroneously show.) Yellow pasque flowers, white moon-daisies and banks of humpy polished and grooved rock precede beautiful Lago Rotondo (2427m), dominated in turn by Cima Mezzana.

Keeping high above the right-hand side of the lake, now beneath true Cima Tremenesca (the 2882m peak west), the path narrows and, heading south briefly, cuts diagonally across a rubble gully before climbing another easy rock wall. Coasting alongside a stream, you emerge at squarish and even lovelier Lago Alto (2575m). The final stretch to the pass follows small cairns, useful in early summer if waymarking is covered by snow. And after a grand total of 4h30mins, you finally reach breathtaking Passo Valletta (2694m), a wide col between Cima Mezzana (east) and Cima Valletta (west). View-wise, north are the valley's seven lakes visible at your feet, then the Zufritt Spitze, while in the distant NE is Austria's snow-capped Gross Glockner. On the southern side of the pass is the marvellous extension of the Presanella-Adamello range running SW, as well as the Brenta Dolomites SE. Superb.

An optional ascent from here is to Cima Valletta (2857m) from the pass (marked, about 30mins) via the crest west, then north - some scrambling over fractured fallen rock masses is involved.

Stage Two: descent via Malga al Campo (45mins), Roncio (1h15mins) to Mezzana (15mins)

From the pass, keeping left at first, the faint path drops steeply south over stone detritus into the ample grassy valley still used for grazing. Keeping to its left-hand side, through marmot colonies and down the flower-scattered slopes, head for the prominent farm, known as both Malga al Campo and Malga del Monte Alta (2106m).

(Should you inadvertently end up near Malga Bronzollo (2084m) - see the Alternative Exit to Menas - remedy by taking the signed jeep track east past another variant descent path for Menas, towards Malga al Campo, and thus rejoin n.121.)

From a junction not far from the farm, n.121 for Mezzana moves east across Valle della Casina (or Val di Spona depending on which map you have), then south again. It drops past another farm (1699m) and has a stretch in common with a vehicle track. The final part cuts through wood past a couple of old houses, to reach the farming settlement of Roncio (1095m). From here it's via road (SW) to Mezzana (940m) on the Val di Sole main road.

Alternative exit via parking area (approx. 1800m) to Menas (2h30mins)
Only recommended in descent for a car link as a long stretch of winding dirt vehicle track is involved downhill from the parking area. During the descent from Passo Valletta, you'll see clearer markings (n.121b) that lead SW into a small pasture plain with a small hut (about 2200m), then around right to a newish farm with a crucifix, near Malga Bronzollo (2084m) (1h from the pass). From here a

recently constructed vehicle track (authorised traffic only) winds downhill, crosses a torrent around 1850m, and reaches a parking and picnic area (about 1800m, 45mins). A dirt road from here comes out at Ortisé, with Menas nearby east. From here the original cart track to Mezzana is still usable, and starts from the fountain. Keep right at the first two forks, then it's signposted (45mins).

TOURIST OFFICE MEZZANA tel:0463/757134
TOURIST OFFICE RABBI tel:0463/985048 seasonal

WALK 21 (see sketch map G, p.116)
VAL DE LA MARE - Rifugio Larcher and Chamois

---

via Peio - Malga Mare car park (2h30mins) - Rif. Larcher (1h45mins) - side trip to La Forcola (2h15mins return) - Lago del Careser (1h25mins) - Malga Mare car park (1h20mins) - Peio (2h10mins) Total walking time: 9h10mins (+ 2h15mins for side trip) - 2 days suggested
MAP: TABACCO No.08 scale 1:25,000

An absolutely brilliant trip with some splendid scenery, this one is well within the reach of family groups - with the exception perhaps of the Forcola side trip, the final steep stretch of which can be tricky and icy. This latter is, however, strongly recommended in good conditions, as the 3032m vantage point gives access to a wonderful vast icescape.

Plenty of wild flowers are guaranteed in addition to the animals, which range from roe deer and chamois to marmots. On the road connecting Peio Fonti with Peio proper is a small-scale open air "area faunistica" run by the Stelvio Park rangers.

By driving as far as the Malga Mare power station car park (9.5km - turn-off at Cogolo, before Peio Fonti) it is possible to do the thus reduced circuit, taking in Rif. Larcher and the lakes, as a day trip (about 4h30mins, excluding the Forcola extension).

As far as walking supplies go, the Val di Sole shops stock tasty local cheeses as well as sausages, while sweet ideas include wholesome

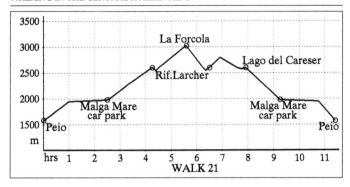

carrot cakes or the speciality "torta di fregoloti", a hard, lumpy, shortbread-like tart made with chopped almonds.

Peio, like other spas and springs in neighbouring valleys, owes it waters to a geological fault, also responsible for the minerals mined in the whereabouts until recently. Traces of the activity remain in place names such as Fucine (furnace). Nowadays a mineral water bottling plant operates near Peio.

ACCESS: the small spa resort of Peio Fonti (also called Pejo Terme) is situated in a side valley off Val di Sole, and can be reached all year round by bus (24.5km) from Malé (train from Trento). Further on (2km uphill) is the actual village of Peio, served by most bus runs.

In summer there are direct coaches from Milan via Passo del Tonale to Peio Fonti.

Stage One: from Peio to Malga Mare car park (2h30mins)

From where the bus leaves you in the mountainside village of Peio (1579m), walk uphill bearing diagonally left to the church (signposting for Malga Saline and Malga Mare). Follow the road up several winds past a late 15th century chapel (S. Rocco) to the start of a dirt track (n.105) heading north, in the proximity of a playing field (15mins). Clear red and white waymarkings lead through meadows dotted with old timber barns and huts, then shady wood. A good 1h from the village is the junction with n.127 (at about 1950m) where you turn right for Malga Mare, with an essentially level path ahead.

132

Alternative Access via cable car and Rif. Scoiattolo

This is a little shorter (by 30mins) than the main route for reaching the above-mentioned junction, but cuts nearly 400m off the ascent. From lower Peio Fonti (1383m), the cable car Funivia Tarlenta 2000 (operates early July to first week of September) and runs as far as 2034m and Rif. Scoiattolo (drinks and meals only). Around behind the building a path (n.127 but unmarked at first) leads down east into a flowered hollow with masses of spotted gentians, and across a stream. Continue through the wood mostly on a level, ignoring the turn-off (10mins) to Malga Saline, and after a brief drop to a small building (and over the underground pipelines from Malga Mare), go left onto the dirt road to where n.105 from Peio village joins up and Malga Mare is signposted (30mins to here).

N.127 heads due north now and is a wide, easy if rather long stroll. There are plenty of distractions in the conifer woods in the form of roe deer and sometimes even chamois in the undergrowth, while the tree tops host noisy woodpeckers, nutcrackers and acrobatic squirrels. As far as flowers go, there are stupendous banks of alpenrose as well as slender white St. Bruno's lilies in open grassy areas, just to name a few. Some way along, following an avalanche-prone slope is a stream crossing, then several small concrete structures for the underground water conduits. Narrowing considerably, n.127 climbs off left to round a couple of rocky outcrops and reach a lookout point towards the upper valley, including Rif. Larcher. Not far now is the Italian Electricity Commission (ENEL) reservoir and small hydroelectric power station, together with the car park at 1983m. (1h30mins from n.127-n.105 junction.)

Stage Two: ascent to Rif. Larcher (1h45mins)

Once through the car park, path n.102 climbs to the long cow shed of ex dairy farm Malga Mare (2031m, 10mins), which has been beautifully renovated and converted into a restaurant. As far as the name "mare" goes, rather than a marine reference ("mare" is Italian for sea), the name comes from the mountain to its west, Palon de la Mare. It in turn is believed to derive from the pre-Roman "lamara" for a heap of stones, while "pala" refers to a particularly steep slope.

The well-trodden path climbs in wide curves through more pink alpenrose shrubs and the occasional larch and Arolla pine to a series of streams amongst open marshy terrain rendered more picturesque by fat yellow globeflowers and fluffy white cotton-grass. The Vedretta Rossa glacier comes into view WSW now, beneath M. Vioz. Its name, "red glacier", came about when the ice was coloured by the tears of blood wept by the mother of Prince Adalberto at his death (see Walk 22 for the Vioz story).

At 2290m, the path enters the immense Pian Venezia, the wide middle section of Val Venezia, equipped with a Park hut, drinking water and a picnic area. At the junction keep to lower path n.102 (NNW). (N.146 climbs to Lago Lungo.) A gradual hour's climb remains up the left-hand flank of the valley, the panorama widening at every step, and Rif. Larcher already visible ahead. A couple of fresh springs are signposted ("sorgente") along the way though your eyes will probably be set on the fantastic sights of the great moraine walls across the valley (west) beneath the ice and snow cascade of multi-crevassed Vedretta de la Mare. In fact once you've arrived at Rif. Larcher (2608m), it's even more spectacular, right opposite the refuge. Dramatic colour tone contrasts are provided by the khaki-brown moraine, lichen-stained green rock, red scree, blue ice and white snow.

The refuge's namesake, Guido Larcher, was a Trentino patriot and chairman of SAT, the Trentino Alpine Club. The original building Rif. Cevedale dated back to 1882 and had separate dormitories for men and women. The spacious new one (inaugurated in 1992), in local red-grey stone brightened by blue and white shutters, occupies the same site and has modern bathrooms with showers (though hot water is another matter). The hearty home-style cooking, on the other hand, is recommended, while the custodian, an alpine guide, and his wife are a mine of information about the surrounding area and glacier and rock-climbing routes. Nb: Rif. Larcher doesn't accept individual bookings (groups only).

Side trip to La Forcola (2h15mins return)

Expect snow and possibly ice on the final approach to La Forcola pass and be prepared to turn back if conditions are unfavourable. Allow a good 1h20mins for the ascent.

From in front of the refuge's kitchen door take the path (n.103 but

Rif. Larcher on its rock perch opposite multi-crevassed Vedretta de la Mare

no numbering at first) that heads slightly downhill (NW) along the valley. (The variant via the chapel is feasible but the faint path soon disappears, leaving you to do a lot of clambering over fallen rock.) It soon ascends in earnest, punctuated by purple dwarf snowbells, perfumed dainty pink primroses (early summer), marmots and timid chamois, not to mention the soaring flocks of alpine choughs and the occasional eagle. Once over a ridge (about 45mins up) you lose sight of the refuge. The final stretch of zigzags is very steep and should be covered with due attention as it tends to be snow-covered and icy well into the walking season. All effort is fully repaid with the incredibly wide-ranging panorama at the ample pass, La Forcola (or Fürkelescharte, 3032m). As well as finding yourself on the administrative border between Italian-speaking Trentino and German-speaking Südtirol, you're right over some vast glaciers, a gentle rolling sea of snow and ice. Below are Martellerhütte and Zufallhütte in Martelltal. Mountain-wise, NNE in the distance is the Similaun, NW Ortler, close-by west is Cevedale, while back SE are the Brenta Dolomites. The crest leading WSW constitutes one of the approach routes for M. Cevedale (experts only).

Return to Rif. Larcher by the same route.

Stage Three: lake circuit via Lago Marmotta (25mins) and Lago del Careser (1h), then descent to Malga Mare car park (1h20mins)

From Rif. Larcher follow signposting for Lago Marmotta (E). Well-trodden n.104 climbs gradually to a ridge where it enters a wide valley echoing with marmot cries, and housing the aptly named lake (2704m). Further on, east, past small sluice gates, ignore the path junction (variant n.146 via Lago Lungo to Pian Venezia) whereas at the next one (where n.104 climbs NE to traverse the Vedretta di Careser) turn right (SE) on n.123. It coasts easily along through flat grassy flowered (spotted gentians and round-headed rampions) terrain to the next small lake, Lago Nero (2624m). In the vicinity are huge black glacier-polished rocks like whales. Azure lake-cum-dam Lago del Careser (2603m) is next, with a discrete series of ENEL buildings on its shores. If the gate to the dam wall is open, you can probably nip over (access is theoretically unauthorised, but the personnel tend to close a blind eye), otherwise keep to the official path which unfortunately drops below the wall in a 20min detour, climbing up again to emerge at the southernmost end of the dam. Here a rest will give you time to take stock of the line-up of giants west over the valley which have accompanied you this far: the twin Cevedale peaks NW, Palon de la Mare WSW, M. Vioz SW.

The pleasant descent path moves SW past another delightful lake (Lago della Lama) and there are views down to Valle di Peio, with flat-topped Cima Presanella-Cima di Vermiglio in the background (SSW). The path winds down easily and pleasantly and into light wood once more, to reach the car park below Malga Mare.

Stage Four: return to Peio (2h10mins)

If you don't manage to hitch a lift down the road to Cogolo (buses), then the return to the valley is as per Stage One in reverse.

RIF. G. LARCHER AL CEVEDALE tel:0463/751770. SAT, sleeps 90 (20/6-20/9)
TOURIST OFFICE COGOLO tel:0463/754345 seasonal
TOURIST OFFICE PEIO FONTI tel:0463/753100

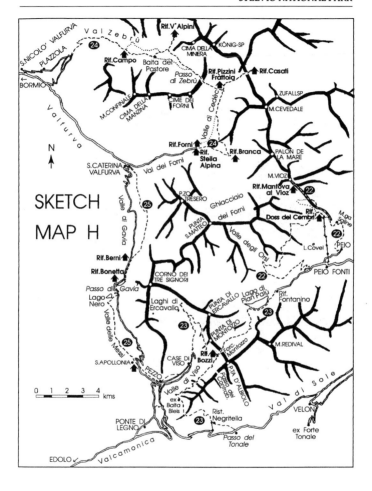

SKETCH

MAP H

WALK 22 (see sketch map H, p.137)
MONTE VIOZ - 3645 metres

---

via Peio - Malga Saline (1h30mins) - Rif. Mantova al Vioz (4h30mins)
[Alt. from Peio Fonti via cable car to Rif. Scoiattolo (10mins) - chair
lift to Rif. Doss dei Cembri (10mins) - Rif. Mantova al Vioz
(3h30mins)] - Monte Vioz (35mins return) - Rif. Doss dei Cembri
(2h15mins) - Sentiero dei Tedeschi - Valle degli Orsi (2h30mins) -
Malga Termenago di sotto (1h30mins) - Peio Fonti (20mins)
Total time: 13h10mins (less 2h10mins if cable car and chair lift are
used in ascent) - 2 days suggested
MAP: TABACCO No.08 scale 1:25,000

Justifiably popular for its spectacular summit views, at 3645m Monte
Vioz on the southern edge of the Ortler Group is the highest point in
this guide. It is well within the reach of all fit walkers who have a clear
head and sure foot. However good conditions are imperative,
including absence of ice on the summit stretch (unless you possess
crampons, ice pick and experience). This route should not be attempted
in adverse weather conditions as it can be extreme and is often
exposed to bitter winds. Clouds, of course, obstruct views. Even
when hot weather in the valleys dictates T-shirts and shorts, walkers
must carry warm windproof and waterproof clothing as well as
energy foods for the strenuous ascent. August-September is probably

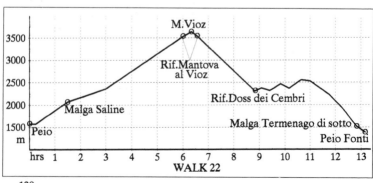

the best period, but conditions will naturally vary from year to year.

Though it is a great pity to miss sunrise from the top if you overnight at Rif. Mantova al Vioz, M. Vioz can be done as a day trip from Peio Fonti in about 7h (see Alternative Ascent). Careful timing is involved to fit in with the cable car and chair lift operating schedules.

Stage Four, although not essential to the ascent of M. Vioz, has been included as an easy variant descent. It is well worth following for the variety of bird and animal life observable, combined with the sweeping views south and east.

As far as the name goes, Vioz was actually a horse, a trusty steed on a desperate journey with his heroic master Adalberto, a young German prince, who perished on the summit for the glory of his homeland.

ACCESS: see Walk 21.

Stage One: from Peio via Malga Saline (1h30mins) to Rif. Mantova al Vioz (4h30mins)

Those opting for the 2066m climb on foot without mechanical aids are best off setting out from the quiet village of Peio (1579m). As for Stage One of Walk 21, from the bus stop, head up left to the church, then around the road to the start of a dirt track (15mins) signposted n.105 for Malga Saline. This climbs north for the most part, through meadows then forest, to the farm, Malga Saline at 2074m.

From here n.105 curves southish across a ski slope (patchy waymarking), close to an erratic block called Sas delle Strie (Witches' Rock, 2219m). Witches were believed to use its (prehistoric) cup-shaped hollows for cooking food and lighting fires for their Sabbaths. It was also the site of a terrible curse - the servants of young Re di Valle (king of the valley - Monte Redival is SW) were turned to stone as they climbed bearing gifts for their master's beloved Donzella (Pala della Donzella, due north).

The path heads north once more in continual ascent. It moves onto a ridge (Filon degli Uomini, the petrified men) where it is joined by the Alternative Ascent following, above Rif. Doss dei Cembrì (some 1h30mins from the Malga at approx. 2360m). NW now it hugs the ridge, but soon crosses over to the eastern flank, often exposed but not dangerously narrow. Fixed cable is provided at times, and some sections require clambering. Stops for getting your breath back and acclimatising provide the chance to drink in the ever-expanding views. After rounding the base of the Dente del Vioz, the path is joined by the variant from Valle della Mite (see Alternative Descent), and this stretch alongside a jagged ridge is known as the "Rastel". After a near vertical aided passage, the climb proceeds steeply, and the regular, effort-saving zigzags reveal their military origin. NE is glittering Lago del Careser beneath its immense flat glacier, hemmed in by a series of impressive peaks, while Rif. Larcher is visible to the north in the underlying valley.

In due course you climb up past the tiny chapel to Rif. Mantova al Vioz (3535m) on the southern shoulder of M. Vioz. Note that the tap water here is not drinkable. (At the time of writing the refuge was only open for refreshments as extensive renovations were under way, with completion programmed for 1996.) Originally a German Alpine Club refuge, later transferred to the Trentino club (SAT), it also functioned as an Austrian garrison during the First World War with a position constantly manned on the summit itself.

Alternative Ascent: via cable car to Rif. Scoiattolo (10mins), chair lift to Rif. Doss dei Cembri (10mins), ascent to Rif. Mantova al Vioz (3h30mins)
At Peio Fonti (1383m) the bubble-like cable car (Funivia Tarlenta 2000) usually functions from early July through to the first week of September as far as Rif. Scoiattolo (2034m, meals only).

It's a further 10mins by chair lift (same operating period) to Rif. Doss dei Cembri (2313m) or Gembri, a reference to the Arolla pines which abound here. In the quiet of early mornings and evenings, chamois are often found grazing on the grassy slopes. The refuge-cum-guesthouse is another great place to stay, and their generous homestyle meals in the Trentino tradition are recommended.

NW from here Rif. Mantova al Vioz (1350m to go) can be seen, dominated by the sharp tooth, Dente del Vioz. Just uphill from the chair lift and refuge the signposted path turns right (SE at first) to cut across the slope and climb steadily in wide zigzags. Larches and grass are quickly left behind and it's soon all scree and rock. Higher up on the crest you merge with the main route n.105 (from Malga Saline) - see the appropriate point in the previous description.

Stage Two: M. Vioz summit (35mins return)

From Rif. Mantova al Vioz the well-trodden path for the final 110m (20mins) to the summit follows the exposed and narrow NNW-running ridge in snow for the main part, in between two sheer ice-bound slopes. Soon after reaching a large cross is the summit, on more level ground and marked by a trig point (20mins). The breathtaking sights need some time to sink in. 13 peaks surround the magnificent Forni glacier at your feet (and when connected constitute a well-followed mountaineering itinerary). The most notable mountains, from north moving anticlockwise, are Cevedale, the nearby rounded Palon de la Mare, far-off König-Spitze NNW, then Pizzo Tresero (WSW) and Punta San Matteo (SW). Southwards on a good day the Adamello and Presanella groups are visible, plus the Dolomites (east) if you're especially lucky. NB: while admiring the view and taking photographs, be careful not to inadvertently move onto snow cornices.

An Austrian First World War front ran from the summit of M. Vioz via several strongholds and southwest along the crests to Punta S. Matteo, and tangled historic barbed wire still litters the slopes.

(It's 15mins back down the same way to the refuge.)

Stage Three: descent to Rif. Doss dei Cembri (2h15mins)

Same route as the Alternative Ascent, with the option of detouring via Valle della Mite, only slightly longer and less frequented, as follows:

Alternative Descent: during the "Rastel" and prior to the Dente del Vioz, path n.138 branches off down right (west) into Valle della Mite. It is rough going at times across the stony slope but the route is clear. You reach the stark valley floor at what used to be a chair lift station (about halfway down Valle della Mite) - ruined by a recent avalanche which evidently wiped out the marmots too. SE down at the valley mouth the path emerges close to Rif. Doss dei Cembri.

Stage Four: via Sentiero dei Tedeschi to Valle degli Orsi (2h30mins) and descent to Malga Termenago di sotto (1h30mins) and Peio Fonti (20mins)

This route (n.139), known as the "Sentiero dei Tedeschi" (Path of the

Germans, presumably a reference to the First World War), is clearly signposted from Rif. Doss dei Cembri. At first there's a brief uphill stretch, then left across the stream and around the corner away from people. On a level over mostly dry terrain on this south-oriented hillside, the route comes complete with heather, bell-flowers, light purple multi-flowered variety of gentians, while chamois, marmots, crag martins and birds of prey are not rare. As far as views go, ahead SW is Punta di Ercavallo, with dark crests swinging around via Punta d'Albiolo in a southerly direction to connect with M. Redival, whereas SE the Brenta Dolomites are still visible.

After about 1h you cross the inner part of a valley below Punta Taviela and south now, three short stretches of fixed cable aid you across rock. An unstable crumbly passage, then around the corner you reach a path junction in a grassy saddle (Colen 2368m, 1h20mins this far).

Alternative exit: as signposted, it's possible to descend at this point via Lago di Covel (1839m), thence Peio.

Keep to the upper branch (marked "Valle Orsi collegamento", meaning link), and climb into the next small side valley. Dominated by moraine crests, the ground here is rockier and frequented by sheep and goats together with twittering ground nesting birds. Further south, on a lookout point (2532m) below Cima Frattasecca, are old stone walls where you look down onto Lago di Pian Palù (50mins from the previous junction).

A clear passage NW follows through fallen boulders in descent now towards Valle degli Orsi. 15mins on, at a signpost (for the bit you've done it says Colen - Rif. Doss dei Cembri - collegamento sent. 139), turn down left into a grassy hollow. Path and waymarking disappear, so head further west over to the nearby torrent that descends from Vedretta degli Orsi. Here, in an ideal spot for picnicking, the path becomes n.122, with signposting for Biv. Meneghello (north). (This part differs from the map, which shows the path further east and not actually touching the stream.) During the First World War Valle degli Orsi (Valley of the Bears) was an essential supply channel for the Austrian strongholds on Punta S. Matteo and the crests eastwards. Fortification work and bombardments were, in fact, responsible for lowering the peak by a good 6m. The name for Punta S. Matteo was given it by Payer who reached its summit on St Matthew's Day (1867).

Don't cross the stream here but turn sharp left for the descent. After a brief rise, a good path (n.122) cuts down the heathered slope. Encounters with vipers are not unusual on this dry terrain - treading heavily to give them time to move off the path seems to be the best policy. Stone ruins such as those you pass at 2349m provide perfect breeding grounds.

Some 30mins in descent is a junction: fork left (n.122) for Vegaia and Peio (right for Malga Giumella and Lago di Pian Palù). Red and white waymarking on the narrow path leads you east, then south again, down into larch, then mixed conifer wood with carline thistles. It is 20mins to a rough vehicle wide track (n.124) where you go left. This is tall shady forest now. At the first corner curve (1794m), a side path leads to a waterfall (Cascata Cadini, then Lago Covel, hence Peio village, but it's rather roundabout). Keep down right following the track. After several wide bends (no short cuts), you finally emerge at the picnic area of Malga Termenago di sotto (1523m, now a Park refuge reserved for groups) and drinking water.

Nearby is the car park, then asphalt road, where you turn left. 20mins around through meadows is Peio Fonti with hotels, shops and buses again.

RIF. DOSS DEI CEMBRI tel:0463/753227. Private, sleeps 28 (1/7-7/ 9)

RIF. MANTOVA AL VIOZ tel:0463/751386. SAT, sleeps 50 (re-open for accommodation in 1996) (1/7-20/9)

TOURIST OFFICE PEIO FONTI tel:0463/753100

WALK 23 (see sketch map H, p.137)
ERCAVALLO-ALBIOLO GROUP -
First World War Remains

---

via Peio Fonti - Rif. Fontanino (1h) - Forcellina Montozzo (3h30mins) - Rif. Bozzi (15mins) - Alt. a) ex Baita Bleis (1h) - Rist. Nigritella (1h30mins) - Passo del Tonale (15mins) OR Alt. b) Laghi di Ercavallo (1h30mins) - Case di Viso (1h45mins) - Pezzo (45mins)
Total walking time: Alt. a) 7h30mins; Alt. b) 8h45mins - 2 days suggested
MAP: TABACCO No.10 scale 1:50,000

The walking involved here is straightforward and suitable for all ranges of abilities - the sole exception being the exposed section at the start of Alternative b) which necessitates extra care and a head for heights. Points of interest include First World War trenches and constructions still visible around Forcellina Montozzo and Rif. Bozzi, as well as the animal life (marmots guaranteed) and clusters of traditional stone houses in Valle di Viso, not to mention some wonderful panoramas.

Geologically it's all metamorphic, but there are striking differences between dark red and flaky silvery-grey mica-bearing rock (schists), alongside light and dark banded (gneiss), and even some white patches of marble.

ACCESS: Peio Fonti (also called Pejo Terme), a small spa resort, is in a side valley running NW off Val di Sole. It can be reached all year round by bus (24.5km) from Malé (train from Trento).

For the Alternative a) exit from Passo del Tonale, either return eastwards to Val di Sole by year-round bus, or descend west to Ponte di Legno by the occasional summer line. Here, at the northernmost reach of Valcamonica, year-round buses run the 19.5km SW to the railhead at Edolo (trains south to Brescia and the Milan-Venice line).

Pezzo, where Alternative b) terminates, is connected to Ponte di Legno (5km south) by minibus (except Sundays).

Stage One: via Rif. Fontanino (1h) to Forcellina Montozzo (3h30mins) and Rif. Bozzi (15mins)

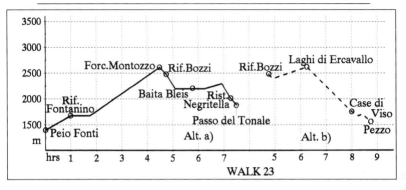

WALK 23

Leave the small resort of Peio Fonti (1397m) along the surfaced road west for the 4km to Rif. Fontanino (1675m) and parking area. Despite its name, Rif. Fontanino is only a restaurant and no accommodation is available there.

A wide track climbs up to the dam (Lago di Pian Palù) and farms, then (n.110) skirts the southern shore to the opening of Val Montozzo. Here at a junction, n.111 starts zigzagging decisively in ascent south through larch forest. The going levels out somewhat once you're in the upper green open pasture area, on the other side from the crest joining M. Redival and the two Albiolo peaks (south). After a final curve round south, you reach wide grassy Forcellina Montozzo (2613m) pitted with First World War trenches. The contested pre-war border between Austria and Italy ran through here and down to Passo del Tonale, and now it marks the administrative division between Lombardy and Trentino. The view back to the distant snowy ridge running NNE takes in Punta San Matteo along to M. Vioz, with Rif. Mantova perched on its eastern flank. On the other side is the triangular form of the Corno dei Tre Signori NW, while SW stands Corno Baitone, part of the Adamello Group.

A wide mule-track (n.2) leads down to a small lake and modest but homely Rif. A. Bozzi (2478m), named in memory of a courageous Italian soldier who lost his life on nearby Torrione d'Albiolo (east) in 1915.

145

Crucifix at Forcellina di Montozzo, with Corno dei Tre Signori behind

Alt. a) via ex Baita Bleis (1h), Rist. Nigritella (1h30mins) and Passo del Tonale (15mins)

Ex-military track n.2 moves off SW and after an inital gradual descent to 2200m, maintains that height. Marmots and spotted gentians characterise the first section, with layers of alpenrose, green alder shrubs and larch later, as you round Cima Bleis. After n.2 (signposted junction) continues SW to drop to Ponte di Legno, n.63 takes over. A short distance south is a ruined hut Baita Bleis (2202m, only important as a reference point). It's a further level 30mins to another signposted junction where a pause is on the cards for serious admiration of the immense panorama before you: south are the immense ice and light grey rock massifs of the Adamello-Presanella groups, while behind you, back NW, is Val delle Messi with its crown of dark grey and reddish peaks.

N.63 goes SE now with several ups and downs and ins and outs, cutting grassy hillsides pitted with marmot burrows. The path is waymarked regularly by paint splashes on stones along the way. After criss-crossing a ski slope, you drop to Ristorante Nigritella (no accommodation) and chair lift (operates in summer and deposits you at the main road some 2km west of the pass proper). On foot, as ski slopes and chair and ski lifts have eradicated the original marked paths, make your way down via the dirt track or slopes to the central area of Passo del Tonale (1883m). Buses stop near the First World War memorial.

Yet another alternative traverse: a further interesting and slightly shorter crossing from Rif. Bozzi to Passo del Tonale is by way of the "smugglers" pass', Passo dei Contrabbandieri (2681m), on path n.111 (2h20mins).

Alt. b) via Laghi di Ercavallo (1h30mins), descent to Case di Viso (1h45mins) then Pezzo (45mins)
From Rif. Bozzi, ex-military route n.2 drops past a series of ruined constructions and terracing dating back to the First World War, and heads NW, then due north, with interesting views down onto the Case di Viso hamlet. The path quickly narrows and becomes a horizontal incision into the steep and friable flanks of Punta di Montozzo. In fact for the good part of the next 1h it is rather exposed with numerous crumbly stretches, only one of which is equipped with a length of (unreliable) chain. After the path widens, you swing around (west) to join the path from the valley floor. Now n.2 climbs easily (10mins) to the first of the Laghi di Ercavallo (2621m) in the vast cirque beneath the Corno dei Tre Signori. This "Horn of the Three Lords" was thus called as the borders of Switzerland, the Duchy of Milan and the Republic of Venice once met there. Another "3" motif is that its glaciers feed three rivers - the Adda (west via Valtellina) and the Oglio (south via Valcamonica), which both end up joining the Po, and the Noce, which flows east into the Etsch (or Adige). While snow lies late here, July walkers will be rewarded by a profusion of alpine snowbells, sticky primroses and daisies. Chamois can sometimes be sighted around the head of this valley. (From here path n.2 continues NW to higher lakes and eventually crosses a south ridge of the Corno dei Tre Signori, involving a brief climb and ice traverse in descent to Passo Gavia.)

For the descent, return to the path junction and take n.59, a good earth path in wide curves down the steep grassy slopes. Apart from the ubiquitous bellflowers, an occasional martagon lily brightens the descent amongst alpenrose and green alder shrubs, though your attention will soon be captured by marmots scampering down their roomy burrows on your approach.

About 1h30mins down (at 1880m) is a car park and picnic area (complete with fireplaces, drinking water and toilet block). (From here n.52, a direct jeep track, climbs to Rif. Bozzi in 2h.)

Short-cut the dirt road downhill and 15mins will see you following the torrent through banks of rosebay willow-herb and the picturesque Case di Viso (1754m). This carefully restored hamlet was built almost entirely in stone, including large slab-tiles as roofing. The huts are mostly summer holiday homes now, though a couple are still used by local shepherds who sell their dairy products, as well as a bar.

To reach Pezzo, take the dirt road on the right-hand side of the torrent above the tiny church and the terraced fields. Some 15mins down where asphalting starts, a worthwhile alternative to the traffic is to turn right up the track to another small hamlet, Case di Pirli (1711m). Once you're past the houses the track narrows and a path (red and white waymarking) heads off down left through woods the locals "revere" in view of the anti-avalanche protection they provide. 20mins bring you out at the interesting old village of Pezzo (1565m). In addition to a panoramic hotel, a couple of shops and bus stop (on the far NW edge, at Bar Stazione), there are several unusual crucifixes decorated with a variety of carved objects in wood, symbolising the Passion of Christ.

(For the footpath to Ponte di Legno, see Walk 25 after Stage Two.)

RIF. A. BOZZI tel:0364/900152. CAI, sleeps 23 (15/6-21/9)
ALBERGO MIRAVALLE (PEZZO) tel:0364/91183
TOURIST OFFICE PASSO DEL TONALE tel:0364/91343
TOURIST OFFICE PEIO FONTI tel:0463/753100
TOURIST OFFICE PONTE DI LEGNO tel:0364/91949

WALK 24 (see sketch map H, p.137)
VALLE DI CEDEC & VAL ZEBRÙ - Glaciers and Wildlife Galore

---

via S. Caterina Valfurva - Rif. Forni (1h30mins) - Rif. Branca (1h) - Rif. Pizzini-Fràttola (1h45mins) - side trip to Rif. Casati (3h30mins return) - Passo di Zebrù (1h) - Rif. V° Alpini (2h30mins) - Rif. Campo (1h45mins) - Plazzola (1h45mins) (S. Nicolò Valfurva)
Total walking time: 11h15mins (+ 3h30mins for side trip) - 3-4 days suggested
MAPS: TABACCO No.08 scale 1:25,000 (except for the very end) or KOMPASS No.072 scale 1:50,000

Simply spectacular, this highly recommended route covers a great range of terrains and scenery within the Lombard slice of the Stelvio National Park. The majority of visitors go either for the ice routes or the wildlife and this walk gives a taste of both. In particular, Val Zebrù (Stages Three & Four) has large populations of ibex (reintroduced in 1968), deer, roe deer and chamois, not to mention the marmots. Eagles nest in the valley and large black grouse feed in the conifer woods. Binoculars are a must.

In good weather this itinerary as a whole rates "average" on difficulty. Gaiters could be useful in early summer for the descent from Passo di Zebrù. However the middle and lower reaches of both

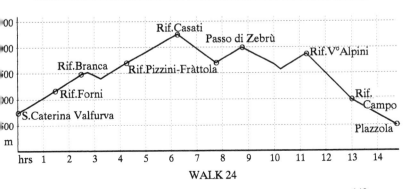

WALK 24

Valle di Cedèc and Val Zebrù mean easy walking on wide tracks and are accessible to all ages and abilities. Making a base in Valfurva or Val dei Forni, Stages One, Two and the side trip are suitable for adaptation as day walks. Similarly Val Zebrù can be visited from Valfurva, though the ascent is very long unless you make use of the jeep taxis (see Stage Four).

The township of Bormio, 13km from the walk's start, is worth a visit for the Stelvio National Park Visitor's Centre as well as several small museums. Furthermore its well-stocked shops offer local gastronomic specialities: ask for "bresaola", thinly sliced dried salt beef, or a local cheese such as sharp "scimud". As well as the valley restaurants, several high altitude refuges on the following route make an effort to serve interesting dishes. Try "pizzoccheri" (pasta made from tartary buckwheat, and mixed with cabbage, potatoes and melted cheese) and "sciatt" (literally "toad" in local dialect, but they're tasty cheese-filled fritters made of grappa-flavoured batter).

ACCESS: from Milan, trains and coaches run NE along Valtellina via Sondrio to Tirano (where the train line turns north for St Moritz), hence coaches to Bormio (195km from Milan). Connections are also possible from Vinschgau via Stilfser Joch (buses from July to mid-September). From Bormio it's a further 13km SE by bus (year-round) to the renowned winter ski resort of Santa Caterina Valfurva. A further access route by car (no public transport) is via Passo di Gavia (only open in summer) from Ponte di Legno and Valcamonica in the south.

The walk exits at Plazzola, above S. Nicolò Valfurva, which is 5km from Bormio on the same bus line as S. Caterina Valfurva - a couple of runs a day are extended up Val Zebrù as far as the "Parcheggio Val Zebrù" (car park) at Plazzola.

Stage One: via Rif. Forni (1h30mins) to Rif. Branca (1h)

From where the bus leaves you at S. Caterina Valfurva (1738m), continue upstream (northeastish) following signposting for Rif. Albergo Ghiacciaio dei Forni (shortened here to Rif. Forni). The road is not always open to private traffic though a small number of jeeps (some owned by alpine guides) are authorised to run a taxi shuttle up to the refuge (10mins) and beyond (on request). On foot it's a pleasant 5.5km ascent. The northern flanks of this valley are covered by a magnificent forest of Arolla pine. At 2061m is Rif. Stella Alpina, which also offers accommodation. Rif. Forni (2178m) is friendly and has good food. The magnificent Forni glacier, the second-largest in the Eastern Alps, is already visible SE, crowned by mountains. As you move east (at first) for Rif. Branca up track n.28a (sometimes painted as 82) the view improves considerably. After a dam the path keeps to the left-hand side of the valley in gradual ascent, to conclude in steeper curves. Rif. Branca (2487m) occupies a magnificent glacier-observing position above Lago di Ròsole. A cosy hut, though rather regimented, it dates back to 1932.

Stage Two: traverse to Rif. Pizzini-Fràttola (1h45mins)

Next to the refuge's metal shed, a narrow path branches up right to a round red metallic marker which labels it as n.8 (though maps show it as n.28c). Sharp right again (painted red arrow and 'R.P.' on rock), then a clamber onto a long pasture flat where both path and waymarking disappear. Head NW across the grassy slopes towards the crest and another round marker pole. Above a wooden hut, 30mins from the refuge, a panoramic point provides views of the Valle di Cedèc (with variant spellings) running north with views of the König-Spitze, cloud permitting. Pizzo Tresero is the snowbound massif standing SW.

Once around the corner the narrow path crosses rocky terrain and picks its way between fallen boulders. The hillside is pitted with marmot burrows, then lower boggy zones have been colonised by fluffy cotton-grass. Down at the torrent level, a bridge leads you over to join the main valley track (n.28) northwards past a spring drinking water point ("Acqua Bona") for the final 40mins in gradual ascent to hospitable Rif. Pizzini-Fràttola (2700m). The backdrop (north) consists of Punta Graglia, then light grey triangular König-Spitze (alias Gran Zebrù) preceded by the unexpected low red mound of Cima Pale Rosse, surrounded by a sea of vedrettas and colourful moraine.

Alternative access: the direct track (n.28) from Rif. Forni takes 1h40mins.

Side trip to Rif. Casati (3h30mins return time)
550m in ascent is involved but on a good day it's very worthwhile. One of Rif. Casati's outbuildings is visible on the ridge NE.

*Signposting for ascent to Rif. Casati, below Monte Pasquale (right)
and its glacier*

Head north on the jeep track. It curves right through a dreary debris landscape enlivened by bright splashes of flowers like glacier crowfoot. Pass the small lake, then short-cut (over bent corrugated iron sheets) across a stream, just down from the loading point for the refuge's cableway (30mins). The actual climb itself takes another 1h30mins and zigzags steadily on an earth base with occasional steep stretches. Watch your step as old cables lie across the path in many places, and your gaze will probably be fixed on the majestic form of the König-Spitze NW. Near the top on the ridge (Passo del Cevedale, 3260m) are rusty entanglements of barbed wire left from the First World War. Nearby is the annex known as Rif. Guasti, and just over the other side is the main part, comfortable, hotel-like Rif. Casati. Built in 1923 by the Casati family to commemorate their fallen soldier son, at 3254m it is one of the highest huts in the group. The staff are helpful and friendly and can provide guides and equipment for glacier traverses - which should not be attempted alone by the inexperienced. The hut also operates in spring for ski tourers. Weekends are best avoided for overnight stays as large mountaineering groups are common. NB: the cold tap water is not drinkable. The panorama is extensive in this exhilarating spot, most notably with the twin Cevedale peaks SE beyond the expanse of ice. 1h30mins should suffice for the return trip the same way to Rif. Pizzini-Fràttola.

Stage Three: traverse via Passo di Zebrù (1h) to Rif. V° Alpini (2h30mins)

This traverse is relatively unfrequented.

Just below Rif. Pizzini-Fràttola is a signpost for the path (n.30) known by its old name of "Tröj dei Pass Zebrù". Though waymarking, mostly on stones, is not always obvious, it keeps to the right-hand side of the stream, then crosses over to head up the grass and shale slope with patches of flowers such as purple sticky primrose and the pinkish bird's-eye primrose. Rock ptarmigans also nest on this mountain side. Maintaining its westerly direction, the path climbs easily through likely late-lying snow to Passo di Zebrù (3001m) and a small wooden bivouac cabin (two rough bed bases only). There is evidence of First World War positions here.

Now you look down into the desolate upper reaches of immense Val Zebrù, flanked by light-coloured Cima della Miniera (NW) with the Cime dei Forni and separate hanging glaciers and distinct cirques opposite (SW). The name "Forni" from furnace is a reference to the flourishing 13th-19th century iron industry connected with the mine ("miniera") lower down. Quiet early morning walkers can expect reward in the shape of the resident herds of ibex and chamois.

The descent (n.30) crosses a couple of small snow fields (gaiters are handy) with a series of poles to follow at first. Some 30mins from the pass is a steep section of chimney with a (loose) cable as aid. From here down now is marmot territory and delightful scenes of romping naïve youngsters are priceless.

The stream crossings that follow can be tricky, especially when rain-swollen, as the crumbly debris banks continue to wash away. Soon you enter a grandiose mini-valley below the retreating Vedretta della Miniera and, several more stream leaps later, climb out to a grey ridge with a signposted path junction (at approx. 2675m and 1h15mins from the pass).

Alternative descent: the left fork leads down 500m to Baita del Pastore, bypassing Rif. V° Alpini. Allow a good 1h.

It was in these desolate surrounds that Johannes Zebrusius, the Lombard feudal lord the valley was named after, is said to have ended his life of unrequited love in 1150. He was crushed by a boulder balanced on larch trunks beneath the glacier.

Continue on the right branch for Rif. V° Alpini (signposted as 29A though maps show 30b) past some benches. As suggested by the orange-shaded rock debris here, the rock has a high iron content and, in fact, you are virtually below an abandoned magnetite (iron ore) mine. Further down, on the other hand, edelweiss and yellow Rhaetian poppies mean calcareous soil, confirmed by the light hues of the surrounding rock.

The path narrows considerably, with brief exposed sections and a rough section of old fallen rocks. It rounds an outcrop (approx. 2650m, signpost) and there are breathtaking views north to Monte Zebrù with its slow spilling glacier petering out into dark moraine and the orange-roofed refuge perched on an outcrop. A brief drop then to an essentially level scree to join up with the main path from Baita del Pastore for the final gruelling 200m in ample zigzags, past the First World War terraces and dry-stone walls, to 2878m and Rif. V° Alpini (V° stands for "quinto" which means "fifth"). In yet another marvellous setting, this refuge (dating back to 1884 but reconstructed in 1928) was occupied by Italian forces for three consecutive winters. Note that the water is not drinkable here as, taken directly from the glacier, it is devoid of salts.

A climb up behind the hut is a must. There's a renowned panoramic trig point at 2943m with Cime dei Forni south, Cima della Manzina SSW, and M. Confinale SW. Not much further up the path (extra care needed) you reach the towering edge of the impressive cracked blue ice masses belonging to the Vedretta dello Zebrù. The heaps of scrap iron are among the First World War odds and ends the retreating glacier is slowly releasing.

(Allow the same time, 3h30mins, for this stage in reverse direction.)

Stage Four: descent via Rif. Campo (1h45mins), Plazzola (1h45mins)

Time permitting, stop as often as possible during this stage for binocular scans of the mountain sides for animals.

Leave the refuge on the same path you arrived on, but continue straight down (right branch) at the first junction (10mins). At the foot of the refuge's mechanised cableway the path widens into a jeep track. Rhaetian poppies dot the scree, which gives way to grassy banks soon with dwarf mountain pines. 15mins on will see you at another fork:

Alternative descent: a path signposted for Rif. Campo branches right (west) and is a feasible alternative, only slightly longer. Less frequented, it stays higher longer, though several tiring ups and downs across rough moraine are involved before it descends the minor Val di Campo.

On the main route, 1h15mins is enough to reach drinking water at the first farm, Baita del Pastore (2168m), and the parking area for the authorised jeep shuttles that connect with Valfurva. Through mixed wood with larches and Arolla pine at this point, 30mins on in the vicinity of old timber huts is Rif. Campo (1989m). The rest of the way down means sticking to the easy track west through pasture areas, each with its own small summer hut or "baita", some of which provide refreshments. Through rich mixed wood the valley narrows with steeper flanks and the torrent is crossed several times.

The first parking area you eventually come to is known as Tre Croci (1610m), and not that much further around a steep hillside is a large parking area, kiosk and bus stop and the hamlet of Plazzola (approx. 1500m).

(Allow 4h30mins in ascent from here to Rif. V° Alpini.)

Should you have to walk the final stretch to S. Nicolò Valfurva (1319m), allow 30mins and keep to the asphalted road.

RIF. V° ALPINI & G. BERTARELLI tel:0342/901591. CAI, sleeps 58 (27/6-27/9)

RIF. C. BRANCA tel:0342/935501. CAI, sleeps 100 (25/6-18/9)

RIF. CAMPO tel:0342/904349. Private, sleeps 25 (15/6-15/9)

RIF. G. CASATI & A. GUASTI tel:0342/935507. CAI, sleeps 280 (25/6-18/9)

RIF. ALBERGO GHIACCIAIO DEI FORNI tel:0342/935466. Private, sleeps 100 (1/4-30/9)

RIF. L. E. PIZZINI-FRÀTTOLA tel:0342/935513. CAI, sleeps 100 (25/6-18/9)

RIF. STELLA ALPINA tel:0342/935388. Private, sleeps 18 (10/3-31/9)

TOURIST OFFICE BORMIO tel:0342/903300

TOURIST OFFICE S. CATERINA VALFURVA tel:0342/935598

WALK 25 (see sketch map H, p.137)
VALLE DI GAVIA & VALLE DELLE MESSI -
Passo di Gavia

---

via Santa Caterina Valfurva - Rif. Berni (3h15mins) - Rif. Bonetta, Passo di Gavia (25mins) - Lago Nero (45mins) - S. Apollonia (2h) - Pezzo (20mins)
Total walking time: 6h45mins - 1-2 days suggested
MAPS: TABACCO No.10 scale 1:50,000 (except the very start) or KOMPASS No.072 scale 1:50,000

The beauty of this easy walk is that it constitutes a pleasant transfer from the northern to the southern sectors of the Stelvio National Park (or vice-versa) via the western edge. There is no public transport for the 30km between the renowned winter ski resort of S. Caterina Valfurva and Ponte di Legno so the route can be extremely useful for car-less walkers.

The road via Passo di Gavia (2618m), built by First World War Italian troops and asphalted relatively recently, is an experience in itself. Narrow with some tight curves, it is only kept open during summer months and is infamous for attracting bad weather and icy conditions even in midsummer. The dramatic photos of the 1960 "Giro d'Italia" cycle race on display at Rif. Berni exemplify this.

As far back as 1200 the pass was used by Venetian merchants for the passage of goods from the Orient en route to Bormio and Germany. As was common in the Alps, last century in particular, a route for salt contraband ("Via del Sale") ran through here. At the pass itself, travellers erected a rough stone pyramid to which they would evidently add the skulls of those who perished during storms and blizzards.

The itinerary only actually touches the road in the vicinity of the

Rif. Denza, looking north, the Redival chain and Ortler Group beyond

At Passo del Maroccaro, view south over Lago Scuro to Vedretta del Mandrone (right), the Lobbie knuckles and Vedretta della Lobbia (left)

Lago Seródoli
From Biv. Festa towards Passo di Gallinera

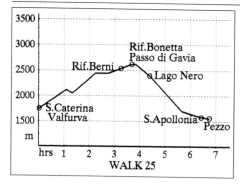

pass, and is suitable for all ranges of walkers. (NB. All path numbers are given as per maps, but in reality they hardly ever appear on the ground.)

ACCESS: see Walk 24 for S. Caterina Valfurva, and Walk 23 for information on Pezzo and Ponte di Legno. (p148)

Stage One: via Rif. Berni (3h15mins) to Passo di Gavia (25mins)

To leave S. Caterina Valfurva (1738m), from the bus stop cross the bridge south and take the secondary road (n.35) left through a brief concrete tunnel and on past the camping ground and Bar Ristorante Cevedale. A dirt track continuation crosses the next stream (Torrente Gavia), then briefly left at a Stelvio Park signboard is a narrow path (n.24a, right) leading (off the wide track) into lovely conifer forest. Beneath the larch, Arolla pines and spruce, thick undergrowth conceals bilberries and wildlife. After some 1h20mins south, joined by a wide track, it turns briefly downhill to Ponte delle Vacche (literally "Bridge of the Cows", 2047m). Still on the left-hand side of the stream, it heads uphill once more in a series of zigzags (n.25b). Two path junctions are passed, then a rough hut Baita dei Pastori (2445m, emergency shelter only). A little further along (n.25a now) is the intriguing natural stone bridge, Ponte di Pietra. Both the bridge and the deep gorge it spans were sculpted out by the impetuous water of Rio del Dosegù which carries the meltwater and silt deposits from the glacier of the same name. The stream is, in fact, a distinctly different colour, and contrasts markedly with Torrente Gavia, which it merges with nearby.

With just 30mins to go, Rif. Berni is soon visible on the roadside ahead, the dark points of M. Gavia behind it. You cross a wooden bridge followed by a marshy zone with masses of soft-tipped cotton grass. Rif. Berni (2541m) was built in 1933 in memory of the heroic

Italian Alpine troop captain, Arnaldo Berni, who lost his life during the defence of Punta S. Matteo in 1918. The refuge looks over to the Ghiacciaio di Dosegù NE, with Pizzo Tresero NNW.

An easy couple of km south past Lago Bianco (white because of the glacier silt it contains) on the road at Passo di Gavia (2618m) is hospitable private Rif. Bonetta-cum-restaurant (excellent minestrone). The graceful pyramid of Corno dei Tre Signori (see Walk 23 for notes on the name) is due east now, while SE is M. Gaviola - a well-known panoramic point, whose 3025m peak is accessible for experienced walkers (allow 2h for the return trip).

Stage Two: via Lago Nero (45mins), S. Apollonia (2h) to Pezzo (20mins)

Opposite Rif. Bonetta, take the path (n.57) that goes around behind the old building, then cuts down across grassy slopes. It turns west to cross the road and follow the dirt access track for Lago Nero (2386m). Lying in a glacial cirque, the lake overlooks Valle delle Messi (meaning "middle valley"). After a brief stretch around the left-hand lake side, the path heads off downwards (south) once more. Thick with flowers such as edelweiss, arnica and purple monk's-hood, and the occasional marmot, it winds quietly down thick grassy banks with views SSE onto the light grey Adamello massif.

Some 1h15mins from the lake (at approx. 1700m) you merge with path n.58 (from Biv. Linge). It's wider from here down, and traverses an active pastoral and dairy zone, with old-style stone and timber shepherds' huts. To your right, the ridge (including Punta di Pietra Rossa, WNW) hosts herds of chamois, whereas eagles are said to nest on the eastern side of the valley.

A camping and picnic area (drinking water, WC) with car park are soon reached. The next group of houses, Case Silizzi (a reference to silicates), was once a site of mica extraction.

The small settlement of S. Apollonia (1584m) on the roadside boasts ferruginous spring water ("Acqua Benedetta"), a modest guesthouse and a chapel to the virgin martyr Santa Apollonia, the patron saint of dentists (she is depicted holding a pair of pliers). She was captured during a pagan uprising in Alexandria, Egypt, in 249 AD, and had her teeth pulled out one by one, before throwing herself onto a fire.

Across the road from the guesthouse is the old cart track (signposted) for Pezzo. It comes out on the edge of the small village near Bar Stazione, the minibus terminal for the infrequent link with Ponte di Legno. Quiet Pezzo (1565m) is worth a visit for its quaint old houses and unusual artistic wooden crucifixes.

Footpath to Ponte di Legno (1h15mins)
In lieu of the bus, this pleasant track leads down south to Ponte di Legno.

From Bar Stazione, take Via A. Berni diagonally downhill (SE) past Albergo Miravalle. On the lower edge of the settlement branch off left on the dirt track to cross the torrent. Further on it joins an alternative dirt road from Case di Viso. Some 30mins from Pezzo (just before Talasso hamlet, 1499m), a narrow path (n.2) turns down steeply through wood and past a holiday house to the main road. A final 20mins of asphalt (the road from Passo di Gavia) will see you in the bustling but traffic-free centre of Ponte di Legno (1257m) with its excellent bakeries and delicatessens. The bus station is a few more minutes downhill across the wooden bridge that gave the town its name.

RIF. A. BERNI tel:0342/935456. CAI, sleeps 70 (1/7-30/9)
RIF. BONETTA tel:0364/91806. Private, sleeps 30 (1/7-15/10)
ALBERGO MIRAVALLE (PEZZO) tel:0364/91183
ALBERGO PIETRA ROSSA (S. APOLLONIA) tel:0364/91311
TOURIST OFFICE PONTE DI LEGNO tel:0364/91949
TOURIST OFFICE S. CATERINA VALFURVA tel:0342/935598

Adamello Nature Park

INTRODUCTION

The area as a whole straddles the major mountain massifs of the Adamello and Presanella Groups that extend south from Passo del Tonale and Val di Sole, bounded by Valcamonica in the west and in the east by Val Rendena. On paper it is actually divided into two, the western section known as the "Parco dell'Adamello" (set up in 1983 under the Province of Brescia, contact Comunità Montana di Valle Camonica, at Breno, tel:0364/320028), while the eastern part, "Parco Naturale Adamello-Brenta", which takes in the Presanella Group, has been under the Autonomous Province of Trento since 1967 (headquarters at Strembo, tel:0465/84637). (The Brenta Dolomites section has not been covered as it is included in *Walking in the Dolomites* by Gillian Price, Cicerone 1991.)

The extensive core is characterised by some high peaks, notably Monte Adamello (3554m), Cima Presanella (3558m) and Monte Carè Alto (3453m) as well as a plethora of other over-3000m summits. They emerge from permanent snow fields and glaciers, such as the Adamello glacier which recent measurements found to be over 18sq km, classifying it as the largest in Italy. The long, wild, glacially modelled valleys that penetrate the massifs offer some excellent walking of all ranges. As well, the Presanella Group in the northeast is well-known for its numerous picturesque lakes.

On the Park's southwestern edge in Valcamonica at Capodiponte is the Naquane National Park of Rock Engravings. A visit is highly recommended (closed Mondays). The graffiti, some of which are thought to be 10,000 years old, were presumably the work of the Camuni people, who gave their name to the valley. On huge slabs of Permian (280-225 million years ago) sandstone, smoothed and deeply grooved by glacier movement, are intriguing scenes depicting rituals and hunting including elk, now extinct there. Information is available in English (tel:0364/42140).

Geologically speaking, the Adamello-Presanella area is quite distinct from its neighbours. The original 230-year-old sedimentary base was penetrated by an enormous mushroom of magma some 50 million years ago. Where the two came into contact, the original rocks were metamorphosed: pure limestones, for example, were transformed into marble, and argillaceous rocks (such as clay and shale) became slate, traditionally used in Valcamonica for roofing (in contrast to the predominance of timber in South Tyrol). The magma itself cooled mostly into granite-like igneous rocks such as quartz-bearing diorite and tonalite (named after Passo del Tonale), the principal component of several major peaks. These rocks are nonporous and coarse-grained for the most part, which means a good grip for walkers, even when wet. However, on the long boulder clambering stretches (particularly on Walk 33) they are very abrasive for hands and boots alike.

Glacier action and atmospheric agents were responsible for the successive external modelling, moulding valleys and exposing underlying rocks.

WALK 26 (see sketch map J, p.162/163)
PRESANELLA GROUP - Princess Presanella

via Velón (15mins) - ex Forte Tonale (1h30mins) - Rif. Denza (1h30mins) - side trip to Vedretta Presanella (2h30mins return) - Passo dei Pozzi (1h) - ex Forte Tonale (2h45mins) - Velón (1h) - bus stop (15mins)
Total walking time: 8h15mins (+ 2h30mins for side trip) - 2 days suggested
MAP: TABACCO No.10 scale 1:50,000

Easily accessible and straightforward (apart from minor difficulties in Stage Two), this loop circuit leads up a glacial valley to a refuge beneath the north faces of the majestic twin Presanella and Vermiglio peaks. There is an extra high detour to a glacier front, then a little-frequented pass with top views.

The area was a First World War Austrian stronghold - the front ran from Passo del Tonale south to M. Carè Alto - and the remains of one of the four strategic forts is touched on. Countless Standschützen

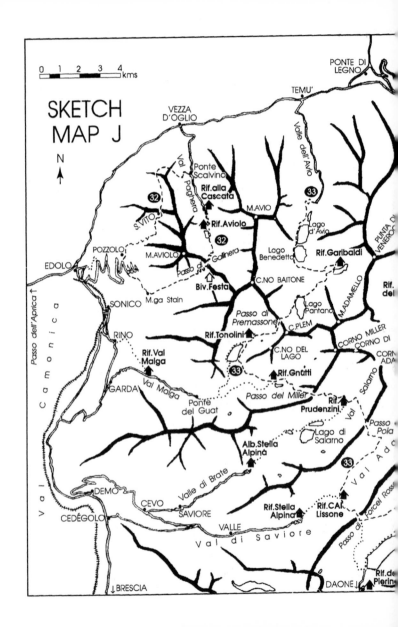

SKETCH MAP J

N

0 1 2 3 4 kms

PONTE DI LEGNO

TEMÙ

VEZZA D'OGLIO

Val dell'Avio

Val Paghera

Ponte Scalvino

Rif. alla Cascata

M. AVIO

32

33

S. VITO

Rif. Aviolo

32

Lago d'Avio

POZZOLO

M. AVIOLO

Galinera

Lago Benedetto

Rif. Garibaldi

PUNTA DI VENEROCOLO

EDOLO

Passo di

Biv. Festa

C. NO BAITONE

M. ADAMELLO

Rif. del

M.ga Stain

Lago Pantano

Passo di Premassone

Passo dell'Aprica ↑

SONICO

C. PLEM

Rif. Tonolini

CORNO MILLER

CORNO DI

RINO

Rif. Val Malga

33

C. NO DEL LAGO

CORN ADA

C a m o n i c a

GARDA

Val Malga

Rif. Gnatti

Ponte del Guat

Passo del Miller

Rif. Prudenzini

Val Salarno

Passo Pola

V a l   d i   A d a

Alb. Stella Alpina

Lago di Salarno

33

Val Adc

DEMO

Valle di Brate

CEVO

SAVIORE

Rif. Stella Alpina

Rif. CAI Lissone

Passo di Forcel Rosso

CEDÉGOLO

VALLE

V a l   d i   S a v i o r e

↓ BRESCIA

DAONE

Rif. de Pierin

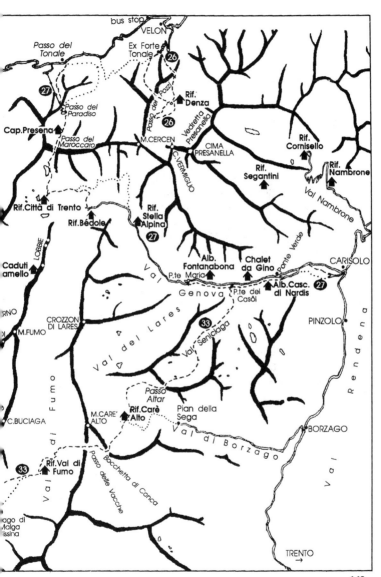

(volunteers) lives were taken by avalanches and the fearful cold, more than those lost in fighting. Most of the soldiers were actually Italian and Ladin speakers, inhabitants of the surrounding valleys, then Tyrol and part of the Hapsburg Empire.

Another tragedy said to have taken place in the same valley involved Presanella, a joyful maiden, child of the stone-hearted king, Presena. Prince Cercen, from a far-off northern land, fell in love with her, but her heart, alas, belonged to a mere pageboy, Vermiglio. A dramatic rescue sequence saw Presanella plait her long hair for her beloved's escape from a high tower prison. They fled, of course, but Cercen, furious, caught up with them at Passo del Tonale, where a curse transformed all three into rock and ice - thus the line-up of linked peaks - Cima Presanella furthest east, Cima di Vermiglio, the western point of the ridge, while Monte Cercen is the next west. The runoff from their snow and ice flows as tears into the Torrent Noce in Val di Sole. The toponymy traces the origin of Presanella from the Latin "prehensa" or grasp. A reference perhaps to the shape of the group - a spindly three-armed octopus reaching down to envelop the valley?

The first recorded ascent of Cima Presenella (3558m), the highest in the Trentino region, was by Freshfield and others in 1864.

ACCESS: the walk starts and ends in Val Vermiglio, the westernmost part of Val di Sole. From the main town Malé in the east (train from Trento), it's a further 24km by bus, past the village of Vermiglio. Just after Hotel Foss, get off at the road fork for Velón (SW). There are also

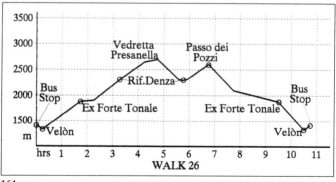

WALK 26

occasional buses from Ponte di Legno (Valcamonica) in the west, via Passo del Tonale to here.

Drivers can proceed through Velón (1340m) and as far as the ex Forte Tonale (1880m) in Stage One - though this second stretch is an old Austrian military road, not always in good condition.

Stage One: via Velón (15mins), ex Forte Tonale (1h30mins) to Rif. Denza (1h30mins)

From the bus stop, on foot downhill by road, 15mins are sufficient to reach the hamlet of Velón (no shops) on the valley floor. Across the river is the Baita Velón trattoria (1354m). Ignore its turn-off and keep on the road around left. 10mins on is a narrow signposted road (n.233) up right into forest. This was constructed as the access and supply route for the fort further up. Walkers can take the short-cuts indicated by red arrows and stripes, climbing through conifers, interspersed with birch and rowan trees later. Both bilberries and raspberries provide excuses for pauses. The way is often steep but clear, with occasional panoramas NE along Val di Sole. You'll need all the 1h30mins to reach the turn-off (1859m) to the left for Rif. Denza.

(Only 100m around to the right, the road terminates with parking space at the dominating position over the valley head of ex Forte Tonale (1880m), alias Forte Pozzi Alti, though its correct name is Forte Presanella.)

N.233 goes SW on a level through a rock tunnel, guarded by the inevitable madonna statue. After several ins and outs across minor valleys, you're joined some 30mins further on (at about 1900m) by n.206 (a longer, less-used path from Stavèl, the neighbouring hamlet to Velón). The refuge comes into sight ahead, dwarfed by Cima Presanella.

With still almost 400m (and a good 1h) in ascent to go, the path climbs in earnest zigzags. Trees thin out, but shrub vegetation continues until high up. Alpenrose and juniper, for example, flourish amidst fallen boulders. Rif. Denza (2298m) stands on a ridge on the westernmost flank of the valley, well above the thundering cascades of the glacier's ablation waters.

Curiously enough the namesake of the refuge, Francesco Denza, was a 19th century Neapolitan friar, astronomer and meteorologist. The dark timber chapel nearby was built (after the Second World

165

War) entirely with timber collected from the First World War fortifications and barracks in the area.

Side trip to Vedretta Presanella (2h30mins return)

This round trip is worth the effort and time as it takes you up to the front edge of the glacier in a desolate morainic landscape in an ample amphitheatre crowned by the north aspect of the twin summits.

Take the unnumbered path (marked by a yellow stripe and red dot) south behind the refuge. A steep but problem-free climb leads up to a crest (1h). The rock surfaces, once beneath the frozen mass, were smoothed by its slow motion. Now reduced in size, and referred to as a "hanging glacier", Vedretta Presanella has a very broad front but is shallow and steep, with folds like an accordion. The faint path keeps to the crest and coasts westish, virtually parallel to the ice front. Purple saxifrage abounds. Some 30mins later, at a point over 2700m, hunt around among First World War timber and barbed wire remnants for red paint marks on rocks indicating the turn-off (right) for the descent. (The ascent continues south across the glacier to 3022m Passo Cercen, a key passage for ascents via Sella Freshfield to the Presanella and Vermiglio summits.)

No path as such is obvious at first, so, with an eye on the waymarking, pick your way north down the rubble valley under the Cresta di S. Giacomo (west). Lower down are grassy terraces and more clambering. A small lake nestles in a silent hollow, then a larger one provides a lovely foreground to Rif. Denza further back. At the path junction on the lake's left-hand shore (2314m), take the right branch to return to nearby Rif. Denza, or go left for Stage Two.

Stage Two: via Passo dei Pozzi (1h) to ex Forte Tonale (2h45mins), exit to Velón (1h) and bus stop (15mins)

Take n.234 heading west from the refuge for "Passo dei Pozzi". After the lake and above-mentioned junction, there's a climb through marmot territory and across enormous fallen boulders, before you enter a steep valley, where chamois sometimes feed. The rather tiring ascent gives excellent views of the Presanella line-up, which is hidden from sight further up.

In rugged surrounds characterised by coarse-grained igneous rocks, mainly tonalite, narrow Passo dei Pozzi (2604m) merits a decent stop for its marvellous sweeping views. Back down in Valle Presanella, the minuscule red-roofed refuge seems threatened by floods of dark moraine. North is the mountain barrier with M. Redival (NNW), beyond which are higher ice-bound M. Vioz (N), Punta San Matteo (NNW) and Corno dei Tre Signori (NW). West, on a good day, Piz Bernina can also be identified.

A sure foot is needed for the long descent. After an initial steep stretch straight down a gully, the path (n.234) bears right under a rock face before zigzagging towards a large bowl-shaped snow-filled depression (Pozzi Alti, about 2050m). On the way, however, both path and waymarking disappear and you're left negotiating tiring boulders, which are very rough on the hands. Down at the bottom, keep to the right of the bowl, and head for the grassy promontory where red paint marks reappear to point you down leftish. Accompanied now by low shrubs (including bilberries) and goats you reach a lovely spot amongst trees, with a small triangular hut. (Equipped with two rough beds and possibly wood, it could be used as emergency shelter. Water can evidently be found in the vicinity.) (1h45mins from Passo dei Pozzi.)

Follow waymarking for Velón (still n.234), with a drop right. Keeping essentially NE coasting through damp wood, it takes another 1h to return to ex Forte Tonale.

From the fort, either pick up your car or walk down to Velón for the bus up on the main road (Stage One in reverse).

Alternative extension to Passo del Tonale (2h30mins)
Though a long extension after the tiring descent, this path connection with Passo del Tonale (1883m, access to Walks 23 & 27) is an easy walk, mostly through wood, never below 1600m.

From ex Forte Tonale, path n.218 (clearly marked all the way) heads west. It drops briefly a couple of times past huts, and rounds the lower part of Roccamarcia through thick forest. Torrente Presena is crossed and you keep right at the turn-off for n.231-18 (which heads up south, then west to Passo del Paradiso and Walk 27). The last leg of n.218 climbs to a forestry track that comes out on the road about 2km below Passo del Tonale.

The bare pass (1883m), once thickly wooded but now a ski resort, has a wide range of accommodation, including some particularly unsightly hotel and apartment blocks.

RIF. F. DENZA tel:0463/758187. SAT, sleeps 90 (20/6-20/9)
TOURIST OFFICE PASSO DEL TONALE tel:0364/91343
TOURIST OFFICE VERMIGLIO tel:0463/758200 seasonal

WALK 27 (see sketch map J, p.162/163)
PRESANELLA GROUP - Val Genova

---

via Passo del Tonale - Passo del Paradiso (2h) - Capanna Presena (30mins) - Passo del Maroccaro (1h15mins) - Rif. Città di Trento (1h15mins) - Rif. Bédole (2h) - Ponte Maria (1h50mins) - Sentiero delle Cascate - Ponte Verde (1h40mins) - Carisolo (45mins)
Total walking time: 11h15mins - 2-3 days suggested
MAP: TABACCO No.10 scale 1:50,000

Passo del Tonale, the starting point, owes its name to "thunder" (tunà) as it was once believed to be regularly visited by thunderbolt-wielding Jupiter, not to mention the hordes of heretic beasts and witches who met with the devil there. In the recorded history of the pass, just about everybody who was somebody passed through, including a procession of Roman emperors - Tiberius in 15BC, Charlemagne (then King of the Franks) in the late 8th century, Barbarossa in the early 12th, and Maximilian at the turn of the 16th. The pass itself is rather unattractive as a series of ugly hotels have substituted the original woods. Of geological interest is the light speckled "salt-and-pepper" igneous rock tonalite, similar in appearance to granite. It took its name from the pass and is a significant component of the Adamello-Presanella Groups.

The itinerary crosses south into the Adamello Nature Park and delightful Val Genova which almost separates the Adamello and Presanella massifs with its deep (east-west) cut. Strangely enough, the valley has no connection with the port city of Genoa but is said to owe its name either to the Celtic for "mouth" or Latin for "knee". Along with devils and witches banished there by the Holy Fathers of the mid-16th century Council of Trent, rare brown bears also inhabited

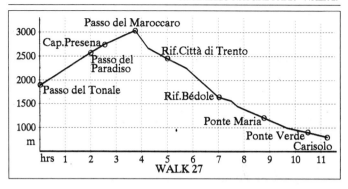

Graph: elevation (m) vs hrs. Points from left to right: Passo del Tonale (~2000m), Cap.Presena (~2500m), Passo del Paradiso (~2500m), Passo del Maroccaro (~3000m), Rif.Città di Trento (~2500m), Rif.Bédole (~1700m), Ponte Maria (~1100m), Ponte Verde (~1000m), Carisolo (~900m). Axis labelled WALK 27, hrs 1-11.

its thickly wooded flanks until very recently, and one was said to have supplied a local hermit with food. Increased traffic and visitors were probably responsible for frightening them into migration east and now, strictly protected, a reduced group roams in the northernmost reaches of the Brenta Dolomites.

Val Genova is also well-known for its waterfalls, indirectly caused by glaciation more than 10,000 years ago. While the slow ice movement carved out the U-shape of the valley floor (successively modified into a 'V' by the river), lateral valleys were left suspended at their original higher level. Hence meltwater from remaining ice and snow pockets has an unusually long and elegant drop for it to reach the Sarca di Val Genova river below.

Important: the 250m climb from Capanna Presena to Passo del Maroccaro (Stage One) traverses the shrinking, crevasse-free glacier Vedretta Presena which is damaged by summer skiing. With decent snow cover, walkers can follow the snow cat tracks, but the absence of snow means exposed ice, making simple walking unfeasible. So unless you are equipped with crampons plan on going early-to-midsummer. The Passo del Tonale Tourist Office can help with information on snow conditions. Otherwise skip Stage One and do it from the Val Genova side. Apart from this section, the itinerary rates an overall "average" as far as difficulty goes.

ACCESS: Passo del Tonale, on the border between Lombardy and Trentino, is served by coach lines from both sides during the summer. From the west: from Edolo via Ponte di Legno (infrequent) (Edolo has trains from Brescia), or via Passo dell'Aprica from Tirano railway station. From the east: a regular year-round service runs along Val di Sole from Malé (trains from Trento), and there are connections with Madonna di Campiglio.

As far as Val Genova and its controversial, partially surfaced 17km road are concerned, private traffic is now restricted during the peak summer period and a shuttle bus runs (21/7-31/8 at the time of writing) between Ponte Verde and Malga Bédole (near Rif. Bédole). NB: the first two runs in the morning actually leave from Carisolo, but return there only in the evening.

At the exit, Carisolo (12km south of Madonna di Campiglio) is on the year-round coach line to Trento (trains).

Stage One: via Passo del Paradiso (2h) and Capanna Presena (30mins) to Passo del Maroccaro (1h15mins)

The cable car a little way west of Passo del Tonale (1883m) only takes 15mins (May to late September). Alternatively, opposite the War Memorial at the highest point of the pass, a path heads SW towards the cable car pylons and line. It winds 700m up a rather uninteresting slope to Passo del Paradiso (2573m) and the Soldanella bar.

(A slightly longer but more interesting route leaves from the same place and heads due east on a level. After about 20mins it joins a dirt track south around the Monticelli ridge. You then turn right on path n.231-18 in a westerly direction in ascent to the pass. Allow 2h30mins.)

Apart from the chair lifts, ski lifts and mazes of cables and pylons, this interesting high valley also hosts the two Monticello lakes and a thought-provoking First World War memorial. Take the wide path (n.209) left around the lakes, then up to the crest and ski chalet Capanna Presena (2738m), at the foot of Vedretta Presena.

If possible head straight up (due south) the (hopefully) snow-covered glacier to the head of the topmost ski lift and the saddle in the light-grey crest. Don't be tempted to try and skirt the ice as there are frequent rock discharges from the dominating crumbly ridges, especially above right, and the last, steeper stretch of permanent ice is unavoidable anyway.

As is to be expected, Passo del Maroccaro (3034m) is a breathtaking lookout point. The name derives from "marocca", debris from mountain sides which crumbled in the wake of the passage of a

*Rif. Città di Trento with Vedretta del Mandrone and the
Lobbie knuckes (left)*

glacier.

Delightful Lago Scuro at your feet has a grandiose frame composed of: SW, Vedretta di Pisgana, walled in by Corni di Bédole, and M. Mandrone (SSE). Adjacent left lies immense Vedretta del Mandrone, separated from the more eastern Vedretta della Lobbia by the knuckles of the three low-profile Lobbia protuberances south. Further east is the point of the Crozzon di Lares (SSE). Back over north are the snowcapped peaks and glaciers of the darker Ortler-Cevedale Group: NE is the flat expanse of Vedretta del Careser, and on rounded M. Vioz (NNE) you can pick out Rif. Mantova al Vioz. Due north is Punta S. Matteo, then Corno dei Tre Signori (NNW).

Stage Two: descent to Rif. Città di Trento (1h15mins)

Path n.212 is straightforward though very steep and loose scree is easily dislodged. After the initial drop it moves left to round a rock outcrop, and soon nears aquamarine Lago Scuro (2668m) (30mins). If you have time to spare, it's only a matter of a short detour down old mule-tracks to its shore, and the good part of a day can easily be spent here - picnicking and swimming (though a single plunge will suffice to understand why it's shark free).

Back on the main path, with wild flowers and grass taking over from the rock debris, you pass another smaller tarn, a signposted turn-off ("Vista su Lagoscuro" up left) and soon reach a panoramic crest (40mins from the pass). The main attraction is icy M. Gabbiolo (ENE), with the light points of C. Presanella and C. di Vermiglio respectively to its left, enhanced by the light grey fluted ridges that drop away from them. At the far eastern end of Val Genova rise the Brenta Dolomites. You also get a glimpse of the orange-roofed refuge, not far away now, down below. The clear path winds down among alpenrose and marmot burrows to well-kept stone and timber Rif. Città di Trento al Mandrone (2449m, often called Rif. Mandrone). Its setting is idyllic - on a high undulating rock plateau with masses of rosebay willow-herb and glittering lakes, the boggy edges of which have been colonised by cotton grass and frogs. Ermine and alpine hares are sometimes spotted in the surrounds of the refuge, and chamois sightings are not uncommon on the higher reaches. South across the valley is the Vedretta del Mandrone glacier and spindly fingers of meltwater emerging from beneath its starfish-shaped mass to combine in a thundering waterfall. As testified by the vast expanse of bare polished rock around it, the glacier has retreated some 2km over the last 60 years, and is reported to be 40m less thick. During the First World War it had a tunnel 2m wide and 5.2km long "dug" through it by the Italians. It was used by mules, donkeys, dogs and soldiers who dragged supply sleds along it. The glacier nowadays, however, is Italy's most extensive (18sq.km), and the Centro Studi Adamello "Julius Payer" was recently set up near the refuge. (Allow a good 2h in ascent for this stage.)

Stage Three: descent to Rif. Bédole (2h)

Past the refuge's cableway, path n.212 leads east to the chapel, and 10mins down is a small war cemetery (brief detour to "cimitero di guerra"). You descend gradually on irregular stone slab steps through grassy terrain brightened by heather, blue bell-flowers and romping marmots. You might find the occasional edelweiss. An easy rock ledge passage is aided by fixed cable, and after a small bridge is a signposted junction (about 2250m, 45mins). Here, experienced walkers can take a longer but more panoramic variant:

Alternative descent via Sentiero Migotti to Val Genova (4h)

Overgrown and rough going in places with exposed and difficult sections (several aided passages with dubiously anchored cables), n.220 is less frequented than the main route, but not recommended for beginners. Named after Migotti, a mountaineer who lost his life while working on it in 1886, it goes (east) along the left-hand flank of Val Genova, and involves lots of ups and downs. 2h15mins should suffice to reach the junction in Val di Cercen (2260m) near an old hut (emergency shelter only). Here n.227 heads valleywards (south) some 700m, with yet more tricky stretches and patchy waymarking. Soon below ex Mandra Pedruc (1567m) you are on the dirt road on the floor of Val Genova, 3km downstream from Rif. Bédole. From here on, see Stage Four.

Walkers following the main itinerary (n.212) continue problem-free down tight zigzags amongst wild roses and springy dwarf mountain pines. A sheer rock face is rounded with substantial fixed cables, and the halfway panoramic point soon reached. There are tall pines as well as silver birches with the inevitable bird life. 50mins or so beneath the previous junction is a waterfall and rustic wooden bridge with a backdrop of the lower edge of Vedretta del Mandrone (SW), dominated by the massive Lobbia Bassa.

Rif. Adamello Collini al Bédole (1641m), mostly simplified to Rif. Bédole (from the Celtic name for birch), is at the westernmost end of Val Genova. (2h45mins in ascent from here to Rif. Città di Trento.) 10mins down the road is Malga Bédole, the departure point for the summer shuttle bus (see ACCESS for details).

Stage Four: via Ponte Maria (1h50mins), Sentiero delle Cascate to Ponte Verde (1h40mins), then Carisolo (45mins)

On foot, you stroll through the grazing areas and farms (dairy products on sale) along the valley floor on the left bank of wide Fiume Sarca di Val Genova. Raspberries, blackberries and bilberries are guaranteed. Just around the corner from the first waterfall, path n.227 (from the alternative descent via Sentiero Migotti) comes out. After a few corner-cuts through wood, the first watering (and eating) hole, Rif. Stella Alpina (1450m), appears (45mins from Rif. Bédole). Inside is a painting of the "King of Val Genova", Luigi Fantoma, a prodigious late 19th century hunter (also a notorious wife beater) who ran up a tally of over 700 chamois and 50 bears, for which he was handsomely rewarded by the Austrian authorities.

A further 45mins along the road will see you at the hamlet of Ragada (1278m), where the road bears east and crosses to the right-hand side of the torrent.

Before the road recrosses the torrent (at Ponte Maria) is signposting for the "Sentiero delle Cascate" (sometimes written as "S d C") at the opening of Valle di Lares, from "larice", larch (and with a magnificent waterfall that drops in stages for a total of 200m). Only slightly longer than the road, this strongly recommended path runs through shady forest parallel to the road, but on the opposite side of the torrent and, as the name suggests, provides close-ups of various cascades on the way down.

(Just stick to the road to reach the guesthouses: quaint Albergo Fontanabona (1092m), 20mins from the path turn-off, or Chalet da Gino (930m), another 25mins down.)

Some 50mins in descent (from Ponte Maria) you reach Val

Seniciaga where path n.215 (and Walk 33) come in. Drop down briefly to the bridge (known as Ponte del Casöl, though not named on maps) over a thundering stretch of torrent.

Another 40mins and you emerge from the forest opposite the valley's most popular waterfall, Cascata di Nardis (100m high). From the small hotel of the same name at 927m, stick to the path on the right-hand side of the valley, and it will bring you out shortly near the car parking areas at Ponte Verde and an ENEL (Electricity Commission) dam. Keep right and 15mins later is a signposted path "Carisolo 3km" (30mins to the camping ground). Otherwise (same length) turn right at the nearby intersection and take the second dirt track right. It leads down to the 14th century church of S. Stefano with its faded frescos (including a 16th century "Danza macabra"). The building is flanked by three tall, bare wood crosses atop a glacially smoothed rock in a commanding position over Val Rendena opposite the Brenta Dolomites, and it's easy to imagine the pagan rites once held here. An old cobbled route continues to Carisolo (806m), where you'll find shops and the bus stop down on the main road.

Just south across the river on the main road to Pinzolo is the Chiesa di San Vigilio, dedicated to the late 4th century bishop and martyr believed to have tamed and ridden a bear. The church has a wonderful, well-preserved 16th century fresco on its southern façade, "Danza macabra" by Simone Baschenis, and is definitely worth a visit.

RIF. CAPANNA PRESENA tel:0463/758299. Private, sleeps 76 (15/6-20/9)

RIF. CITTÀ DI TRENTO AL MANDRONE tel:0465/51193. SAT, sleeps 100 (20/6-20/9)

VAL GENOVA refuges/guesthouses:

ALBERGO CASCATE DI NARDIS tel:0465/51454. Sleeps 6 (15/5-30/9)

RIF. A. COLLINI AL BÉDOLE tel:0465/51405. Private, sleeps 36 (7/6-7/10)

ALBERGO FONTANABONA tel:0465/51175. Sleeps 18 (15/5-7/10)

CHALET DA GINO tel:0465/51360. Sleeps 12 (1/6-30/9)

RIF. STELLA ALPINA tel:0465/51216. Private, sleeps 40 (20/6-20/9)

TOURIST OFFICE PASSO DEL TONALE tel:0364/91343

TOURIST OFFICE PINZOLO tel:0465/51007

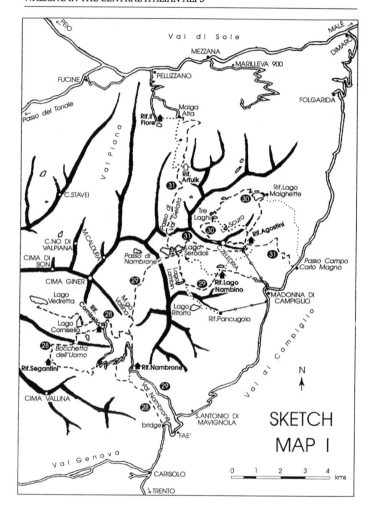

WALK 28 (see sketch map I, p.176)
VAL NAMBRONE - Behind the Presanella

via Faè - Sarca di Nambrone bridge (15mins) - Rif. Segantini
(4h15mins) - Bocchetta dell'Uomo (1h) - Rif. Cornisello (30mins) -
side trip to Lago Vedretta (3h30mins return) - Rif. Nambrone (2h)
- Faè (45mins)
**Total walking time: 8h45mins (+ 3h30mins for side trip) - 2 days
suggested**
MAP: TABACCO No.10 scale 1:50,000

Val Nambrone, with its two upper branches Amola and Cornisello,
was glacially shaped, and smoothed rock surfaces can be seen in the
higher reaches. In contrast, lower down, the action of water from the
torrents has since cut a V-profile. These affluents of the Torrente
Sarca, identified by the name of the valley they flow down, join the
main torrent in Val Rendena and continue on a tortuous course to end
up in Lago di Garda.

The itinerary is a very interesting loop circuit, the only "difficulty"
being the long 1400m climb in Stage One. Several feasible variants are
outlined, beginning with a half-day stroll. Quiet valleys and
picturesque tarns are encountered, and many points provide sweeping
views east to the Brenta Dolomites.

ACCESS: Val Nambrone branches NW off Val Rendena some 7km

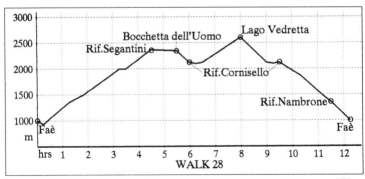

below Madonna di Campiglio, served by year-round coaches (from Lago di Garda, south, Trento, SE, as well as summer connections from Val di Sole, north). A bitumen road actually runs up the northern side of Val Nambrone (official brown Nature Park signposting at its start), whereas the walkers-only path is slightly lower on the southern side. Of the nearest bus stops, one is in the township of Carisolo (806m), giving you 2.5km of main road uphill to the bridge over the Sarca di Nambrone torrent (938m), where the path starts, and the other, slightly closer one, further uphill at the Faè camping ground (before the next village of S. Antonio di Mavignola). The walk is timed and described from Faè.

Convenient points for drivers to park, and thus slot into the itinerary and do shorter round trips, are either 3km up Val Nambrone at Rif. Nambrone, 5km further up at the 1911m road fork referred to later, or a further 2km at Rif. Cornisello. The narrow road, surfaced all the way to the refuge, was originally constructed for ENEL (the Italian Electricity Commission) dam work. When the project was abandoned the road was opened to the public some 20 years ago. Most of the valley's malga-summer farms are likewise deserted and reduced to dark timber ruins, though still marked on maps as useful reference points.

Stage One: via Sarca di Nambrone bridge (15mins) to Rif. Segantini (4h15mins)

From the bus stop near the Faè camping ground (1000m) it's about 15mins down the main road to the bridge over the Sarca di Nambrone torrent (938m). Path n.211 heads NW up the valley as a wide track, later becoming a path. It climbs easily from forest to cow pasture areas, never far from the torrent. A good 1h on, after abandoned stone buildings, a level stretch and an old hut at 1351m, a red painted arrow on a huge fallen boulder (with Rif. Cornisello and Rif. Segantini painted in large letters on the reverse side) points you left (west) away from the torrent.

Alternative access from Rif. Nambrone (15mins)

If you leave your car at Rif. Nambrone (1355m), cross over to the ice-blue torrent. Take the path left and down, following faint signs for Malga Amola. After four bridge crossings in rapid succession you reach the large boulder path junction mentioned above, and turn right around it to link up with the previous path.

Waymarking is faint on the next stretch so keep your eyes peeled. The path goes briefly left, then swings back to climb through mixed wood with plenty of raspberries and bilberries. However it is overgrown and can be very scratchy going, with insidious stinging nettles. Conifer wood follows, then a hut in ruins (1500m) and a bridge over the Sarca d'Amola. Here views east to the graceful dolomite Brenta peaks start. 15 steep mins later and you come out on the road. Several worthwhile short-cuts are indicated by arrows painted on the road surface, and some pass through banks of alpenrose. Others, unused, have eroded away. By road, it's just under a 1h slog to a road fork at 1911m (right branch for Rif. Cornisello), where you go left. (Total 3h to here.)

(Drivers can park in the vicinity and make the Rif. Segantini-Rif. Cornisello circuit a worthwhile day trip.)

With only 1h30mins to go now, path n.211 cuts up off the road keeping to the right bank of the torrent, and leads above the tree line, into the wide deserted rubble valley with a meandering torrent (at about 2000m). You stay up right, above the loading point for Rif. Segantini's cableway. After a small bridge over a rushing torrent, there are two possible ascents marked with metal commemorative plaques: slightly longer Sentiero Mattasoglio proceeds west up the valley, whereas Sentiero Collini climbs in zigzags to a lovely crest. Here, with a couple of ups and downs, it runs due west, amongst gentians, perfumed pink striped splurge-laurel and sticky primroses, and yellow pasque flowers. The refuge buildings are soon visible ahead in a setting of grey-green glacier-smoothed rocks and a background of mountains including C. Quattro Cantoni (west), pointed M. Nero (WNW) with the Presanella slightly further back (NW).

Rif. Segantini (2371m), recently extended and renovated, is an important base for Presanella (3558m) ascents. Meals here include tasty local specialities such as Canederli dumplings, not to mention Teroldego, a recommended Trentino red wine.

Stage Two: via Bocchetta dell'Uomo (1h) to Rif. Cornisello (30mins)

Go north from the refuge (n.216 - Sentiero Dallagiacoma) following the red stripes (not the large red dot) over the smoothed rocks. You soon reach a balanced plank crossing over a frothy torrent which descends from a beautiful desolate amphitheatre. This is seen better slightly further around, flanked by M. Nero, C. Presanella (WNW), C. d'Amola and C. Cornisello (NW). The path curves around in an easterly direction to run parallel beneath a ragged weathered crest. Waymarking is clear, but as the path twists and turns unpredictably, check regularly that you're on the right track. Spotted gentians thrive here. It's 1h to the wide saddle Bocchetta dell'Uomo (or Om, 2350m), the reference being to the sharp rock gendarme (ie. uomo/om, man) belonging to the Crozzi dell'Uomo (east). The pass affords lovely views down onto the incredibly turquoise Lago Cornisello and the smaller contrasting dark Lago Nero, your next destination.

An easy descent takes you north to a signposted path junction where n.216 continues directly down to Lago Cornisello and the path for Lago Vedretta (see side trip). Turn right (n.238) to the shores of Lago Nero (2238m) (out-of-date maps don't show this path). Here on a good day you can picnic on the gentian-studded shore and contemplate the elegant light-coloured towers of the southern Brenta range. Like most others in this valley, this pretty lake is a trout fishing reserve (permits on sale at the refuge or valley resorts). The path passes on the left-hand side of the lake, then climbs down steeply over grass, earth and rock to a dirt road. You might surprise the occasional rock partridge in this area, and if the light brown-patterned female has young to protect, she will fly away from the nest to distract you. Nearby is a blocked tunnel entrance, witness, together with the incongruous idle cable car around to the right, to the aborted dam plans. The track leads you quickly down to the new family-run Rif. Cornisello (2120m), with more wide-ranging Brenta views. The original building, an ENEL prefab, burnt down after being struck by lightning several years ago. Tap water here is classified unsuitable for drinking purposes as it is devoid of mineral salts (meaning it is likely to cause stomach cramps). Times have changed - legends say the nearby lakes came into existence to assuage the thirst of San Vigilio during his crossing from Val di Sole to Val Rendena to convert its pagan inhabitants, who subsequently martyrised him.

Side trip to Lago Vedretta (3h30mins return)
This recommended side trip climbs nearly 500m to a desolate area,

suited to the shy chamois observable there.

From Rif. Cornisello descend briefly to the underlying road junction and turn left up to the large lake. Skirt its right shore, cross the torrent and continue round to a western-climbing valley with waymarking for n.239 for Lago Vedretta (30mins this far). (The connecting path from Lago Nero joins up here.) The path ascends easily but steadily on the left-hand side of the stream. Some 30mins up, as you glimpse a small glacier west, it crosses over right to climb more steeply up the flowered northern slope accompanied by marmot alarm whistles. You reach a desolate rubble valley, then follow the crest westwards again, climbing steadily, towards far-off marker poles and the lake at 2612m, usually iced up well into the summer. Allow a good 1h30mins in ascent from the start of path n.239 at Lago Cornisello. The surrounding mountains include C. Laghetto (SW), followed by C. Cornisello next to it up-valley, and C. Scarpaco at the valley head, with Corni di Venezia (NW). The return route, the same way, is particularly panoramic.

Stage Three: descent to Rif. Nambrone (2h) and Faè (45mins)

A few minutes below Rif. Cornisello at the intersection, leave the rough road and go straight down onto the rock slabs following the red arrows for n.238. It takes you down, detouring to the right of the ruined farm huts and through the first of a number of patches of gigantic nettle and dock leaves. Waymarking is clear and you wind your way south at first through delightful banks of alpenrose intertwined with blue alpine clematis flowers. Some 35mins on in light wood is a brief narrow passage where the path has crumbled away, but it is easily detoured. Soon are the first views of the beautiful Cornisello waterfall, better further down though. The mixed wood (larch, rowan and beech) thickens, then becomes more shady with pine trees whose needles make it softer going underfoot. Twittering birds abound and roe deer are known to inhabit the area. The ruined hut at 1863m, called ex Mandra dell'Orso, is a reference to the presence of bears there once ("orso" means bear). You finally emerge at another hut not far from the foot of the waterfall, where a wooden bridge crosses the Sarca di Nambrone at 1485m (1h40mins this far).

(From here n. 217 heads north up to Passo di Nambrone - see Walk 29.)

Turn right on n.217 down the left-hand side of the torrent, and you soon join the final stretch of road from Rif. Cornisello. It's an easy 20mins to Rif. Nambrone (1355m).

To exit to the main road, the shortest route is the 3km ashphalt road (n.217) SE. Once at the road junction, the nearest bus stop is briefly downhill (right) at Faè camping ground.

RIF. CORNISELLO tel:0465/57150. Private, sleeps 16 (20/6-20/9)
RIF. NAMBRONE tel:0465/57323. Private, sleeps 10 (1/6-30/9)
RIF. G. SEGANTINI tel:0465/57357. SAT, sleeps 64 (20/6-20/9)
TOURIST OFFICE PINZOLO tel:0465/51007

WALK 29 (see sketch map I, p.176)
PRESANELLA GROUP - Some Picturesque Lakes

---

via Faè - Rif. Nambrone (1h) - Malga Vallina (1h) - Passo di Nambrone (2h45mins) - Lago Seródoli (30mins) - Lago Lambin (45mins) - Rif. Lago Nambino (1h) - Madonna di Campiglio (45mins)
Total walking time: 7h45mins - 1-2 days suggested
MAP: TABACCO No.10 scale 1:50,000

This is a cross-over from Val Nambrone to Madonna di Campiglio. Though it is rather lengthy, no technical difficulties are involved and there's a good chance you'll have the valleys to yourself. The route crosses an eroded rock crest and connects valleys once filled with long tongues of ice that crept downhill from the Val di Sole glacier. This ice mass retreated in stages and left a series of armchair-like cirques in steps. Their lower rims became obstructed by debris that then trapped the melt-water, thus giving rise to the numerous and delightful lakes encountered on the walk.

ACCESS: see Walk 28.

Stage One: via Rif. Nambrone (1h), Malga Vallina (1h) to Passo di Nambrone (2h45mins), Lago Seródoli (30mins)

From the Faè camping ground bus stop (1000m), it's 15mins up the main road to the signposted turn-off ("Val Nambrone") at 1080m.

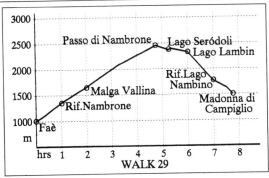

3000
2500 — Passo di Nambrone Lago Seródoli
          Lago Lambin
2000
1500 Malga Vallina
      Rif.Nambrone   Rif.Lago
                          Nambino
1000 Faè   Madonna di
 m   Campiglio

hrs 1   2   3   4   5   6   7   8
              WALK 29

You can either drive or walk the 3km in gradual ascent through thick wood with purple orchids to the small guesthouse Rif. Nambrone (1355m).

Keep straight on up-valley until the road crosses to the left of the torrent and your path n.217 branches off right. It's about 25mins to the wooden bridge over the Sarca di Nambrone torrent (1485m) where n.238 from Rif. Cornisello joins up. Keeping to the right-hand side, take the wooden steps uphill on n.217. It's a steep climb through the tall conifer forest next to the crashing torrent which is crossed higher up to reach a summer shepherds' hut, Malga Vallina (1660m). Its herd of goats seem fond of following walkers, but apart from them, you'll probably have the valley to yourselves. Now mostly on a level the path traverses immense fields of secondary growth, witness to previous human activity. The pass (not Passo di Nambrone yet) visible at the head of the valley (north) appears deceptively close and low now, but it takes over an hour to reach. A narrow passage leads into a wonderful spacious amphitheatre called Busa dei Spini (2079m). (2h15mins from Rif. Nambrone.)

Across grass and rubble with the occasional tongue of snow you proceed with clear waymarking NE across marmot territory. It's another 380m (1h30mins) over some tiring steep terrain with loose detritus, the occasional crumbled-away part and clambers over fallen rocks, but nothing exposed or difficult under normal conditions. You keep to the right-hand side of the valley, and climb up to a corridor, probably filled with snow and chamois tracks at the start of summer. If Passo di Nambrone (2460m) isn't doing its favourite trick of channelling clouds, it's a revelation and some beautiful lakes are housed in the cirque at your feet. The first, Lago Gelato (meaning iced), is guaranteed true to its name with blue ice at the start of summer.

The descent path is an improvement on the ascent, and n.217 turns right (due east) and down steeply to skirt the next lovely lake, Lago Seródoli (2370m). Crag martins perform acrobatic zooms and skim the surface. 30mins down from the pass will see you at a small hut (unusable for shelter) on a panoramic rise.

Alternative exits:

a) From here the shortest way to finish the itinerary is via path n.217 (marked "Lago Nambino") in descent via Malga Buca dei Cavalli (Horses' Hollow) to Lago Nambino and its restaurant and refuge (allow a good 1h15mins).

b) A little longer, with tiring ups and downs, is the higher route east (marked "Pradalago" and "5 Laghi"). It climbs initially, then moves around and down again to the Pradalago cable car station (2082m, descent to Madonna di Campiglio) or Rif. Agostini, for a good meal and night's rest (1h30mins at the most). See Walk 30, Stage One in reverse.

Stage Two: via Lago Lambin (45mins) to Rif. Lago Nambino (1h) and descent to Madonna di Campiglio (45mins)

Just below the hut at Lago Seródoli is a path junction (yellow and red waymarking) - take the route (n.232) due south (marker pole) across rock and with a brief climb at first. Next are 45mins coasting, taking in sweeping views of the valley floor and opposite, a good part of both the north and south sections of the spectacular Brenta group, and you reach another pretty tarn, Lago Lambin (2324m), hidden away.

Just around the corner are three successive marked path junctions for the descent to Lago Nambino (n.269). It's a gentle grassy 1h east with clumps of spotted gentians on the first stretch. The path moves down right into a valley, partially buried by tongues of snow even in July. Heading NE now, it soon reaches wooded zones, then peaceful Lago Nambino (1768m), visible from some time above. According to a legend these waters, now infested by alpine charr (like trout), were once inhabited by a horrible dragon that spat both fire and poison.

Evidently some locals believe it to be a gigantic trout still lurking at the bottom of the lake. As far as the refuge (Rif. Lago Nambino) on the lake shore goes, accommodation is reasonable, but the restaurant, while good, is rather over-priced.

The final stretch to the fashionable resort Madonna di Campiglio (1510m) is by way of path n.263 via Malga Nambino (1634m). Allow about 30mins to the malga, then path and road.

Alternatively, from Lago Nambino, walk up to Rif. Agostini Pradalago. The path (n.266) turns left at the eastern end of Lago Nambino and moves up into the squirrel-infested wood. It passes under the cable car and chair lift, then follows a bare ski slope uphill to join the access path from Madonna di Campiglio before the final stretch west (1h15mins).

Day Trip - Giro dei Cinque (5) Laghi (3h)
To do this classic popular itinerary, the 5 Lakes Tour, from Madonna di Campiglio take the Funivia 5 Laghi (cable car) to Rif. Pancugol (no accommodation). Path n.232 passes Lago Ritorto and leads to Passo Ritorto, then Lago Lambin and Lago Seródoli with nearby Lago Gelato, before descending to Lago Nambino and Madonna di Campiglio (3h total).

An extension east from Lago Seródoli takes advantage of the Pradalago cable car in descent, so timing is about the same. Paths are well-trodden and well-marked, but cable car operating periods (usually late June to early September, but subject to variation) should be checked with the Tourist Office.

RIF. AGOSTINI PRADALAGO tel:0465/41200. Private, sleeps 15 (20/6-20/9)
RIF. LAGO NAMBINO tel:0465/41621. Private, sleeps 25 (1/6-30/9)
RIF. NAMBRONE tel:0465/57323. Private, sleeps 10 (1/6-30/9)
TOURIST OFFICE MADONNA DI CAMPIGLIO tel:0465/42000
TOURIST OFFICE PINZOLO tel:0465/51007

WALK 30 (see sketch map I, p.176)
CIMA ZELEDRIA - Sentiero Bozzetto

---

via Rif. Agostini - Cima Zeledria (50mins) - Tre Laghi junction (1h)
- Rif. Lago Malghette (1h40mins) - Rif. Agostini (1h)
Total walking time: 4h30mins - 1 day suggested
MAP: TABACCO No.10 scale 1:50,000

The first part of this highly recommended itinerary follows a length of the airy Sentiero Bozzetto (the Bozzetto Path), a partially aided climb of medium difficulty, with some fixed cable and ladders. "Constructed" between 1979-1984 with some recent additions, it was the idea of Italian cartoonist Bruno Bozzetto and dedicated to his family. Some experience is recommended. It should not be attempted in anything but guaranteed good weather conditions as its exposed tracts are slippery when wet, and of course cloud cover would spoil the views. An easier variant is given to avoid this first section.

(Details on the other sections and difficulty of the Sentiero Bozzetto are available on request at Rif. Agostini - the alpine guide on the staff was involved in preparing the route.)

Later on, after descending via some lovely tarns with splendid backdrops, there is a scenic crossing opposite the splendid Brenta Group.

ACCESS: see Walk 31.

Stage One: ascent to Cima Zeledria (50mins), then descent to Tre Laghi junction (1h)

From Rif. Agostini Pradalago (2085m, meaning meadows at the lake), signposting for Sentiero Bozzetto indicates the way due west up the hillside, above the right-hand side of the lake. The ascent is problem-free, if a little steep, and features alpenrose and cawing alpine choughs. The Italian flag (always "flying" as it's metallic) on the summit of Cima Zeledria (2427m) is soon at hand, along with wonderful all-round views. You look down onto the nearby lakes nestling in their cirques, west to the minor peaks belonging to the Presanella Group, further behind, NW, to the snowy Ortler-Cevedale

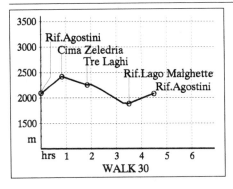

3500
3000
2500
2000
1500
m

Rif.Agostini
Cima Zeledria
Tre Laghi
Rif.Lago Malghette
Rif.Agostini

hrs 1   2   3   4   5   6
WALK 30

Group, not to mention the Brenta Dolomites SE.

Follow the narrow path west along several aided passages (fixed cable) and some crumbly exposed stretches - a sure foot is necessary. Take care your rucksack doesn't catch on jutting rocks. For the most part you follow the jagged crest and in 15mins reach a signposted junction (another Bozzetto variant heads left for Lago Serodoli - 2h), you take the right-hand fork in gradual descent. More cable follows, occasionally frayed but on the whole in good condition. 20mins will see you at a long metal ladder down into a rubble-strewn amphitheatre. The path is wider and easier from now on across fallen rocks, then a wide gully, possibly choked with snow in early summer. Keep on beneath M. Nambino (west) and over a couple of easy crests with expanses of classic blue gentians and the larger yellow spotted variety. After a total of 1h from the summit is a path junction on a wonderful knoll above the delightful isolated mini-valley with the Tre Laghi (three lakes) down to the left, and Lago Scuro down right.

Alternative access to here (1h20mins)
From Rif. Agostini take path n.265 past the chair lift on a level in a northerly direction. After 15mins turn left in ascent to a nearby saddle (ski run) and over to another fork - the left branch (another section of Sentiero Bozzetto but not aided as not necessary) leads west to Lago Scuro (2160m) in about 25mins. From here it's a 150m climb to the path junction mentioned above.

Stage Two: via Rif. Lago Malghette (1h40mins), return to Rif. Agostini (1h)

There's a brief descent to the largest of the three lakes (2257m), then with yellow and red waymarking up to the middle-sized one and

Final aided stretch on Sentiero Bozzetto

along a crest right to the smallest. After another rise the path (not shown correctly on maps) drops to Lago Alto (2158m, 35mins) and skirts its right-hand shore, in yet another cirque. The lower lake and Rif. Lago Malghette come into sight far below, and virtually due east over the valley appears the red, iron-like shape of Sasso Rosso, the atypical northernmost outpost of the Brenta Group. According to legend, its dramatic colouring is the spilt blood of a wonderful deer hunted for its golden hoofs.

N.277 is a lovely path down through larch and Arolla pines, banks of alpenrose with loaded bilberry shrubs, not to mention the wine-red martagon lilies in July. Fallen trees are easily detoured. Past a turn-off for the mountain hotel Orso Bruno (NE) the path curves high around the lakeside to bar-restaurant Rif. Lago Malghette (1890m, no accommodation). As the lake's water is used to supply the valley, swimming and other aquatic activities are strictly forbidden.

Alternative exit route
It is possible to reach Passo Campo Carlo Magno from here in 50mins.

The return route to Rif. Agostini climbs steadily (200m in all) and though mostly in sweet conifer wood, gives you ample chances to appreciate the graceful pale towers and massive peaks of the northern Brenta. The wide flat expanse of Passo del Grostè is SE, adjoining which (northwards) is Pietra Grande and its horizontal stratification. Then follows a graceful series of peaks, the highest, C. Flavona partly enclosing a small glacier at the head of Val Gelada.

Some 40mins around past the turn-off for Lago Scuro (the alternative access in Stage One), and the path crosses open pasture land and pistes, before a final brief uphill section to a chair lift and lakeside Rif. Agostini once more. Even if you don't overnight here it's worth a stop for a plate of the delicious pasta they serve.

RIF. AGOSTINI PRADALAGO tel:0465/41200. Private, sleeps 15 (20/6-20/9)
TOURIST OFFICE MADONNA DI CAMPIGLIO tel:0465/42000

WALK 31 (see sketch map I, p.176)
PRESANELLA GROUP - Val Gelata

---

via (Madonna di Campiglio) Passo Campo Carlo Magno - Rif. Agostini
(1h) - Lago Seródoli (1h45mins) - Passo di Val Gelata (45mins) - Rif.
Artuik (2h) - Malga Alta (1h) - Pellizzano (1h)
Total walking time: 7h30mins - 1-2 days suggested
MAP: TABACCO NO.10 scale 1:50,000

This route starts out in the Nambino area above (NW) Madonna di
Campiglio. The road pass was named after Charlemagne (Carlo Magno
in Italian). Legend has it that he passed this way in the late 8th century
(as King of the Franks), soon after he conquered the Lombards. As he
allegedly did in the Val di Sole (and other alpine valleys on his path),
he went about sacking the castles of pagans and Jews and hanging the
inhabitants who refused to surrender and be baptised. This was
undeniably more successful than the evangelising efforts of San Vigilio
nearly 400 years earlier - he was stoned to death for having dared
overturn a statue of Saturn in the then Roman dominion.

After a scenic traverse and climb past lovely tarns to an easy pass,
the route descends a desolate valley, more often visited by chamois than
walkers. A bivouac hut breaks the descent of nearly 1600m to the Val di
Sole and the historic village of Pellizzano.

ACCESS: the resort centre of Madonna di Campiglio (1510m) is 76km by
year-round coach NE of Trento (trains). Some buses continue the 2.5km
as far as Passo Campo Carlo Magno. Connections are also possible from
Lago di Garda in the south and, as well, there is a summer line from the
Val di Sole, north.

As far as the end point, Pellizzano, in Val di Sole goes, regular buses
connect it all year round with the railhead Malé 15km to the east (train
to Trento). For those wishing to return to square one, there is a summer
line via Dimaro back to Madonna di Campiglio.

Stage One: ascent to Rif Agostini (1h) then via Lago Seródoli (1h45mins) to Passo di Val Gelata (45mins)

From Madonna di Campiglio, the Pradalago cable car will cut 45mins
off the ascent. Otherwise, on foot from the road pass, Passo Campo
Carlo Magno (1702m), follow track n.265 west via Malga Zeledria. After

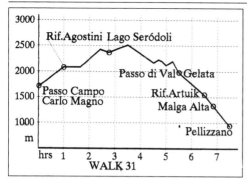

the initial woods, the higher part is rather uninteresting as the terrain is continually modified for winter ski runs. However the view east over the valley to the Brenta Dolomites brightens it considerably.

From Rif. Agostini Pradalago (2085m) take the wide path up to the cable car station and restaurant. From here follow "Sentiero Bozzetto" signs up the crest to a nearby junction and take the left branch to traverse the grassy mountain side coloured by martagon lilies and alpenrose blooms at the start of summer. Some 40mins along west is a fork - turn up right on the "5 Laghi" path. There's a consistent climb, then it resumes the traverse with long tracts of old rock falls. You have a wide-ranging outlook over the valley. It's a further 45mins to where the long variant of the aided climb from Cima Zeledria joins up (Sentiero Bozzetto "alpinistico") - keep straight on past an exit route for Madonna di Campiglio (off left). After a small lake and marmot burrows you descend somewhat to reach Lago Seródoli (2370m) and the (unusable) hut there on a rise.

Now, ignore path n.217 for Passo di Nambrone and go straight down to the lakeside to briefly skirt the left (southernmost) shore. The faintly marked path, not always obvious, crosses the narrow strip of land before the next small lake and then coasts its edge. Cross a low stone wall (clear red waymarking here) at the end of higher and larger Lago Gelato (2393m). Head along its shore then straight up the first (unlikely looking) gully on the right (virtually due north). Though rock-choked, it's problem-free and waymarking soon reappears - red paint splashes on the left-hand side (path n.203). You climb up to a small cairn and a saddle. The pass is visible north, not far away up a grassy slope. Stones have been heaped up as markers for the final stretch in ascent, and you make your way up to the right-hand part of wide Passo di Val Gelata at 2515m (sometimes referred to as Passo di Nambino). Late-lying snow is usually patterned with the tracks of chamois who might materialise if you're in the vicinity early in the morning.

Stage Two: descent to Rif. Artuik (2h) Malga Alta (di Sopra) (1h) and Pellizzano (1h)

Hunt around for a large red painted blob to find the way down. N.203 plunges into the icy realms of wild Val Gelata which runs due north. The view is clear all the way down to the woods and villages in Val di Sole. Scree flows from Cima di Val Gelata (west) are usually snow-covered until late in the season, but the path keeps to the right-hand slope, avoiding them. A couple of tricky crumbly stretches, however, are involved. Occasional tiny clumps of purplish sticky primroses, pink alpine snowbells and white alpine buttercups thrive on meagre patches of earth. After a tiny lake the terrain becomes grassier and easier and soon passes a huge isolated boulder. A little further down again and you bear right over rocks with a stream flowing underneath. A short climb follows, then a veer right into a sort of corridor. A well-prepared path winds up eastish through mixed rocky terrain amongst alpenrose and juniper shrubs, the occasional dead larch sentinel to a grassy hollow. More "up" to a ridge and over into a neighbouring sub-valley. Descend to a stream and then ascend (the last ascent) to a path junction (right-hand branch for Lago Azzurro) (about 1h45mins from the pass).

Now it is a mere 15mins through wood into the wide pasture area with long cow sheds, a drinking fountain and recently restored Rif. Artuik (or Artuich, 1976m). It is, in fact, a roomy unmanned bivouac hut - one room (containing table, benches and wood stove) is always left open. Users are requested to leave the premises clean. A well-equipped kitchen and upstairs sleeping area are locked, but should you be ascending from Pellizzano, the key can be collected from (and returned to) the Local Council Office (Comune di Pellizzano).

From here, with 1000m left in descent, two routes of similar length are feasible to reach Malga Alta:
a) take the path west at first through wood and down to Lago di Stablò, then the hut (for private use only) Rif. Regina del Bosco (1639m). Resuming the descent, the path joins the rough track described in the following alternative near Malga Alta (also referred to as Malga di Sopra), at 1546m. Allow about 1h this far, or
b) follow the rough forestry track (n.203) north. After a cow gate (please shut), it descends in curves through a tall pine forest to Malga Alta in 1h. (In the opposite direction you can drive this far from Pellizzano - 3kms.)

Now, for the rest of the way to Pellizzano, there are two more possibilities to choose from:

c) a signposted path leads across the fields to romantic Lago dei Caprioli (1307m) where there's a small hotel. Not far down the road from the lake, at Fazzón, is private Rif. Il Fiore (also known as Rif. Fazzón and Rif. Alpino). From here the rest of the way down is via the road with several possible steep short cuts through forest, to the village of Pellizzano (937m) (hotels, buses, shops - even open Sunday mornings in summer). Otherwise,

d) from Malga Alta, with the same timing, stay on the rough road and 20mins will see you at the junction with the road from Fazzón. Turn down right, in common with c).

The church in the village square, with its elegant Renaissance portico, was reputedly founded by Charlemagne on his "crusade" through the area, and was originally decorated with frescos (no longer visible) depicting the "holy slaughter" of Jews and pagans who refused to convert. The impetuous Torrente Noce that runs through the village was used for the 1993 World Kayak Championships.

RIF. AGOSTINI PRADALAGO tel:0465/41200. Private, sleeps 15 (20/6-20/9)

RIF. ARTUIK Bivouac hut. Contact tel:0463/751128. Comune di Pellizzano, sleeps 10. Keys available on request from Council Office.

RIF. IL FIORE (FAZZÓN) tel:0463/751515. Private, sleeps 20 (15/6-15/9)

TOURIST OFFICE MADONNA DI CAMPIGLIO tel:0465/42000

TOURIST OFFICE PELLIZZANO tel:0463/751183 seasonal

WALK 32 (see sketch map J, p.162/163)
UPPER VALCAMONICA - The Yellow Bivouac Hut

---

via Vezza d'Oglio - Ponte Scalvino (1h) - Rif. alla Cascata (30mins) - Rif. Aviolo (1h30mins) - Passo di Gallinera (1h15mins) - Malga Stain (2h) - Pozzolo (1h) - Ponte Scalvino (3h30mins) - Vezza d'Oglio (45mins)

Total walking time: 11h30mins - 2 days suggested

MAPS: KOMPASS No.71 scale 1:50,000 or Carta dei Sentieri di Vallecamonica (Comunità Montana) scale 1:50,000 (available locally)

A versatile itinerary, lending itself to several interesting variations to suit your time availability and fitness. If walked in its entirety as a circular route it takes you on a circumnavigation of M. Aviolo (2881m, climbable from the west side). Those with a car can park (limited space) near Ponte Scalvino for the round trip (cutting some 1h40mins off the total time). Otherwise, it's possible to drive as far as Rif. alla Cascata and do a worthwhile day trip (suitable for families) to Lago d'Aviolo in its magnificent setting, and even as far as Passo di Gallinera and bright yellow Biv. Festa, returning by the same route (approx. 4h30mins total).

A useful alternative exit to the railhead of Edolo is also given.

Various interesting landscapes and habitats are encountered, ranging from woods of broad-leafed trees and conifers to high-altitude lakes and marshes in the shadow of severe ice-bound tonalite peaks. There's also a wild southern valley (Val Gallinera, a nature reserve) characterised by dry vegetation types.

The name "Aviolo", commonly found in this area in a variety of forms, is believed to derive from pre-Indo-European words for either water, landslide or eagle.

ACCESS: Vezza d'Oglio, in upper Valcamonica, is 5.5km west of Temù - see Walk 33 ACCESS.

Stage One: via Ponte Scalvino (1h), Rif. alla Cascata (30mins) to Rif. Aviolo (1h30mins)

From the main road at Vezza d'Oglio (1080m) Corno Baitone is visible

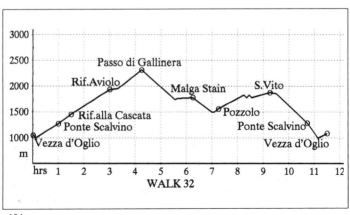

WALK 32

SSE with its small glacier above a spacious cirque. From the bus stop in the village, take the nearby narrow road south, signposted for Rif. Aviolo and Val Paghera. After crossing the River Oglio it swings around left, then heads south up Val Paghera. This name comes from "pagher", dialect for spruce, plentiful here in thick woods which host roe-deer and hare.

Allow 1h as far as Ponte Scalvino (3km, 1278m) where the road crosses to the right-hand side of the torrent (parking area) and narrows somewhat. Pleasant family-run Rif. alla Cascata is a further 30mins up at 1453m. The waterfall ("cascata") the refuge took its name from is but a trickle of its former self due to the ENEL (Electricity Commission) dam and huge underground conduits upstream which now carry the bulk of the water to the power station at Edolo.

Take path n.21 - it soon joins the road which quickly ends at the ENEL cable car station. Signposted, the path begins its steep climb out of the wood. There are two long series of rock steps up gullies, the second with a hand cable. Take extra care in the wet as it can be slippery. You emerge onto a grassy platform with several buildings. For the final not-so-steep 30mins, after a brief ridge diagonally left, the path passes through low wood and leads to welcoming Rif. Aviolo (1937m). There are views back to Vezza d'Oglio and north up Val Grande, while M. Avio is east, the Baitone group south, M. Aviolo SW and Corno Plaza west.

Stage Two: via Passo di Gallinera (1h15mins) to Malga Stain (2h) then Pozzolo (1h)

From the refuge, a couple of minutes further south at Lago d'Aviolo, are better views of the point of Corno Baitone SE, joined to a series of peaks, all around 3000m.

Path n.21 coasts the left bank of the lake with its glacier-smoothed flanks, and leads to a beautiful upper valley with a stream meandering through marshy cotton grass zones. It's not far to ruined stone huts (Malga Aviolo, 1955m) from where, past marmot hide-outs, you go back and forth across the torrent. The climb (SW) up a gully is accompanied by a surprising variety of rock types (including speckled grey tonalite) which testify to the fault line of Passo di Gallinera. The pass itself is a wide grassy saddle at 2320m, SE from M. Aviolo. The name is derived from the dialect word "galiner" used for a place frequented by black grouse. Shy chamois sometimes graze amongst a riot of wild flowers (some endemic).

Intriguing prehistoric engravings on a glacially polished rock surface at
Naquane National Park of Rock Engravings, Capodiponte

The yellow metallic hut (Biv. Festa) perched on a spur 5mins around to the left off the main path is always open and is equipped with bunk beds and blankets (but no water or stove). Its backdrop is a dramatic wall of ice and snow descending from Roccia Baitone.

From the pass, the clear path (n.21) leads down the steep grassy slopes into the wild domain of Val Gallinera, with Valcamonica in the distance. This relatively unfrequented stretch is steep and knee-destroying at first, not to mention slippery when wet. Once down at the torrent, you stick to the thickly wooded (and often overgrown) right-hand side of the valley and after a series of ups and downs come to a signed path junction at about 1745m (1h30mins from the pass). (Connection via Forcella Bombiano to Rif. Tonolini - though rather long and tiring at 5h30mins, and not recommended for beginners, it could be used as a link into Walk 33.) In slight ascent through the ever present rowan trees and wild strawberry patches, n.21 reaches ex Malga Stain (1780m), a great lookout point with sweeping views over Valcamonica, taking in Piz Bernina NW. Though the buildings here are abandoned, they can be used for emergency shelter and have a fireplace, wood and some basic furniture.

Heading NW and narrowing now, the path drops, then coasts through areas of heather and carline thistles, laden raspberry and bilberry shrubs beneath M. Foppa. Soon after crossing two enormous conduits, you join the quiet winding road that climbs from Edolo. Down at the next curve take the turn-off right past the parking area along the dirt track. After 10mins, before the buildings (there's a fresh spring down left), fork right and up through the fields to climb around to a shady but panoramic picnic/bbq area known as Pozzolo (1560m).

Stage Three: via S. Vito (2h) to Ponte Scalvino (1h30mins) and Vezza d'Oglio (45mins)

After passing the n.34 branch up east for the M. Aviolo climb, n.72 continues in ascent NE, to approach two granite towers. Val Finale (nature reserve well-known for deer and roe deer) is crossed, and is followed by a further climb, steep in parts. It brings you out at a clearing and a chapel dedicated to S. Vito and S. Anna (1877m), site of local festivities the last Saturday in July. A restful level stretch goes around north to farms at Iclo (where n.72b forks off right to proceed via Corno Plaza to Rif Aviolo - exposed in parts). Now it's in gradual descent past a series of small farm houses and huts, through meadows and woods, ending with a wide curve around east, then south to emerge at Ponte

Scalvino in Val Paghera.

From here on foot via the road, allow 45mins back to Vezza d'Oglio.

Alternative exit: via Pozzolo turn-off to Mu (1h15mins) then Edolo (15mins)
At the Pozzolo turn-off mentioned towards the end of Stage Two, keep on the asphalted road west for Edolo. There are several feasible short-cuts, but none is signposted. One guaranteed alternative to the road is the old track, concreted in parts, cobbled in others, to be found some 25mins and several winds downhill. Once you're actually on it it's easy to follow. Hopefully many dense and fruitful raspberry jungles later, you'll reach the picturesque village of Mu (780m). Past the imposing church, you cross the River Oglio to Edolo's (690m) main square, inclusive of bus stop and extremely helpful Tourist Office. The railway station is further on, down left.

RIF. AVIOLO tel:0364/76110. CAI, sleeps 60 (15/6-20/9)
RIF. ALLA CASCATA tel:0364/76185. Private, sleeps 10 (1/6-15/9)
BIV. VALERIO FESTA bivouac hut. CAI, sleeps 15
TOURIST OFFICE EDOLO tel:0364/71065
TOURIST OFFICE VEZZA D'OGLIO tel:0364/76131 seasonal

WALK 33 (see sketch map J, p.162/163)
ADAMELLO GROUP - The Adamello Tour

via Temù - Malga Caldea (1h30mins) - Rif. Garibaldi (3h15mins) - Bocchetta del Pantano (50mins) - Passo di Premassone (2h40mins) - Rif. Tonolini (1h30mins) - Passo del Gatto (1h5mins) - Rif. Gnutti (40mins) - Passo del Miller (2h15mins) - Rif. Prudenzini (2h) - Passo di Poia (2h) - Rif. CAI Lissone (2h30mins) - Passo di Forcel Rosso (1h45mins) - Rif. Val di Fumo (3h) - Passo delle Vacche (2h30mins) - Bocchetta di Conca (1h) - Rif. Carè Alto (1h) - Passo Altar (2h30mins) - Ponte del Casöl, Val Genova (2h40mins) - Carisolo (1h35mins)
Total walking time: 36h15mins - 7-8 days suggested
MAPS: TABACCO NO.10 scale 1:50,000 (excluding parts of some exit routes) or Carta dei Sentieri di Vallecamonica (Comunità Montana) scale 1:50,000 (available locally, useful as far as Forcel Rosso)

This long, tiring and extremely rewarding route starts off in Lombardy,

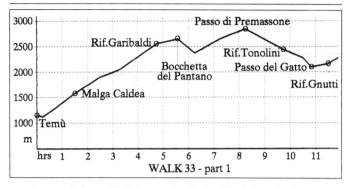

WALK 33 - part 1

running south down the Valcamonica flank of the Adamello Group and Nature Park, then curving east into the Trentino region, with a final stretch northwards, ending up in Val Genova (close to Madonna di Campiglio). Constantly high up between 2000-3000m, it crosses the high mountain ridges that radiate out like octopus tentacles from the central body of the Adamello massif, to connect some wonderful rugged unspoilt valleys, each with a well-placed refuge. The area is well known for its higher level glacier itineraries, but the ice-free paths described here are relatively untrodden. Accommodation only needs to be booked ahead on weekends and in August to be on the safe side. Many refuges are run by helpful Alpine Guides, who can be consulted about weather forecasts and glacier or mountain itineraries.

All the refuges can be reached from an external valley and road, so exit routes are given from each, including public transport. The Stage Six exit (from Rif. Val di Fumo) is the only long and inconvenient one. Many villages also have a taxi service which will meet you at the start of the motorable road - ask refuge staff for details. Exit routes can also be used to make chunks of the Tour into shorter sections or day trips, but they are too long to be feasible for a dash down to a village to stock up on food. Most refuges will prepare packed lunches at reasonable prices if you opt not to carry extra weight for the whole trip.

The itinerary is not suitable for absolute beginners as there are several exposed and tricky rock stretches (Passo di Premassone - Stage Two, Passo del Miller - Stage Four) and a couple of snow fields are traversed (Passo del Miller - Stage Four, Passo di Poia - Stage Five and between Passo delle Vacche and Bocchetta di Conca - Stage Seven). Adverse weather or late snow cover could add further difficulties.

Under normal conditions (good weather and non-icy snow) no extra equipment such as crampons or ice pick is necessary, though gaiters could be useful in soft snow. While a week is possible (if Stage Three were combined with either Two or Four), a rest day is recommended - it could easily be spent exploring the higher reaches of any one of the beautiful valleys encountered.

A final note: with a couple more days to spare, this itinerary can be extended into a complete circuit of the Adamello, returning to Temù. Either catch the shuttle bus or walk up Val Genova to Rif. Bédole, and do Walk 27 in reverse, coming out at Passo del Tonale. From there some irregular stretches of path descend west to Ponte di Legno.

ACCESS: Valcamonica runs north from Lago d'Iseo (between Bergamo and Brescia) and the village of Temù, the starting point for this itinerary, is in the northernmost part (3.5km west of Ponte di Legno). It can be reached in three ways. A private train line connects Brescia with Edolo, then you continue by bus. Secondly, from the west and the railway station at Tirano (Milan-St. Moritz line), buses run via Aprica to Edolo. Temù can also be reached via Val di Sole in the east (connections from Madonna di Campiglio or from Trento by train via Malè), with the rare bus via Passo del Tonale and Ponte di Legno.

For the final exit, Carisolo (12km south of Madonna di Campiglio) is on the year-round coach line to Trento (trains), with connections possible for Lago di Garda.

Stage One: via Malga Caldea (1h30mins) to Rif. Garibaldi (3h15mins)

Temù (1155m) has a modest First World War museum (Museo della Guerra Bianca), a collection of relics and photographs of the terrible "white war" fought on the Adamello's glaciers. On the main road almost opposite the Pro Loco (local Tourist Information) is signposting for Rif. Garibaldi, pointing you south down Via Val d'Avio and across the River Oglio. After following several signposted turnings into the Valle dell'Avio, keep left up the asphalted road through wood. It's a good 3km (45mins) to a junction at 1300m (signpost) where you leave the bitumen to the ENEL (Electricity Commission) vehicles and fork left up a dirt track on n.11. Another easy winding 45mins will see you at the abandoned farm buildings of Malga Caldea (1584m) (end of car access, limited parking space).

A roughly asphalted track, occasionally used by vipers for sunbathing, now zigzags up through scrubby vegetation and blue round-headed rampion flowers to ENEL buildings at 1904m (drinking water, cold beers and soft drinks available) (under 1h from car park). Mostly on a level now, n.11 leads due south above the right side of the first artificial lake to the second, Lago d'Avio. About halfway around its shore, the path climbs away from the vehicle track to reach more buildings and Lago Benedetto, fed by several cascades. The scenery becomes decidedly more interesting now with the first sight of the crisp clear ridges and triangular point of M. Adamello (SE). After a climb around and across cascades at the far end of the lake, you emerge onto a beautiful plain (2044m) where fluffy cotton grass grows in the marshy zones. Despite the preponderance of pylons and overhead cables, the views are magnificent and also include the Corno Baitone (WSW).

With only 1h30mins to go now, past the junction for Rif. Tonolini, n.11 bears left (east) to cross the grey torrent and climb an old military mule-track through larch and alpenrose. The long final stretch, known as the "Calvario", takes you up a steep rocky slope past stone ruins, and can seem endless, particularly in the presence of swirling mist. On arrival near the dam wall at the western end of Lago Venerocolo, keep left past the commemorative First World War chapel. Rif. Garibaldi (2550m) soon comes into sight on the lake shore, at the foot of the north face of M. Adamello (3554m, first ascended by J. Payer in 1864). Just over the ridge of peaks and stretching east and south lies the immense Adamello glacier.

As you'll gather from the photos inside this family-run refuge, the previous hut, now beneath the waters of the artificial lake, was originally the infirmary building and supply base for higher Italian positions during the First World War. During lulls, the alpine soldiers worked on perfecting their skiing techniques - the record for the descent from Passo del Venerocolo (3136m, east) was 2mins50secs, incredible considering the equipment of the time.

Rif. Garibaldi is an important base for glacier crossings and mountain ascents, but booking is only usually necessary on weekends, late July-August.

Stage Two: via Bocchetta del Pantano (50mins), Passo di Premassone (2h40mins) to Rif. Tonolini (1h30mins)

Visible SW from Rif. Garibaldi is Cima Plem, and this stage heads for the key passage to its right, Passo di Premassone (slightly SE of Passo dell'Avio, shown instead on some maps). Go back down the path to the dam wall and follow signs across it for "Alta Via Adamello", n.1. Large yellow daisy-like arnica, with medicinal properties, grow along the way. There's a brief climb over an old moraine crest into the valley beneath the Vedretta del Ven-erocolo with its dark debris-covered front and melt-waters, then south past marmot burrows up a wide gully to the saddle, Bocchetta del Pantano (2650m, 50mins). The descent is in tight zigzags. The old iron rods are neither necessary nor well-anchored. Unfortunately you "lose" nearly 300m in height and move left in traverse to the next dam, Lago Pantano (2378m). The name is a reference to the original boggy nature of the area. (Total 1h30mins to here.)

Make the most of the panoramic stroll across the dam wall, as there's a stiff 500m climb ahead. Well signposted, n.1 turns decidedly up the steep grass and earth slope dotted with violet alpine asters and spotted gentians. It bears steadily SW, traversing boulders and crossing streams. Views over to M. Adamello and its surrounding summits and dazzling glaciers improve step by step, and your attention is drawn by regular thundering ice and rock falls. Even in midsummer the last steep 200m (1h) will probably be snow covered, and extra care is needed. You'll have to pick your way over fallen boulders to follow the red and white waymarking heading up right to the rock face. There's a fixed cable up a short rock passage, then an earth path, and more cable for a further brief climb. The final stretch goes left along a narrow, somewhat exposed ledge to Passo di Premassone (2847m) with several cairns. Views back north now include the long crest with Punta S. Matteo. Nearby is imposing Cima Plem, whose name aptly derives from precipice.

The descent (south) is well marked and problem-free. It crosses several smooth rock slabs heading for Lago Premassone and the delightful solitary valley below. After the lake the path continues south, then west. There are often tracts of late-lying snow to cross, but these are nowhere near as tiring as the rough rubble valley ahead to be negotiated. However the refuge is already in sight.

Set on a panoramic outcrop above azure Lago Baitone, due south of Corno Baitone, is recently extended grey stone Rif. Tonolini (2437m). Regular visitors are the docile marmots who come from the nearby lake shores and seem to be unusually fond of the soap the refuge uses.

Exit route: descent via Malga Premassone, Ponte del Guat (1h45mins), Rif. Val Malga (Ponte Faet) (40mins), Sonico (1h15mins)

Take path n.13 down the right-hand side of Lago Baitone amidst wafting sweet daphne (Mezereon) to the dam wall. Keep right, then traverse flowered slopes past more ENEL buildings to conifer wood. You come out at the vehicle track and bridge at Malga Premassone summer dairy farm (1585m) on the floor of Val Malga, whose woods are known to host roe deer. On the left-hand side of the torrent the track soon reaches Ponte del Guat (1530m) (limited parking space, *no* refuge here, though maps show otherwise). (Time in ascent from here 2h45mins.)

4km (40mins) further down the narrow asphalt road is privately-run Rif. Val Malga (1130m, drinking water) at Ponte Faet (from "faggio", beech). The chaotic state of the Torrente Remulo bed is due to the 1987 flooding which seriously threatened the underlying villages. The road heads off left across the bridge, but walkers can take the old paved road that cuts down to the village of Rino (673m). The rare bus comes this far from Edolo, otherwise it's less than 2km to the train line at Sonico (the name is from the German for honey). Allow nearly 4h for the entire descent.

By car, a combination of this exit route with Stage Three and the next exit route results in a worthwhile round day trip: from Malonno or Sonico in Valcamonica, drive up Val Malga as far as Ponte del Guat, then walk Malga Premassone - Rif. Tonolini - Passo del Gatto - Rif. Gnutti - Scale del Miller - Ponte del Guat.

Stage Three: via Passo del Gatto (1h5mins) to Rif. Gnutti (40mins)

Take n.1 left down a brief easy rock passage, then a clear path. It keeps to the left-hand side of the valley and Lago Baitone, and passes some interesting glacially smoothed rock. There are clumps of gentians and pink hairy primroses. Some 45mins will see you at the dam wall (2283m), where n.1 turns left, then drops down to an abandoned railway track and buildings. At the madonna shrine take the lower path branch which winds down amongst alpenrose shrubs, heading SE. Some 20mins from the dam is Passo del Gatto (Cat's Pass) (2103m), actually a protected ledge with fixed cable, cutting around Corno del Lago. The narrow path continues east with several exposed but not difficult stretches, some aided. There is a surprising range of wild flowers, in particular the delicate white St. Bruno's lily, purple orchids and saxifrage in the rocky crannies. After a gradual climb past stone ruins, modest but welcoming Rif. Gnutti (named after a valorous Alpine lieutenant and funded by his family) greets you on its lakeside at 2166m in Val Miller (the eastern extension of Val Malga). Apart from a helicopter drop when the hut opens, supplies are usually backpacked up here. The dominating peak in this valley, NE from the refuge, is

Corno di Miller, an important corner support for the Adamello glacier on the other side.

Curiously enough, the name Miller did not belong to an early British mountaineer exploring the zone, but is believed to originate from "mill", the local name for a type of kite. The birds were once

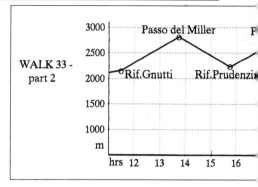

WALK 33 -
part 2

plentiful in the valley and exacted as live tax when Valcamonica was subject to the bishop of Brescia in the 9th century.

There is plentiful evidence of glacial polishing on the rock surfaces here, and the refuge itself was built on a "roche moutonée". Evidently there used to be a 700m-long, 150m-thick glacial tongue here.

From Rif. Gnutti a rewarding side trip can be made to the higher reaches of beautiful Val Miller, known for its lakes, mist and marmots. The path is easy, though not always clear. Allow a good 2h return time to take in the highest lake, Pantano del Miller (2423m).

Exit route: descent via Scale del Miller, Malga Premassone, Ponte del Guat (1h30mins), Rif. Val Malga (Ponte Faet) (40mins), Sonico (1h15mins)
Below the dam wall, n.23 crosses marshy ground then follows the torrent down the grazing plain some 30mins to a crucifix and path junction on the left-hand side. Keep straight ahead to the start of the Scale del Miller, a rough rock staircase that drops some 200m to the valley floor and Torrent Remulo. If you are tempted to complain that it jars your knees, spare a thought for the poor shepherd who has to drag and push his cows up and down here every June and September. Continue down, more gradually now, through light wood to abandoned farm buildings (Malga Frino, 1695m) and a madonna shrine on top of an enormous boulder. A wide track leads down quickly now across the torrent to Malga Premassone with its taciturn shepherds and noisy dogs. Not far down you come out onto the asphalted road and the bridge, Ponte del Guat. See the exit route, Stage Two, for further details. (In ascent allow 2h15mins.)

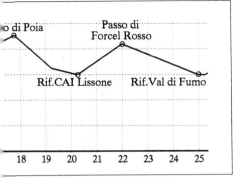

It's a good idea not to start off late on this stage as midsummer sun can make the snow field soft and wet going.

Go back to the small bridge and path junction at the end of Stage Three, then take n.1 up-valley on the left-hand side of the lake. There's a path junction after 10mins and you keep right, well below a hut. The torrent is forded and the climb starts in earnest SE up the opposite flank, leaving behind alpenrose and yellow arnica. You cross several streams and climb easily beneath a rock spur that descends from Cima Prudenzini (east). About 1h30mins on you enter a cirque at 2600m, the edge of a permanent snow field. There may be some surprising "snow mushrooms" here - stone caps atop snow stems. Mountains visible now include Cima Plem (NW), Cima del Laghetto (NNE) with Corno Miller to its right (north). The pass ahead can be identified by a marker pole and weird stone obelisk, resembling an Easter Island statue. If the snow is firm to the tread, it's easier to go straight up than keep left as the official route does. When the snow becomes too steep, icy or soft, move over left to the loose rocks and the red and white waymarking. It's tiring work clambering over fallen rocks up the ever-steepening slope. The final short stretch, to be taken with care, is a climb up a short rock gully leading to Passo del Miller (2818m), where hardy glacier crowfoot flowers somehow thrive. A new valley, Val Salarno, opens up east now with several lakes. (Its name is believed to be derived from pre-Latin words referring to its water courses.)

The descent begins on grassy terrain, but soon deteriorates to leaps and clambers over large, coarse-grained irregular boulders, hard on the hands. There is no path as such, but red and white indications clearly show the way. The route goes north on a level for a while, then, finally back on an earth base again with bright clumps of gentians and fresh alpine moon-daisies, crosses a vast ridge (Coster di Destra) that runs parallel to the valley floor, before descending more decidedly. The refuge is soon in sight but the path, easy-going now, bears a little up-valley to avoid a recent landslide, before the final curve down. The sturdy grey stone building of Rif. Prudenzini (2235m), named after a local magistrate and mountaineer, stands on a grassy flat next to the stream. The horse and mule that graze here help bring up supplies from the lower cableway.

At the head of this magnificent valley is Corno Miller, left of Corno di Salarno (north) and its overspilling glacier. Right, at Passo di Salarno, stands a yellow bivouac hut, Biv. Giannantoni at 3168m, on the edge of the glacier which provides access for M. Adamello ascents and traverses to the strategic Rif. ai Caduti dell'Adamello.

Exit route: descent via Malga Fabrezza (1h45mins) to Saviore di Adamello (40mins)

Path n.14 takes you SW past two lakes and several summer dairy farms, then steeply down Valle di Brate, keeping to the right-hand side of the watercourse until the final section. Due south below M. Marser stands the small guesthouse Alb. Stella Alpina near Malga Fabrezza (1424m) (from here in ascent 2h30mins). As well as a lovely waterfall, there are cars and some asphalt on the next narrow 3.5km to the village of Saviore di Adamello (1210m) for bus connections with Cedégolo in Valcamonica and the train line. The parish church of S. Giovanni Battista has paintings attributed to Palma il Vecchio and Palma il Giovane, 15th-16th century Venetian artists.

Stage Five: via Passo di Poia (2h) to Rif. CAI Lissone (2h30mins)

Signposting behind the refuge points you up-valley to the wobbly ingenious bridge across the torrent, then marshy terrain towards the water storage tanks. You walk NE up the easy grassy flowered slope, then southish, with improving views. After crossing an upper amphitheatre (45mins), there's a climb into a higher cirque with year-round snow. The remaining ascent (all snow) is still long and steepish but presents no particular difficulties under normal conditions. Extra care will obviously be needed with ice, otherwise dig your toes in well and plod on towards Passo di Poia (2775m), identifiable by its signpost, under Cima Poia.

Find a perch for a rest amongst the stone walls left by First World War soldiers. In addition to the panorama of mountains at the head of Val Salarno, M. Adamello can be seen behind them, NNW. On the opposite side of the new valley, Val Adamè (east), are some wonderful jagged crests and peaks, including Cima Buciaga (SE). Beyond is the point of M. Carè Alto (ESE).

In descent, the initial short stretch climbs down a rock face with plenty of hand and foot holds. Continuing south, there's some grass, then the inevitable boulder clambering once more in slow descent. You swing left towards an area of snow and rocks inhabited by marmots. Some 45mins from the pass will see you at the edge of the upper valley and on a much more decent earth path. Now it's a steeper but problem-free descent down the grassy mountain side with the occasional juniper and flowering alpenrose shrubs. On the valley floor, near a ruined shepherds hut (Cuèl del Manzoler, 2130m) are scattered fallen boulders (1h30mins from pass). Another wonderful solitary valley, enclosed to the north by a dark rock crest with Corno di Adamè, the secondary summit of M. Fumo with its dark underlying ridges of moraine, then Cima delle Levade. A red bivouac hut (Biv. Cecco Baroni) is visible on a crest NNE. Time permitting, continue north up-valley to the base of the small Adamè glacier (not included in total walk time).

At the signposted path junction on the valley floor, turn right and follow delightful Torrente Poia southwards. (It was this water course that gave its name to the pass and peak, and in the dialect of Brescia means "a clearing where twigs and branches are burnt to make charcoal".) It's 15mins to a path junction (keep straight down) and shepherds' huts. Plenty of picnic or bathing spots present themselves as the valley widens into a plain and the torrent meanders across a thick green, yellow and white carpet of grass, dandelions and cotton grass. Goats graze high on the rocky slopes. Very soon after a larger summer farm, Malga Adamè, complete with cows and pigs, the path crosses to the left-hand side to 2005m and Rif. CAI Lissone (1h from Cuèl del Manzoler). The modern comfortable building (hot showers available) stands on the edge of a sheer drop, where Val Adamè becomes Val di Saviore.

Should you wonder, Lissone is a place on the outskirts of Milan, whereas the name Adamè comes from the Latin "ad hamae (acquas)", used for the marshy plain up-valley, exploited by shepherds for many centuries. The name Adamello, on the other hand, was evidently suggested by the priest from Saviore to French map-makers in the late 18th century, for the mount of Val Adamé.

Exit route: descent via Scale dell'Adamè, Malga Lincino (45mins) to Valle (1h45mins)

Take n.15 signposted for Valle. It drops steeply down the right-hand side of the valley on innumerable zigzags and rock steps (the Scale dell'Adamè) to Malga Lincino (1621m). Here you join a wider track, asphalted soon, an easy route through wood. At 1316m is private Rif. Stella Alpina with limited car parking (ascent time from here is 1h45mins). Below is an area called Le Croste, probably a reference to its enormous glacially polished rock slabs. Official car parking is at the lower hamlets of Forame and Rasega, where reinforced river embankments were constructed to prevent repeats of the disastrous 1987 floods. The historic village of Valle (1208m) is under 1h away now on rougher road, and has a bus service to Cedégolo (railway station) in Valcamonica.

Stage Six: via Passo di Forcel Rosso (1h45mins) to Rif. Val di Fumo (3h)

From here on the route bears eastish and no longer follows the Alta Via Adamello (n.1) (which continues on to Rif. Brescia, Maria e Franco in 6h, then Rif. Rosa in 4h30mins, and involves difficult rock passages). This stage is even less frequented than the previous ones, and while long, is not difficult.

Facing downhill, take n.24 left along the wide track. After 10mins it departs from n.1 and turns up left (signpost). The climb, in tight curves SE, traverses banks of alpenrose for a good way. Red and white waymarking is frequent and leads you across tracts of snow and rock. About two-thirds of the way up it becomes quite steep on a multicoloured scree and earth base. This was a contact zone where intrusive magma metamorphosed sedimentary rocks, later exposed by uplifting and erosion. There is a brief stretch on the right-hand side of the wide gully where you can help yourself up using hand-holds in the rock, before returning to final zigzags up the middle to ample grassy Passo di Forcel Rosso (2601m) ("rosso" refers to the predominance of iron-red rock). Here are extensive Italian First World War fortifications and a couple of precarious tunnels (possible shelter in bad weather). Running south, then SW from M. Fumo, the crest once constituted a border between the Veneto Republic and the Principality of Trento, then between pre-First World War Italy and Austria and nowadays between Lombardy and Trentino. One explanation, in fact, for the name of Val di Fumo (it literally means valley of smoke, mist), relates it to "fines" or boundary.

(Signposting indicates a good path, n.245 (right) in gradual descent southwards to Lago di Malga Bissina (1789m, 1h45mins) where there is a private refuge. This could be used as an escape route, and joins up with

First World War fortifications at Passo di Forcel Rosso

the next exit route.)

Instead, take the left branch of n.245 above an upper valley with marmots and tiny spring gentians. Now a very gradual descent begins, coasting the grassy eastern flank of Val di Fumo, high above the glittering expanse of Lago di Malga Bissina. Soon, NE above a jagged ridge, the great elongated triangle of M. Carè Alto comes into sight. The descent is a pleasant scenic walk, highlighted, with any luck, by the sight of the soaring golden eagles which nest in the valley. More numerous inhabitants are alpine choughs (large yellow-beaked, red-footed crows), flocks of which have been known to attack the eagles.

A rocky crest is rounded, followed by a huge protruding granite-like slab, with views onto the upper valley and refuge. A traverse over fallen rock takes you down more decidedly into a valley where you may surprise ground-nesting rock partridge. Areas of white cotton grass indicate bogs - detour. Arolla pines cling to some unbelievable rocky points, and amidst the first larch trees are pink and purple orchids and wine-red martagon lilies. Though the direction is clear, the path itself disappears at times. There's an unexpected brief climb around another small valley where you descend a thickly flowered sunny slope with chocolate-scented black vanilla orchids, white St. Bruno's lilies and several varieties of cactus-like house-leeks amongst juniper shrubs. A welcome respite in a shady wood follows. Beware of hidden holes in the overgrown path. You finally stagger out near the bridge (not corresponding to the maps) in the peaceful pastoral valley. The horses and cows belong to Malga Val di Fumo, on your left, where tasty cheeses can be purchased (try the "spressa"). Now lovely old-style Rif. Val di

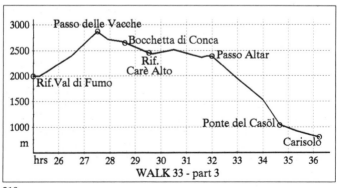

WALK 33 - part 3

210

Fumo (1997m), in a picturesque setting on a rise, is only 5mins across the Fiume Chiese.

It provides free hot showers (the refuge's power is supplied by a low-cost water-driven turbine), imaginative cuisine, and a wide selection of wines, including the excellent full-bodied Trentino red, Teroldego.

Exit route: descent via Lago di Malga Bissina (1h) to Daone (4h)
Allow about 1h SW past Rif. Alto Chiese (refreshments only) to the dam wall of Lago di Malga Bissina (1780m). Private Rif. da Pierino (also known as Rif. Malga Bissina) (1699m) is just 2km in tight curves down the road (from this point in ascent allow 1h45mins). From here the valley changes name - lovely Val di Daone extends for 22km to the village of Daone (767m) (4h should do), where occasional buses (except on Sundays) run the 7km to Pieve di Bono in Val Giudicarie (connections via Tione to Trento or via Baitoni to Riva, Lago di Garda).

Stage Seven: via Passo delle Vacche (2h30mins), Bocchetta di Conca (1h) to Rif. Carè Alto (1h)
Path n.222 follows the river valley north for some 15mins on its right-hand side, before starting its serious climb east (right). The path is good, though somewhat overgrown, and it tends to double as a stream bed during rain. There's a grassy hollow above the tree line, then you head north up to a good lookout point (1h30mins to here). The pass is clearly visible east. Over rock and thinning grass you approach a huge boulder where "R. Carè Alto" in red points you right. Guided by red stripes, spots and heaps of stones you continue climbing over rock slabs with rivulets underneath. There may be snow on the later stretch. A red arrow shows the final rock path up and left past scattered (Austrian) First World War barbed wire to Passo delle Vacche (2872m) (Pass of the Cows). Should you be caught out by bad weather here, 5mins round to the right past the stone wall is a tunnel, which could be used for temporary shelter. You might see chamois on this desolate terrain. M. Adamello (NW) with Corno Miller (to its left) should be visible.

Across the valley due east is your next destination, the Bocchetta di Conca. The ex-military supply path (marked RCA) keeps left alongside a rock flank, then winds down easily on stone steps into a sheltered snow-filled cirque beneath a small glacier. Heaps of stones function as markers and supplement the faint painted waymarking to guide you across the snow, then cut up the other side. There are several brief ups and downs, easy walking over non-slip rounded slabs, and you reach

2674m and the Bocchetta di Conca pass where deep blue trumpet gentians grow.

Around left (NE), after an initial descent, the refuge can be seen ahead. Marmot cries echo across the vast rubble slope. The rest of the traverse, in slight descent, is on mixed grass, rock and earth brightened by masses of chamois ragwort and moon-daisies. Due to the many streams flowing down from melting snow and glaciers, the path has crumbled away in a couple of places, but nothing more than a careful detour is necessary. Though it seemed deceptively close, Rif. Carè Alto is actually a good 1h from the pass. The last stretch, across marshy mountain side, leads past a small chapel (the work of Russian POWs in 1917) to the previous Austrian stronghold where Rif. Carè Alto now stands. The refuge was built at 2459m on the ridge running down due east from M. Carè Alto (3463m), which attracts the mountaineers who besiege the hut on July-August weekends. Weekdays are quiet though, when you'll hopefully have the chance to taste the "Risotto al Teroldego" concocted by the cook-cum-guide. (Week-long courses in rock and ice technique as well as ski touring are held here.)

The name Carè - the same root as the village of Carisolo - is derived from Carex, or sedge grass, commonly found in the lower marshy area.

Exit route: descent via Pian della Sega (Val di Borzago) (2h30mins) to Borzago (1h30mins)

The descent path (n.213) drops quickly in tight zigzags down a steep grassy-stony slope to a sharp bend left about 1h down. Alpenrose and bilberry shrubs concealing the occasional black grouse characterise the following 50mins up to a Himalayan-type bridge across the torrent in the vicinity of several waterfalls. Then through waist-high stinging nettles and mixed undergrowth you wind down to a wide track near the refuge's cableway loading point. Take the short-cut down right - it rejoins the jeep track and in 20mins, through tall mossy forest, brings you to where the road is barred at a parking area (Pian della Sega, 1270m). (In ascent from here 3h30mins.)

With luck, further down this peaceful valley there'll be views back up west of M. Carè Alto with the Vedretta di Niscli right. Now it's 7km (1h30mins) which soon become asphalt, past summer holiday cabins to Borzago (640m) in Val Rendena - transport as per Carisolo (see ACCESS), 9km north.

Stage Eight: via Passo Altar (2h30mins) to Ponte del Casöl, Val Genova (2h40mins), Carisolo (1h35mins)

Relatively unfrequented, this stage is problem-free (weather permitting) and offers a rewarding finish to the tour with a descent into delightful Val Genova.

N.215 passes in front of the refuge, then drops down left on a series of cut stone steps guided by a cable. The path curves around and climbs little by little NNW across the vast and splendid Conca di Niscli amphitheatre. The path is clear but snow-covered in early summer. 35mins will see you at a cable-slung crossing (if released by snow) of an impetuous grey torrent which comes from the Vedretta di Niscli. The climb continues to approx. 2520m (1h) over rock smoothed by the passage of ice, and in the vicinity of a prominent boulder, n.215 for Passo Altar forks decidedly right (east) and drops. (Left continues NE to the Pozzoni and glacier routes.) It coasts across stark debris terrain beneath crests and minor peaks that are riddled with First World War caverns and fortifications (Cima degli Obici north, for example, is "Howitzer Peak"). The final stretch is a narrow earth path that climbs to Passo Altar (2385m) where concrete sentinels testify to a wartime cableway. Resting time here can easily be occupied by eagle or chamois watching, or, cloud permitting, admiration of the majestic form of M. Carè Alto WSW now from this superb vantage point. The Brenta Dolomites are NE.

Though long (approx. 1400m total in descent), the way is easy and well marked (n.215), NE down Val Seniciaga. Easy zigzags down the grassy slope amongst alpenrose and spotted gentians lead down into its pretty upper basin inhabited by marmots and where a meandering stream feeds several small lakes bordered by characteristic cotton grass. Heaps of stones mark what used to be shepherds' huts (ex Malga Altar, 2150m). The valley narrows and you cross fallen stone blocks, then thick bushy undergrowth before reaching a hut in sea of nettles and dock leaves (1h, Malga Seniciaga Alta, 1950m, emergency shelter possible). The snowcapped point of the Presanella can be glimpsed north, with M. Nero to its right.

Further down, after a couple of stepping stone stream crossings, is yet another abandoned pasture zone. After a stretch of shady wood alongside the cascading torrent is a long cow shed and summer farm, Malga Germenega Bassa.) A further 10mins on (total 2h from the pass) is drinking water at Malga (or Baito) Seniciaga Bassa (1536m). Though converted into a bivouac hut, it is kept locked (at worst the wood shed could be used for shelter).

5mins downhill past a modest Austrian First World War memorial is a cattle-proof gate and turnstile. The descent is much steeper now and zigzags through a beautiful beech and conifer forest in earshot of the cascading torrent right. It's a good 40mins all the way down to the wooden bridge (Ponte del Casöl, 1046m - not usually shown on maps) where you can join the Val Genova road. However it's infinitely more pleasant to follow the "Sentiero delle Cascate" (waterfall path) which branches off downstream (west and unsigned at first), a few path winds back uphill before the bridge. You go via the beautiful Nardis waterfall and guesthouse (40mins), then proceed to Carisolo (806m). See Walk 27 (Stage Four) for details as well as shuttle bus information.

Val Genova, however, with its pleasant shady forests, numerous cascades and modest guesthouses, lends itself to (well-earned) resting aided by local gastronomic delights. These include "strangolapreti", literally "priest stranglers" as the southern versions made with rough millet were said to "strangle" the priests used to softer foods. They are potato-spinach gnocchi (small dumplings). "Capriolo con polenta" is also popular - a rich spicy stew of venison (roe deer, usually imported frozen from Eastern Europe) served with "polenta", corn purée.

RIF. CAI LISSONE tel:0364/638296. CAI, sleeps 60 (15/6-30/9)
RIF. CARÈ ALTO tel:0465/801089. SAT, sleeps 96 (1/6-30/9)
RIF. G. GARIBALDI AL VENEROCOLO tel:0364/94436. CAI, sleeps 108 (20/6-20/9)
RIF. S. GNUTTI AL MILLER tel:0364/72241. CAI, sleeps 40 (20/6-20/9)
RIF. DA PIERINO (MALGA BISSINA) tel:0465/674625. Private, sleeps 10 (1/6-15/10)
RIF. P. PRUDENZINI tel:0364/634578. CAI, sleeps 100 (1/6-30/9)
ALBERGO STELLA ALPINA (MALGA FABREZZA, VALLE DI BRATE) tel:0364/634386. Private, sleeps 40 (Easter-31/10)
RIF. STELLA ALPINA (LE CROSTE, VAL DI SAVIORE) tel:0364/638297. Private, sleeps 15
RIF. F. TONOLINI AL BAITONE. CAI, sleeps 36 (30/6-30/9)
RIF. VAL DI FUMO tel:0465/674525. SAT, sleeps 52 (1/6-30/9)
VAL GENOVA guesthouses - see Walk 27 for listings
RIF. VAL MALGA (PONTE FAET) tel:0364/75340. Private, sleeps 8 (20/6-15/9)

TOURIST OFFICES:
DAONE tel:0465/64999 seasonal
EDOLO tel:0364/71065
PIEVE DI BONO tel:0465/64744 seasonal
PINZOLO tel:0465/51007
SAVIORE DI ADAMELLO tel:0364/634131 seasonal

TEMÙ tel:0364/94152
VALLE tel:0364/64669

GLOSSARY

ITALIAN	GERMAN	ENGLISH
Aiuto!	Zu Hilfe!	Help!
Albergo	Gasthof	Hotel, guesthouse
Alta Via	Höhenweg	High level walking route
Alto	Hoch, hohe	High
Baita, malga	Alm	Alpine hut for shepherds, sometimes a farm or refuge
Bivacco	Biwakschachtel	Bivouac hut, unmanned
Bocchetta, forcella, giogo, passo	Joch, Jöchl, Scharte	Pass, saddle
Caduta sassi!	Steinschlag!	Falling rocks!
Castello	Schloß	Castle
Cima, vetta	Gipfel	Peak, summit
Corno	Horn	Hornlike peak, pinnacle
Cresta, crinale	Kamm	Crest, ridge
Difficile	Schwierig	Difficult
Est	Osten	East
Facile	Einfach	Easy
Fiume	Fluß	River
Funivia	Seilbahn	Cable car
Ghiacciaio	Gletscher	Glacier
Gola	Schlucht	Gorge
Lago	See	Lake
Maso	Hof	Alpine farm, sometimes a refuge
Montagna, monte	Berg	Mountain
Nord	Norden	North
Ovest	Westen	West
Paese, villaggio	Dorf	Village
Pericoloso	Gefährlich	Dangerous
Ponte	Brücke	Bridge
Posto di ristoro	Jausenstation	Refreshment station
Punta	Spitze	Point (mountain)
Rifugio	Hütte, Schutzhaus	Refuge, mountain hut or inn providing food and accommodation
Rio, torrente	Bach	Mountain stream
Scorciatoia	Abkürzung	Short-cut
Seggiovia	Sessellift	Chair lift
Sentiero	Steig, Weg	Path, route
Soccorso alpino	Bergwacht, Bergrettung	Mountain rescue
Sorgente	Brunnen	Spring
Sud	Süden	South
Val, valle	Tal	Valley
Vedretta	Ferner	Hanging glacier
Via ferrata	Klettersteig	Aided climbing route
	Waalweg	Path alongside irrigation canal

REFERENCES

The following were consulted:

Bersezio, L. & Tirone, P. (1988) *Andar per Rifugi*, Istituto Geografico de Agostini, serie Görlich, Novara.

Bezzi, Q. (1988) *Lungo le Rive del Noce*, Centro Studi per la Val di Sole.

Bonacossa, A. (1915) *Regione dell'Ortler*, Guida dei Monti d'Italia, CAI, Milano.

Buscaini, G. (1984) *Ortles-Cevedale, Parco Nazionale dello Stelvio*, Guida dei Monti d'Italia, CAI/TCI, Milano.

Comunità Montana di Valle Camonica, Regione Lombardia *Percorsi Didattici in Valle Camonica* (leaflets).

Consorzio Turistico Alta Vallecamonica (1990-91) *A piedi alla scoperta dell'Alta Vallecamonica* (series of brochures).

Gadler, A. (1985) *Guida alpinistica escursionistica dell'Alto Adige*, Panorama, Trento.

Gadler, A. (1989) *Guida alpinistica escursionistica del Trentino Orientale* (5a ed.), Panorama, Trento.

Gambillo, C. (1882) *La Valle di Rendena*, SAT, Rovereto.

Höhne, E. (1981) *Ortles*, Athesia, Bolzano.

KOMPASS (1991) Guida escursionistica *Val Venosta, Gruppo dell'Ortles*, Bolzano.

Lichem von, H. (1990) *Gebirgskrieg 1915-1918 Ortler-Adamello-Gardasee*, Athesia, Bozen.

Merci, L. (1986) *Le più belle leggende dell'Alto Adige*, Manfrini, Calliano (Trento).

Ongari, D. (1978) *Presanella*, Guida dei Monti d'Italia, CAI/TCI, Milano.

Provincia Autonoma di Bolzano Alto Adige (1986) *Parco Naturale Gruppo di Tessa* (booklet).

Sacchi, P. (1986) *Adamello Vol. II*, Guida dei Monti d'Italia, CAI/TCI, Milano.

Saglio, S. (1939) *Alpi Venoste, Passírie, Breónie dal Résia al Brénnero*, Guida dei Monti d'Italia, CAI/CTI, Milano.

Saglio, S. & Laeng, G. (1954) *Adamello*, Guida dei Monti d'Italia, CAI/TCI, Milano.

Various other pamphlets and maps kindly supplied by local Tourist Offices.

Printed by CARNMOR PRINT & DESIGN
95-97 LONDON ROAD, PRESTON, LANCASHIRE, UK.

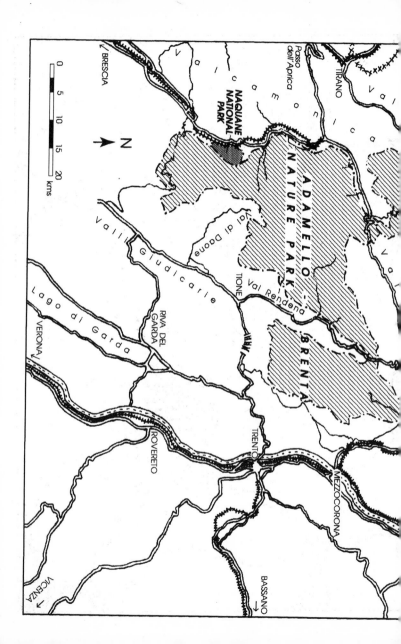